Corey Lindsey

7-12-04

From: Mamaw

THE GAME ACCORDING TO SYD

The Theories and Teachings of Baseball's Leading Innovator

Syd Thrift
AND
Barry Shapiro

SIMON AND SCHUSTER
New York London Toronto Sydney Tokyo Singapore

Simon and Schuster
Simon & Schuster Building
Rockefeller Center
1230 Avenue of the Americas
New York, New York 10020

Designed by Levavi and Levavi/Carla Weise
Manufactured in the United States of America

10 9 8 7 6 5 4 3 2 1

Library of Congress Cataloging in Publication Data

Thrift, Syd.
The game according to Syd: the theories and teachings of
baseball's leading innovator / Syd Thrift and Barry Shapiro.
p. cm.

1. Baseball—United States—Management. 2. Baseball—
Economic aspects—United States. I. Shapiro, Barry.
II. Title.
GV875.7.T47 1990   89-77867
796.357'0973—dc20   CIP

ISBN 0-671-68410-8

To my wife, Dolly,
to my sons, Jim and Mark,
and to all people of
great vision

CONTENTS

ACKNOWLEDGMENTS

My coauthor and I would like to thank the many people who gave of their time and knowledge: Hal Baird, Alan Blitzblau, Steve Boros, Jim Bowden, George Brett, Dave Buccolo, Cynthia Busis, Michael Callan, Mickey Cobb, the late Joe Consoli, Larry Doughty, Bob Drury, John Garver, the late A. Bartlett Giamatti, Jim Gott, Mike Hall, Dr. William Harrison, Brad Hines, Al Kasprowicz, Ewing Kauffman, Buzzy Keller, Sam Ketchman, David Levine, Jim Leyland, Dr. Eric Margenau, Tom Martin, Joe McIlvaine, Hal McRae, Ray Miller, Dr. John Nash Ott, Lou Piniella, Bob Rich, Dom Scala, Mackie Shilstone, Dr. Warren Sipp, Dr. Tony Stellar, Gene Stephenson, Jim Thrift, and Dr. Joseph Trachtman.

Our thanks to Jay Acton, our literary agent; Jeffrey Neuman, our editor; and Linda Sullivan and Peter Jamieson, who transcribed our mountains of spoken notes. And our love and gratitude to Dolly Thrift and Allison Shapiro, who inspire us every day.

1 MY QUEST FOR ANSWERS

I am a baseball maverick. For more than 30 years I have refused to accept the rationale spouted by a long-standing faction in Major League Baseball who say, "The game is fine the way it is. There's no need to change it."

Whenever I hear about the quantitative gains baseball has made over the past 30 years—more teams, more postseason games, more fans in the seats, great appreciation in the value of baseball franchises, bigger television contracts, more million- and two-million-dollar player salaries—I retort, "But has the quality of the game improved? Is the product as good as it can be?"

The answer is, no. Today we have fewer .300 hitters, fewer 20-game winners, fewer players who execute fundamental plays consistently. Why? More often than not, our methods of player instruction are antiquated and impersonal, and our front offices are so focused on marketing, promotions, and external sources of revenues that the training and development of our players are taken for granted.

Some 50 years ago Branch Rickey, a baseball executive with the St. Louis Cardinals and Brooklyn Dodgers, blazed a trail that has yet to be duplicated. Rickey dared to fail where other general managers were afraid to try. He may be best remembered for breaking baseball's color barrier by bringing Jackie Robinson to the major leagues, but Rickey was also a great teacher who believed that well-trained players and scouts were the keys to building perennial contenders.

During his years with the Cardinals, Rickey introduced a minor league farm system so more players could be signed, trained, and developed instead of being bought from independent operators. And Rickey devised such teaching aids as sliding pits for base runners and car tires suspended by rope for pitchers to throw pitches through.

Rickey's farm teams produced so many good young players that he could make trades from a position of strength. To those who accused Rickey of being lucky to have so many prospects, Rickey would counter, "Luck is the residue of design."

Since that time, the truly great teams that contend year after year have won championships because of an abundant supply of well-trained talent in their farm systems. However, far too many baseball franchises have done little to improve the quality of their scouting and player training.

In the past two decades some franchises have even cut back on their number of scouts and minor league teams, arguing that those systems cost too much and yield too little. So how do those teams become competitive? By signing high-priced free agents to multimillion-dollar contracts. You tell me, is that saving money? I see free-agent signings as a declaration of failure; the organization has failed to develop its own players and must throw its player payroll out of whack to make amends.

And now there are a few owners who in the last three years have overreacted to their weakness in player development. They have decided to take away their general manager's authority in this area and hand it to their directors of player development, leaving the general managers to deal only with the major league team. This course of action destroys continuity, and continuity is among the most important aspects in training and developing players. See, your program of training and development should come from the top of the organization, not the bottom. After all, the general manager bears the ultimate responsibility for the success of the organization. Can you imagine a company in any business having sales offices where each branch used different sales and marketing techniques? What if every McDonald's franchise owner decided to use a different recipe for his hamburgers?

Without consistency and uniformity in its scouting staff and farm system, a franchise winds up with a collection of one-dimensional players no other team wants, because players who are willing and able to learn a broad variety of skills don't get the training they need to develop beyond what they know naturally. That's when baseball, a game of speed, power, and grace, a battle between time and space, becomes boring.

I've always followed a simple philosophy: If something can be seen it should be measured, and once it is measured you can then improve upon it. With the superior technologies available today, we can make more precise measurements and evaluations and employ better teaching aids than before. The war of capitalism is won with advanced technologies.

Just look how some countries in recent years have used new technologies to make impressive strides in Olympic sports. You may have read Frank Deford's article, "Sports in China: The Birth of an Athletic Power," in the August 15, 1988, issue of *Sports Illustrated* about the gains of the Chinese in swimming, crew, tennis, gymnastics, and women's basketball. You will certainly remember how the U.S. Olympic basketball team was defeated by the Soviet Union's squad in the 1988 Summer Games in Seoul. The common thread is improved technique, which comes from better teaching, better training, and the incorporation of advanced technologies.

Many coaches in college baseball have been employing new and better training methods over the last 15 years. But in pro baseball I still encounter "baseball people"—managers, general managers, and coaches who've been in the game for 30 years and are using the same techniques they learned 30 years ago—who seem threatened by the doctors, scientists, psychologists, and physiologists I invite into every organization I work for. I can't tell you how many times I've heard coaches make the comment, "Babe Ruth didn't need these techniques." Those people remind me of the 30-year history teacher who taught the same history lesson 30 times.

Being an advocate for excellence in a closed-minded community is a daily battle. I have been characterized at different times by different people as a visionary, a compassionate person, a motivator, a mad scientist, an overprotective paternalist, and a stubborn mule. I see myself as an inquisitive, unconventional, adventure-seeking soul on a quest for answers.

I was born on February 25, 1929, in Locust Hill, Virginia, the first of Lucy and Sydnor Thrift's three children. The name Thrift is Scottish. My grandmother's maiden name was Maclachlan, so I tell people I'm a cross between a lowland and a highland Scot.

My mother, a schoolteacher before her marriage, is a sincere and passionate woman. She never met a stranger. I've never seen anyone with more friends in a variety of age groups than she has. And she has a remarkably positive outlook on life. Everything she sees and every person she meets is the greatest.

My father, who owned a general-merchandise store next to our home, was a man of few words, a demanding disciplinarian who believed in personal integrity. He always told us, "Be honest, and pay all your debts." He detested the bigotry in the segregated South and would not tolerate anyone who made racial slurs. During my school years my father's health deteriorated because of diabetes. If you've ever lived with a diabetic, you've probably learned more about this disease than many physicians. Diabetes initially attacks the smallest veins—in the fingertips, toes, and eyes. In time it weakens the secretory systems. The person suffers mood swings, depending on his blood-sugar content. He is forced to pay strict attention to every single morsel of food he eats. I developed a great empathy for my father and others who live and cope with debilitating diseases.

Even though there were no kindergarten classes in this rural area, my opportunities for education abounded. My mother taught me how to read, write, and do arithmetic when I was four. When I entered the first grade, my teachers discovered I was already ahead of the rest of the class, so they had me meet with the school's guidance counselor. The guidance counselor gave me books to read and asked me to explain to him what I read. Five days later I was promoted to the second grade.

During my free time I'd visit my father's store, which was like a town hall of sorts. His customers would congregate around a potbellied stove and discuss the political scene, religious issues, and events of the day.

Ever since I can remember, my favorite question has always been "Why?" Whether it was my mother teaching me something or a neighbor making a statement during a discussion at my father's store, I'd ask, "Why is that? Why can't it be another way?" Once it was explained, I'd ask, "Can you prove it to me?" These are electrifying questions; they make people think. They're also provocative, challenging questions. I know I used to drive my mother crazy peppering her with question after question.

One person who never tired of my questions was a high school principal named J. H. St. Claire Walker. Professor Walker, a black gentleman who had served as a lieutenant in the Spanish-American War, was a great educator and became one of my best friends. My parents had hired Professor Walker to tutor my sisters, Lucy and Louise, and me. He was fluent in every subject you can name, from English to physics to the arts to history, and he imparted his knowledge simply and concisely. As a tribute to Professor Walker's skills as an educator, a local high school was later named in his honor.

When he wasn't tutoring us or some of the other children in the neighborhood, Professor Walker would sit in front of my father's store and read one book after another. If I came by the store carrying a book in my hand, he would ask to read it, and then we would discuss its meaning. To further my education, he loaned me many of his books. In return, I gave him my copies of *The Sporting News*, because he was an avid baseball fan who committed every player's statistics to memory.

I became a baseball fan in 1936. That year my father took me to a doubleheader between the New York Yankees and Washington Senators. The Senators were a pretty good team, winning 82 games that year and finishing fourth. They were led on offense by left-handed power-hitting first baseman Joe Kuhel, shortstop/outfielder Cecil Travis, and outfielder Ben Chapman, who'd been acquired from the Yankees in June. On the mound, the Senators had right-handers Pete Appleton, who was third in the league in ERA, Bobo Newsom, and Jimmie DeShong.

The Yankees, who went on to win the World Series that year, were in a class by themselves. They had Lou Gehrig, the league's Most Valuable Player; Tony Lazzeri; Bill Dickey; and Red Ruffing. And they were joined by a 22-year-old rookie named Joe DiMaggio.

I was so captivated by the great players I saw that I wanted to become a baseball player myself. I pitched and played first base on the neighborhood teams, and I supplemented my knowledge of the game by reading about it, by listening to Arch McDonald re-create the Senators games on radio—every time the Senators hit a home run McDonald would ring a gong, and I'd holler, "Bong . . . bong . . . bong . . . bong"—and by going with Professor Walker to games. During those five-hour round-trip car rides to Washington, Professor Walker and I would discuss the strengths and weaknesses of every player and the intricacies of the game.

I will never forget the hateful looks Professor Walker and I got from others who saw this black gentleman and this white boy driving together and sitting together, talking and laughing in public, with no regard for the difference in the color of their skins. I realized how pointless, how backward bigotry was, because I could not understand how anyone could find fault with a man of Professor Walker's talents, accomplishments, and character. I developed a prejudice against narrow-minded people that I carry to this day.

By the time I reached seventh grade I had grown to six feet in height, which caught the attention of my school's principal. One day he pulled me out of class and told me to report to the varsity baseball team. Our team didn't have a full-time coach, so a Methodist minister named Steve Cowan, who had been a fine semipro baseball player, volunteered to work with us. Reverend Cowan taught me how to throw a change-up as a complement to my fastball and curveball. Knowing how to change speeds helped me win every game I pitched in my high school career.

One of Reverend Cowan's sermons convinced me to pursue a career in baseball. He preached a sermon on the parable of the talents, which made an everlasting impression on me. The message was that the Creator gives each of us special talents and gifts, and it is up to us to use them to the best of our abilities. I believed my gifts were in baseball.

I entered Randolph-Macon College in Ashland, Virginia, at age 16. In my freshman baseball season I made the all-state first team as a left-handed pitcher. The all-state right-handed pitcher was the University of Richmond's Lew Burdette, who would later win 203 games in 18 major league seasons.

My college coach, Taylor Sanford, also played professional baseball at the time. When our games ended, he would drive to Richmond and play for the Richmond Colts. Sanford knew how to hit. In my freshman year he batted .340 in the Piedmont (Class B) League. Because he was a pro, he grounded us in the fundamentals of the game, which gave our practice sessions a professional flavor. I became so engrossed in baseball that I stopped going to my regular classes. Deep down, I knew that wasn't the brightest thing to do. I used to dream that I came into the classroom, and suddenly the teacher was handing out a test; I hadn't studied, so I couldn't come up with a single answer. I would awaken in a cold sweat. The only thing that got me through my classes was my ability to remember information in detail after a single reading.

After my graduation Sanford took me to Norfolk, where one of the Yankees' farm clubs played, for a tryout before some of the organization's scouts. Following Norfolk's doubleheader, the scouts asked catcher Gus Triandos to stick around and catch me. He was real angry about it, since he'd caught both games of the doubleheader. As if I wasn't nervous enough, now I was pitching to a hostile professional catcher. Thankfully, I showed enough to be offered a contract for the Yankees' farm team in La Grange, Georgia. The funny thing was that even though I was a college graduate,

I couldn't sign the contract until I got my father's permission, because I was only 20 years old, still a minor.

The following winter the Yankees invited me to Phoenix, Arizona, where they were holding their first instructional school, to my knowledge the first such program ever held in baseball. Yankees manager Casey Stengel was on hand to supervise the program. Since I was a first baseman/pitcher, Johnny Neun tutored me on my fielding and Jim Turner worked with me on my pitching. All the young Yankee stars of the future were there, like Mickey Mantle and Hank Bauer. My roommates were Jackie Jensen and Billy Martin. I was so awestruck that I really don't remember how well I played or how much I learned.

The next season the Yankees assigned me to their farm team in Amsterdam, New York. I started off with a bang, but then I pulled a muscle in my back fielding a ground ball one rainy night and was put on the disabled list. I *hated* being on the disabled list; sitting around doing nothing made me crazy. I got so ticked off that I left the team in August and went back home. The Yankees decided to release me from their organization.

A month later I joined the baseball coaching staff and also taught American literature at Middlesex County High School in Virginia. After I completed two years of military service, I taught U.S. government and history at Mount Vernon High School in Alexandria, Virginia. I really enjoyed the interaction with the students and learned a lot from them. They helped me realize that, no matter how old or how young you are, there's always going to be someone out there who knows something you don't.

I'd enlisted in the Army in January 1951 and was stationed in Fort Eustis, Virginia. For two years I earned $80 a month as the player-manager for our company's baseball team, the Fort Eustis Wheels. Vernon "Deacon" Law, a talented 21-year-old pitcher with the Pittsburgh Pirates, and Joe Lonnett, a catcher with the Philadelphia Phillies organization who later became an outstanding major league coach, were also on our team. When the one and only Willie Mays of the New York Giants joined us, everyone stopped calling us "the Wheels" and simply referred to us as "Willie Mays's team."

In 1953 I signed with the Oakland Oaks, a Triple A team. But in spring training I hurt my arm and couldn't throw without excruciating pain. Though the doctors couldn't diagnose my injury, I now suspect that I damaged my rotator cuff. In those days, teams didn't have injury rehabilitation programs. Either you could play or you couldn't. I couldn't, so the Oaks released me. Later that year I attempted a comeback with a Class B club in West Palm Beach, Florida, and then a Class D team in Leesburg, but it was no use. Surgery was not an option back then, because if a doctor did operate on your arm there was little chance you'd play again anyway. So at age 24 I found myself looking for a new career.

Scouting seemed like a natural progression, since I'd spent so much time studying baseball's fundamentals during my playing career. I continued to teach and coach at Mount Vernon High, but also did some part-time scouting for the Yankees. Of the players I scouted that summer, the one I liked best was a catcher named Bob Uecker. He didn't hit much, but he was good defensively and had a strong throwing arm. Uecker decided to sign with the Milwaukee Braves, his hometown team, and went on to fame and fortune, though not for the skills I'd spotted.

In 1956 Rex Bowen, a scouting supervisor for the Pittsburgh Pirates who covered the mid-Atlantic area, hired me as a part-time, special-assignment scout. Bowen, now retired and living in Florida, is a bright, strong-willed man who earned two college degrees. Bowen had the greatest influence on my ability to scout and evaluate players. He was a truly great scout, a master at evaluating players, organizing tryout camps, and managing his territories. Before joining the Pirates, Bowen had worked for the Dodgers and became a disciple of Branch Rickey, and he passed all of his knowledge to me.

The first player I signed for the Pirates was Donn Clendenon, a 6-4, 200-pound first baseman. Clendenon was one of some 80 players recommended by the organization's scouts and brought together in a tryout camp. We set up four teams of 20 players on a side; Clendenon was one of the players on my team.

Clendenon struck out a lot, but he could run like a deer. We timed him at 6.5 in the 60-yard dash. In a scouting meeting that night I recommended we sign him to a contract. Because Clendenon had been on my team, Bowen allowed me to sign him. Clendenon became a successful major leaguer with the Pirates and won the Most Valuable Player award in the 1969 World Series for the New York Mets.

In 1957 I became a scouting supervisor, and in subsequent years I scouted and signed such players as outfielder Al Oliver, pitcher Woodie Fryman, first baseman Bob Robertson, and third baseman Don Money. Oliver and Robertson would later help the Pirates win two World Series and six division titles during the seventies.

Before the 1960 season began I needed to see my lawyer to go over some legal matters for my father. While I was waiting in his office, I struck up a conversation with his legal secretary, a shy young girl named Dolly Wilson. Talk about love at first sight! During our very first conversation we both thought to ourselves, This is the person I'm going to marry. I made the lawyer's office a regular stop on my weekly rounds, and in November 1961 we were married.

Throughout our marriage Dolly has been extraordinarily supportive, even in our lean times, when my baseball salary barely covered our bills. She has great intelligence, warmth, and concern for the welfare of others. She is a wonderful mother to our children and a meticulous homemaker. It takes a special person to keep a marriage growing when her spouse is away from home 200 nights a year, but she has done just that.

Our first son, Jim, was born in 1962, and our second son, Mark, was born in 1965. What happened to Mark changed our lives in more ways than we can count.

As an infant Mark was a beautiful child, with smooth, unblemished skin and a beautiful expression. But as the months went by we realized something was wrong with him. For one thing, he had trouble keeping his food down. Also, his body just wasn't pliable. I kept saying to Dolly, "The difference between Mark and Jim is that Mark is so stiff, so rigid."

We saw doctor after doctor and were given one diagnosis after another. When Mark was 17 months old we took him to the Children's Hospital in Washington for an examination. Doctors there tested Mark and researched his brief medical history thoroughly. They discovered Mark had suffered severe brain damage at birth because his umbilical cord had wrapped around his neck five times and cut off the supply of oxygen to his brain. To compound the problem, Mark had a hiatal hernia, which prevented him from swallowing his food and caused malnutrition. Our obstetrician had never told us about these very significant facts.

While deciding what to do next, I recalled studying in college a technique called "patterning," used on brain-damaged people by the Institutes for the Achievement of Human Potential in Media, Pennsylvania. In their research, the institutes' director, Glenn Doman; his brother, Dr. Robert Doman; and Drs. Carl Delacato and Temple Fay had discovered that every person must go through the initial stages of life—moving their arms and legs, crawling, creeping, and walking—for proper physical and mental development.

Creeping, which entails lifting the body off the floor and moving forward one arm and one leg at a time, requires more coordination than crawling, in which the hands and knees drag the body along the floor. Only creatures with midbrains can creep.

Dr. Fay had used the term "cross pattern" in his studies of the movements of lizards and alligators, two creatures with midbrains. Those creatures do not need to reason their movements; they do them instinctively. From this Dr. Fay wondered, if a child with an injured midbrain could not use his arms and legs to creep, could he learn to do so if others moved his arms and legs for him, in the exact pattern the midbrain was designed for? Could these inherited instincts be awakened by external means?

They tried this test, using three adults to administer it in smooth, rhythmic movements. One adult turned the child's head, while the adult on the side where his head was turned extended his arm and flexed his leg. When the child's head was turned, the adult on the other side did the same thing. With consistent, rigid repetition in the same time pattern each day, the child learned to creep. Once creeping began, if the child's cortex was well, walking would follow. They later developed successful procedures to pattern other areas of the brain.

We went to the institutes and met with Dr. Eugene Spitz, an eminent physician who had invented the V-shunt tube, which is now routinely implanted by surgeons in children to drain excess brain fluid. He examined Mark and helped us set up a program of physiotherapy.

Each day a rotation of three volunteers per hour came to our home in Richmond for 12 hours a day, starting at 7 A.M. Together with Dolly, they would train Mark at precisely the same minute each day to learn the basic skills he needed for his development.

The routines were simple, but required many hours of patient, persistent repetition. Mark would be put into a crawl box, an eight-foot-long, one-foot-high plywood box. The box's floor was carpeted to prevent his hands and knees from bruising. A weave of ropes at the top of the crawl box prevented Mark from standing up. The volunteers would help Mark move his muscles to crawl to the other side, where Dolly was waiting with a treat of some kind.

In other drills Mark would chew peanut butter to train his tongue movements; blow out a candle to coordinate the movement of his lips; pick up pennies from the floor or turn pages of a magazine using his thumb and forefinger to develop his motor skills; follow a light shined in his eyes to improve his visual acuity; take saltwater baths, during which Dolly would vigorously rub the salt water into his skin to increase his sensitivity to hot and cold, a tactile sensitivity brain-damaged people do not usually have.

And every drill was conducted in a particular order to keep him from developing too quickly. To keep Mark from standing up and walking before he finished learning to crawl and then creep, Dolly put furniture coasters with hard plastic teeth in his shoes. We did not allow Mark to listen to music or watch TV until he could speak, since brain-damaged people tend to sing before they speak.

Mark has since learned to function to his fullest capabilities. He lived in our home for nine years and is now in the Northern Virginia Training Center, where he receives the kind of specialized care and constant attention Dolly and I could not give him. He walks properly, dresses himself, and feeds himself, and is responsible enough to leave his dormitory room without supervision. He received an education equivalency degree from the center, which is affiliated with the Fairfax County public school system. As part of his training, Mark has a job at a recycling plant that is part of the institute's complex. Mark's job is to take the aluminum cans that have been crushed and put them in bags.

Every day that Dolly, Jim, and I see him we are thankful for the talents and gifts we have. Before I was married I gave pep talks to players and students about talent, commitment, and excellence. Those qualities became even more important to me and my family because of Mark.

"There are things in life we think are so terrible," says Dolly. "We wonder why they happened to us. We are not happy that Mark was born this way, but we are so grateful for what we have learned from him. Someone once said, 'It's not so bad to die. What is worse is not to live.' You look at life and tell yourself, This is wonderful. Every day brings a new adventure.

"And because of Mark's situation we found the Lord sooner than we would have if we'd had two normal children. I think that's the greatest thing that came out of this for us."

During Mark's years of training, I read extensively and spoke with scores of medical people about a person's ability to learn. Watching Mark's development, I became more aware of the importance of body control and balance in a gifted athlete, who is on the other end of the spectrum.

Also, Mark's patterning program emphasized to me the importance of precise repetition in learning and teaching athletes. Players don't spend enough time practicing their bunting, fielding, and baserunning to achieve perfection. Too often, practice is imperfect; players go through the motions blithely.

But even the most diligent practice has no value if the training methods do not serve as pathways to the brain. What is the single factor that allows a hitter, a pitcher, a runner, or a fielder to be successful? You hear people talk about the hands or the life in his pitches or his first running step or his footwork. The answer is the brain. Every single performance skill is controlled by the brain, the part of our bodies doctors know the least about.

The concept of training the brain was the key to the Kansas City Royals Baseball Academy, the most stimulating baseball environment I have ever been a part of. During my three years as the Academy's founding director, I felt like I was on a planet apart from the other planet called "Baseball," and we were pulling ahead.

The idea for the Academy, which opened in Bradenton, Florida, in August 1970, came from Royals owner Ewing Kauffman, a dynamic man of creative genius who loved to tackle problems. Kauffman, a pharmaceutical salesman who built Marion Laboratories into a multimillion-dollar firm, had purchased the Royals, an expansion franchise, in 1968. What he got in return for his $5.25 million investment were 30 players the other major league teams didn't want. That limited his trading ability. He also felt restricted by the other avenues of acquiring players—the June amateur draft, the December draft of unprotected minor leaguers, and the signing of free agents; those would take a lot of time and money and luck.

The short-term goal of the Academy was to increase the supply of talent to the Royals' organization by finding unsigned athletes—even those who hadn't played baseball before—and molding them into successful baseball players through extensive training and instruction. Kauffman also wanted these players to develop as people, so he paid for college classes they took weekday mornings at nearby Manatee Junior College.

Each year we worked with 40 athletes over a 16-month period. To find those athletes, we conducted tryout camps throughout the United States each summer between mid-June and late July, and over the three years evaluated more than 23,000 high school graduates. Two men superbly coordinated and promoted all our tryout camps: Sam Ketchman, the retired athletic director of Ferris State College in Ohio; and the late Harold "Spike" Claasen, formerly the sports editor of the Associated Press, who'd trained such sportswriting legends as Joseph Reichler and Milton Richman.

Our most famous Academy graduate, Frank White, who

went on to become a seven-time All-Star second baseman with the Royals, had played only basketball and football at Lincoln High School in Kansas City, because Lincoln had no baseball team; he was, however, a reserve outfielder on teams in the Connie Mack, Ban Johnson, and Casey Stengel leagues. White's background was almost conventional compared to the others in our first-year class: a former New Mexico high school wrestling champion, a two-time Missouri high school sprint champion, a pole vaulter from Wichita State, a young man who played no high school baseball at all but excelled in bowling and weight lifting, and a quarterback from Topeka, Kansas, who set his school's record in the javelin throw.

Before we conducted the first tryout camp, Ray Reilly, a clinical psychologist whom Kauffman brought in, helped us establish the norms we would be looking for in identifying the physical and mental skills needed to play baseball. We did this by testing some 150 players in the Royals organization, recording their vision, psychomotor responses, and psychological makeup.

The key to measuring general athletic ability, we discovered, is running speed. Raw speed is the best indicator of muscle twitch—how quickly the muscles react to the acetylcholine that comes through the muscle fibers. Fast-twitch fibers produce the quick reactions needed in baseball. (Slow-twitch fibers are more important for endurance runners.)

Speed is also the one physical tool used on offense and defense, even more so in recent years because of the number of fast artificial playing surfaces used in baseball. To survive defensively on an artificial surface, you need quick players who have good lateral movement at your key infield positions—second base and shortstop—and in the outfield. Otherwise, too many balls will skip by.

In order to be a fast runner you need good body control and coordination, which are essential in batting and fielding. To be a good hitter, the movements of your feet, mid-section, and hands should be in balance. In the field, body control and coordination allow an infielder to charge a ball at top speed, pick it up at his shoe tops, and throw without losing his balance. A well-coordinated outfielder can make a shoestring catch without falling down, which prevents runners from tagging up and taking an extra base.

The second most important requirement in measuring a baseball player is his throwing arm. Obviously, arm strength is necessary for pitchers. But consider how players who possess strong, accurate throwing arms and good running speed affect the other team.

Say the opponent has a runner on second base. The batter hits a single up the middle. Pirates center fielder Andy Van Slyke, blessed with a powerful arm and good speed, charges the ball and reaches it quickly, without losing his balance. The opponent's third-base coach stops the base runner at third, since he knows how strong and accurate Van Slyke's throws are.

Van Slyke's ability to stop the runner from attempting to score—without his making a throw to home plate—is worth a great deal. Van Slyke is human; who's to say his throw home would have been on line? But if he had only a marginal arm, the third-base coach would have made him throw by sending the base runner.

When I think of infielders who combine speed, quickness, and arm strength, Frank White immediately comes to mind. White gets to more balls than a second baseman of marginal speed and quickness, and his arm is so strong that he has thrown out runners at first after ranging to the shortstop side of second base to field the ball.

Of course, there are players in the major leagues who are not fast or do not have strong arms. They compensate by having extraordinary skills in other areas. But for our purpose at the Academy we determined that candidates had to have at least an average major league arm and run 60 yards in 7.1 seconds—the major league average—or less.

The Academy's 121-acre campus afforded us a baseball laboratory. We had five baseball diamonds built to the exact measurements of the Royals' major league stadium, a weight-training room (we were the first in baseball to employ weight-training and conditioning programs), a vision-training lab, and motel-style dormitories. We also had the latest technology, such as videotape equipment, radar guns, closed-circuit televisions in our lecture halls, and nine pitching machines.

My staff was composed of topflight instructors from varying backgrounds who were always available to the players for personalized instruction. The staff included former major league managers Johnny Neun and Jim Lemon; Chuck Stobbs, who had pitched for 15 years in the majors; Joe Tanner, a stockbroker who had played nine seasons— all at Triple A—for the Boston Red Sox; Steve Korcheck, who'd been a catcher for the Senators, a baseball coach at George Washington University and is now the president of Manatee Junior College in Florida; Bill Easton, the track coach at the University of Kansas; and Wes Santee, a former U.S. Olympian known during the fifties as America's greatest miler.

Our team's manager was Carlton "Buzzy" Keller, who had been coaching on the college level in Texas. Our trainer was Mickey Cobb, who had majored in athletic training at Georgia Southern and had received a master's degree in health and safety from Indiana University. Cobb, who in 1978 became the trainer of the Royals' major league team, helped institute training, stretching, and rehabilitation methods that at the time hadn't been used in baseball.

Others from the Royals organization participated in our program whenever they could, including Jack McKeon, who managed the Royals and currently is the field manager and

vice president of baseball operations for the San Diego
Padres; Galen Cisco, a longtime major league pitching
coach; and Dodgers assistant field coordinator of minor
league operations Steve Boros, who managed the Royals'
Waterloo (Double A) team from 1970 to 1972 and has since
managed the Padres and Oakland A's. Incidentally, one of
the batting-practice pitchers I hired was Dick Balderson,
who later became the general manager of the Seattle Mariners and is now the director of scouting for the Chicago
Cubs.

We also invited an array of scientists, psychologists, physiologists, vision experts, photographers, and inventors
whose theories and inventions we tested and, if they were
proven worthwhile, implemented. One of our guests was Dr.
William Harrison, an optometrist who played college baseball at California-Berkeley. His fascination with the visual
prowess of Hall of Famer Ted Williams in seeing and tracking a baseball prompted him to study a science that has
come to be known as "visualization"—creating and con-
centrating on detailed, purposeful mental images of a physical act before doing it.

Dr. Harrison also submitted each of our students to thorough, 90-minute vision tests and hand-eye coordination
tests, and worked with them on drills to improve their sensory responses.

While the students were in their college classes, our staff
met for two- to three-hour think-tank sessions. As Steve
Boros recalls, "We'd have a discussion, almost a free association, about things to look for in a ballplayer, ways to
develop their skills, ways to improve their eyesight, their
concentration, their arm strength, their ability to steal
bases—you name it."

We came away with a host of discoveries that are still
being used in baseball today. Among these techniques,
which I will discuss later in my "baseball tutorial," are the

two-strike hitting approach, the 45-degree-angle bunting method, and the timed, measured baserunning lead. Our time-motion studies showed a three- to four-mile-per-hour difference in the velocity of a fastball thrown with the "four-seam" grip, held across the widest spread between the seams, and the conventional "two-seam" grip, held along the stitched seams. This meant that a pitcher could increase the speed of his fastball simply by changing the way he holds it. We found ways to improve players' reflexes, fielding range, and running speed, debunking old baseball "wisdom" along the way.

Along with the aforementioned topics, there were many other baseball "firsts" spawned at the Academy. Under the direction of Mickey Cobb, we were the first to implement a stretching program for every player. Cobb also incorporated into his rehabilitation program exercises done in a swimming pool. "Until that time," says Cobb, "it was felt that players shouldn't work out in a pool, because swimming took too much out of them. But water provides resistance without putting weight on the injured area. If an injured player needed to run, for instance, we had him run in waist-deep water. If he needed to strengthen his shoulder, we had exercises done in the water for that, too."

Cobb also teamed with the late G. V. Bourette, who had developed an innovative resistance training method, a scheme of resistance using rubber bands that is now used nationwide by orthopedists and physical therapists. Bourette, a retired physical education teacher and Big Eight college football referee from Kansas City, had been invited to the Academy by a former pupil—Ewing Kauffman.

Bourette, Cobb explains, "had the idea of cutting the inner tubes of truck tires into sections and linking them together in a chainlike fashion. Players with sore arms, legs, feet, even fingers, would stretch and pull on the tubes.

"I'd had thoughts about resistance training before coming

to the Academy. I had seen some tubing while I was in graduate school at Indiana University. But the tubing didn't hold up as well as Bourette's chain of rubber."

Bourette designed rubber chains for specific physical activities. "We felt a pitcher should be conditioned in throwing a baseball," Cobb says. "So Bourette would make a chain and tape a baseball to the tubing. The pitcher would then go through his motion in front of a mirror using proper technique.

"For hitters, he would tape one end of a heavier piece of tubing to a bat, the other end to a pole, and have the hitter go through swings, which strengthened his swing and built up his wrists."

Looking through my notes from the Academy, I see that in 1970 and 1971 our staff had a series of discussions about alcohol and drug abuse problems of the future and what we could do to cope with them. We had officials from governmental drug enforcement agencies give lectures to our students about those forthcoming problems. This was two decades ago! You think we were ahead of our time?

Unfortunately, some members of the Royals front office did not share our enthusiasm for the Academy. When I decided the Academy should field a team in the Rookie League, they thought we were wildly optimistic. They said we would embarrass ourselves and the entire Royals organization. But we went ahead and proved them wrong. Our team, known as the Royals Academy, played 200 games a season and posted excellent records each year. In our first season we went 96-13 (a winning percentage of .756) in exhibitions against college and junior college teams from across the nation; 10-4 in a 17-day Latin American tour against all-star teams from Costa Rica, Panama, Nicaragua, and Colombia; and as the Royals' Single-A team in the Gulf Coast League, 40-13, winning the league title by the largest margin in its history while setting a team stolen-base mark and never being shut out. In succeeding years we defeated the team that represented the U.S. in the 1971 Pan American Games, won a Citrus League pennant, and took a share of the 1972 Gulf Coast League crown.

The better the Academy team played, the more the Academy became a source of friction among the Royals brass. It was as if we were in competition with the team's player-development system, instead of being a complement. As a result, only 14 Academy graduates were signed to pro contracts. I became so frustrated by this that I resigned from my position at the Academy in 1972, and a year later Ewing Kauffman closed the program altogether.

"My own people running the Royals didn't approve of the Academy," Kauffman recalls. "They thought they could spend the money more wisely on the minor leagues and the scouting systems. So I said to them, 'Okay, you go ahead and run the Royals and I'll run the Baseball Academy.' I gave them the money in 1970 to hire 22 scouts, but I spent additional money for the Academy.

"Of all the people in baseball, only Bob Howsam of the Cincinnati Reds thought the Academy was a good idea. He offered to share expenses and share results. Of course, I wanted all the results to myself and I turned him down, which probably was a mistake.

"At the time I owned the Royals myself. We were playing in an old stadium. During the third year of the Academy, the Royals and the Academy lost something like $3.4 million. I had to cough that up to keep the team going. The Academy was costing me $600,000 a year, so I thought I'd better cut it back.

"Although our team in Kansas City has done very well since then, if I'd known then what I know now, I would have kept the Academy and we would have created a dynasty."

Yet the Academy lives on through the fertile minds who continue to have an impact on the game. When Steve Boros, who helped develop the timed, measured lead, managed the Royals' Class A San Jose team in 1974, his club stole 372 bases, a minor league record in modern-era baseball. During his years as a coach with the Montreal Expos, Boros developed some of the best base stealers in the game, like Tim Raines. And in his current capacity with the Dodgers, Boros says, "A day doesn't go by where I don't use the things I learned at the Academy. It's the foundation for the way I evaluate a player."

Buzzy Keller brought his base-stealing expertise to the St. Louis Cardinals organization as a minor league manager in Johnson City from 1976 to '78, and later joined me as director of the Pirates' player development.

Bill Harrison's services have been solicited by teams in many different sports. Over the years he has helped such baseball players as George Brett and Lou Piniella, and set up a team program for the Pirates from 1986 to 1988.

One of our students at the Academy, a left-handed pitcher named Hal Baird, has been the head baseball coach at Auburn University for the last six years. Baird, whose studies in player conditioning have made him an innovator in his own right, teaches his players all the things he learned at the Academy. Baird taught the four-seam fastball to right-hander Gregg Olson, who has since become a top relief pitcher with the Baltimore Orioles. Baird also has his players use the visualization techniques Dr. Harrison pioneered.

When I went to work as the minor league director and special assistant to Charles O. Finley in Oakland between 1975 and '76, I was able to use some of the Academy's practices in a modified form (severe budgetary constrictions limited the operation of the entire franchise). One manager who was exposed to our base-stealing principles was Milwaukee Brewers manager Tom Trebelhorn, who in 1976 managed the A's Boise club in the Northwest League; one of his players there was Rickey Henderson. Since 1987, Trebelhorn's first full season as the Brewers' manager, his teams have led the American League in stolen bases each year.

I didn't stay with Oakland for long, because the climate

in baseball had swung toward signing free agents and away from player procurement and development. I knew baseball was headed down the wrong path, and I also realized the owners had no idea how high and how quickly salaries would escalate once they played the free-agent market.

Those owners who couldn't afford free agents were forced to sell their teams. Just look at what happened to Finley. The players his organization had drafted and developed during the late sixties—players like Reggie Jackson, Rick Monday, Catfish Hunter, and Vida Blue—led the team to five playoff appearances and three World Series victories between 1971 and 1975. When I came to the A's, Finley still had some good prospects in his minor league system, like pitchers Mike Norris, Steve McCatty, and Brian Kingman, and outfielders Dwayne Murphy and Denny Walling. During my tenure with the A's I helped procure Rickey Henderson, who had gone unnoticed by the Major League Scouting Bureau. One of our scouts, Jim Guinn, who saw Henderson play in high school, tried him out two days before the amateur draft and immediately called me. After I saw Henderson's explosive speed and superior all-around athletic ability, I selected him in the fourth round of the June 1976 Free Agent Draft.

But because of free agency I watched Finley lose his best players with nothing to show in return. Being a great proponent of player development, I felt like General George Patton must have when the Army decided to cut off his supplies while his troops were sweeping through France. So at age 47 I walked away from professional baseball and embarked on a career in real estate.

I had already obtained a license to sell real estate during the sixties and had worked at it during the off-seasons. In real estate, as in scouting, you have to manage your territories efficiently and always be on the lookout for new and exciting properties. And you spend your days working for owners who have specific goals. Since Dolly also had a broker's license, we opened a real estate firm together. By 1985 Syd Thrift and Associates had 30 agents selling and managing many properties.

One of the nicer aspects of this venture was that I was able to spend time with my son Jim. Until then I had spent most of my life with other people's sons. I hardly knew Jim; Dolly had served in my frequent absences as both mother and father. Now I could put my family ahead of baseball.

Baseball was a big part of Jim's life. I followed his career closely as he rose from Little League to Babe Ruth League to high school to the college ranks. I worked with him in any way I could to help him become a better player. I came to realize that he was helping *me* even more.

Because of Jim, I became totally involved with baseball on the amateur level. Jim's teammates became an extension of my family. His coaches welcomed me to work with them in practice sessions, because they knew I was interested in the development of every player on the field, not just Jim.

I was in a pure baseball environment, free of blemishes, helping players in their baseball infancy who were thirsty for knowledge. It's always exciting to go back to the beginning of something. I felt like the Pied Piper. Everywhere I went on the field, the players followed me. I would hit ground balls and fly balls to them for hours. This was great therapy for me.

During Jim's playing career at the University of North Carolina, I got to see many excellent players in the Atlantic Coast Conference who have graduated to the major leagues, including catcher B. J. Surhoff of the Milwaukee Brewers, shortstop Walt Weiss of the Oakland Athletics, and pitchers Scott Bankhead of the Seattle Mariners, Dan Plesac of the Brewers, and Jimmy Key of the Toronto Blue Jays. I reacquainted myself with the scouting directors and farm directors who came to see the games. And I found the level of teaching in college baseball refreshing and progressive, ahead of the pro game in many ways.

I was also involved in baseball on the amateur level. I conducted baseball clinics in the U.S. and in Sweden, Denmark, and Finland as a member of the commissioner's office and the U.S. Baseball Federation. Coincidentally, one of the American players on the tour was an outfielder named Bobby Bonilla. I was convinced that Bonilla had the physical skills to play pro baseball, so I called the Pirates and recommended they sign him.

During the 1985 World Series, shortly after we moved our company into a new, larger office space, I got a call from Joe Brown. Brown, the Pirates' general manager from 1956 to 1976, had come out of retirement and taken over the general manager's job temporarily after the team dismissed Harding Peterson. He asked me to recommend a candidate. "What type of person are you looking for?" I asked. He turned the question around: "If you were me, what type of person would you be looking for?"

I told him, "It's very simple to me. First, I'd look for the most knowledgeable person in the world in the areas of player procurement and development. That's what it's all about. Your team has tried to sign and trade for high-salaried stars. What happened? You finished dead last and lost millions of dollars.

"Second, you need a crusader, a missionary, because the team's play and the recent drug problems have given your team a really bad image. You need a strong leader to set a new course, revive the fans' interest, and plant a winning spirit."

I wasn't talking about myself. That was the farthest thing from my mind. Over those years I'd had a few itches to return to pro baseball, but I didn't believe I could fit into a traditional setting. I figured the teams that could really use me didn't realize it, and the teams that couldn't use me were the ones that thought highly of me. Besides, I was more than happy to stay in real estate and continue my involvement in amateur baseball.

Brown loved my answers and asked me if I was interested in the job. Dolly was in my office listening to the conversation on our speakerphone. She jumped up and mouthed the words, "Say yes!" I put Brown on hold for a moment. I said to Dolly, "Now wait a minute. We just spent $30,000 setting up these new offices. We just signed a two-year lease. How on earth are we going to get out of it?"

"Say yes!" Dolly insisted. "Say yes!"

"Come on, Dolly, you know Joe Brown is a pretty good practical joker. He's probably pulling my leg."

"Say yes! Say yes!"

Brown told me that if the team was interested, Malcolm Prine, who was then the team president, would call me. I came back home and decided to go goose hunting with a few friends. I wasn't going to wait around for the phone to ring. I thought, Only a team with real guts is going to hire someone who's been out of professional baseball for nine years. When I returned, Prine asked me to come to Pittsburgh for an interview. He told me to pack a change of clothing in case I had to stay over. After a series of interviews with many of the team's owners, I accepted the job of vice president and general manager for baseball operations. Dolly stayed behind and continued to run our business.

The timing was right, because a growing number of teams, including the Pirates, were realizing that player procurement and development is crucial to long-term success, both on the field and on the balance sheet. And the Pirates' situation provided me with a great challenge.

The Pirates' major league club, which had lost 104 games during the 1985 season, was stocked with high-priced, unproductive players. The minor league system had been neglected. And while a coalition of corporations and private businessmen had purchased the club a month earlier and promised to keep it in Pittsburgh, the fans, fed up with the team's apathetic play and still hurt by the well-publicized cocaine trials that year, stayed away from Three Rivers Stadium in droves.

Under the terms of the sale, we had $26.25 million to work with over a five-year period. In 1986 we lost $7 million. With the team payroll and the payments we were making to the unproductive players we released, we were left with $16 million. The ownership group wanted to stem those losses by keeping our operating budget at a bare minimum. So while in theory I could have adopted the "five-year rebuilding plan" that other teams talk about when changing management, in reality the franchise would have lasted in Pittsburgh only two more years if no changes were made. All the marketing in the world would not have brought the fans back if all they were going to see was mediocrity.

So I had a dual problem: I had to improve a team and save a franchise. That, my friends, is where the rubber meets the road.

I relied on all the things I had learned to turn the Pirates around. Once I hired Jim Leyland, the third-base coach of the Chicago White Sox who'd paid his managerial dues in the minor leagues, to manage the major league club, I upgraded our farm system by hiring the best managers and instructors; revamped our scouting department and their reporting procedures; traded veterans of established market value for young prospects; expanded our studies of player performance; and with the help of my staff turned our front office into an efficient nerve center, one that could obtain, digest, and implement all the information our managers, instructors, and scouts were providing. We also brought in experts in such areas as vision training, finance, and conditioning to help our players maximize *their* net worth.

The results were gratifying. On the major league level, the Pirates improved from 64 wins (sixth place in the National League's Eastern Division) in 1986 to 80 (fourth place) in 1987 and 83 (second place) in 1988. In our minor league system, in 1987 all six of our teams played at or above the .500 level and three reached the playoffs—both accomplishments occurring for the first time in the Pirates' 100-year history. During the December 1987 draft a record seven players were selected from our organization by other major league teams. And in 1988 we added a seventh minor league team and still finished with a combined record of .500.

My reward was a pink slip, handed to me by the Pirates' team president two days after the 1988 season. I wasn't surprised by the dismissal, because in today's baseball climate—where the real pressure comes when your team is doing well and everyone wants to take their bows and bask in the spotlight—I don't think anyone can truly be surprised by anything. The basic reason I left the Pirates was the difference in perception among the team president, the chairman of the board, and me about the authority of the general manager. They had created a bureaucracy that made it impossible for the general manager to do his job effectively. And because the Pirates are owned by a coalition with no majority owner, I never knew who I worked for or was supposed to report to.

Five months later I accepted a new challenge when New York Yankees owner George Steinbrenner hired me as his senior vice president for baseball operations. The only baseball position I would have taken was with a team deeply committed to winning, and, listening to Mr. Steinbrenner's recruiting pitch, he made me believe there was no one in baseball more committed to that goal than he.

As it turned out, the Pirates job was a dress rehearsal for the pressure I faced each and every day with the Yankees. The farm system was barren and the major league club was overstocked with designated hitters and off-speed pitchers. My job was to wheel and deal on the major league level— and to get us into first place ASAP.

Though I made some good trades—acquiring such players as right fielder Jesse Barfield, designated hitter Steve Balboni, pitchers Eric Plunk, Greg Cadaret, Walt Terrell, and third baseman Mike Blowers—my primary contribution was a steadfast insistence that we give young players like center fielder Roberto Kelly, shortstop Alvaro Espinoza, catcher Bob Geren, and pitchers Chuck Cary and Clay Parker a chance to play instead of trading them away, as the Yankees had been doing all through the eighties. But that was lost in the turmoil—internal disputes argued through the media, managerial changes, coaching changes—that always engulfs the Yankees.

My adventures in baseball management underscore how fleeting success can be. Though we at the Pirates worked day and night to build a winning organization, once I was dismissed the baseball operation fell apart. The team hierarchy decided it could put the franchise on cruise control, so many of the techniques I instituted were ignored or abandoned. As a result of this corporate masturbation, the work ethic changed, slowly but steadily. When a slew of injuries hit and decisive action was called for, second-guessing abounded. The personal touch our organization had become known for turned to finger-pointing and political posturing. As the major league team plummeted in the standings, my successor, Larry Doughty, who'd been my assistant general manager, came under fire from both the media and team management for not being me. That was totally unfair, since management had previously decided they didn't want me around anymore.

With the Yankees, I learned roughly 36 hours after accepting the job that no matter what I did, the team is, was, and always will be George Steinbrenner's team, bound to his whims. I decided to resign in August 1989, 10 days after Steinbrenner changed managers for the 18th time in 17 years, because I believed the vicelike pressure he applies on his employees—late-night telephone tirades, demeaning personal attacks—to produce to his ever-changing expectations is counterproductive, particularly to someone like me who feels strongly that a positive atmosphere is a vital ingredient for a winning organization.

You've heard that cliché about a team firing its manager or general manager because you can't fire the players. The truth is, anyone can be fired *except* the owner. I figure the best way for me to leave a legacy of baseball excellence is to buy a baseball franchise, but that probably won't happen, unless this book becomes a runaway best-seller. But this book allows me to create a positive, free-thinking environment where I can be an owner, introduce you to teachers and experts from a variety of fields, and show you not only how a baseball franchise runs, but how it can and should be run.

I've long believed in synergy, that two people working together can achieve more than two people apart. I want to share this accumulation of baseball knowledge to prick your imagination, to get you to question what you read. I hope you will see the game as I do and be spurred into studying, testing, using, and refining the methods we present. Now let's get to work on building our world championship-caliber organization.

2 INNER VISIONS

When I watch a baseball game, my concentration is so great that I get into an altered state where things move slower, allowing me to understand them better. I visualize what might happen before it occurs, the way an artist envisions a completed painting before he picks up a brush.

My mind is like a videocassette recorder, storing mental images I will replay over and over again. My eyes are my camera, giving me a wide-angle view of the hitter's hands, the torque action of his midsection, the angle of his bat. I capture the base runner's lead, speed, and footwork. I focus on the pitcher's mechanics in his delivery and the movement of each pitch in flight. I zoom in on the body control and balance the fielders' display.

The mental tapes I make give me a spectrum analysis of the team, its players, the way the game is played, and how it can be improved.

To give you a sample of the things I see, let me tell you

what I saw and thought while seated behind home plate for a game at Shea Stadium on September 6, 1989, between the New York Mets and St. Louis Cardinals.

On that day both teams were in the thick of the National League's Eastern Division race, the Mets 3½ games behind the division-leading Chicago Cubs and the Cardinals, despite injuries to key players, only a game behind.

On the first pitch of the game, Cardinals left fielder Vince Coleman leads off with a drag-bunt single. If you didn't see it, you missed a thing of beauty. First of all, the Mets infielders were just settling in; they weren't ready for Coleman's bunt and couldn't make a play. Second, Coleman's execution was excellent. As the ball came into the hitting zone, Coleman, a left-handed hitter, crossed his left foot over his right foot; as his left foot hit the ground, the ball hit the bat simultaneously; the head of the bat was out in front of him, angled from third base to shortstop; then his right foot hit the ground and he was off to first.

I watch the distance of Coleman's lead and how his feet move as Mets pitcher Ron Darling delivers the ball to home plate. Whether the right-handed Darling throws home or to first, Coleman knows exactly how big a lead he can take. A few pitches into the count and a few pickoff throws later, Coleman has figured out the amount of time Darling takes delivering the ball home and to first, so he is ready to steal whenever he has the green light.

These are the components of the "timed, measured lead," an art we refined at the Academy that I will explain in a later chapter.

On the 3-1 pitch, Coleman takes off. As it turns out, catcher Gary Carter's throw sails into the outfield, allowing Coleman to advance to third, but even if the throw had been on target Coleman had enough time to steal second base successfully.

Now comes the most decisive moment in a ball game, the situation that makes or breaks a team: a runner on third base with less than two outs. In this situation there are six ways the runner can score: on a hit, a deep fly ball, a ground ball to the right side if the infielders are playing back, a bunt, a balk, or a wild pitch. Manager Whitey Herzog has the option of putting on the contact play, in which the runner will head for home as soon as the batter makes contact, unless it's a ball hit to the pitcher.

If the defense prevents the run from scoring, however, the momentum of the game swings their way.

The batter, Ozzie Smith, is jammed by Darling's next pitch and pops out to shortstop.

The next batter is second baseman Jose Oquendo. Oquendo typifies my definition of a "winning ballplayer," one who works hard, gets the most from his abilities, and contributes all the little things—the intangibles—needed for winning baseball. Oquendo, a great fielder, was rushed to the major leagues at age 19 by the Mets, who at the time were desperate for a good shortstop. He couldn't handle big league pitching and was later traded to the Cardinals. Through hard work and the help of Cardinals batting coach Johnny Lewis, the switch-hitting Oquendo remade his stances from both sides of the plate and developed into a fine hitter. From 1986 to 1988 Herzog deployed Oquendo as his jack-of-all-trades, moving him all over the diamond. Toward the end of the '88 season Herzog made him the starting second baseman. In 1989, Oquendo and Ozzie Smith were the best double-play combination in the National League.

The Mets have positioned their corner men on the grass and their middle infielders back, so all Oquendo needs to get Coleman home is a ground ball toward the middle of the infield. On the 1-0 pitch, Oquendo drives a fly ball to right field, deep enough to bring home Coleman and give the Cardinals a 1-0 lead.

Cardinals starting pitcher Ricky Horton, a left-hander, is making his warm-up throws before the bottom of the first. Horton has a deceptive motion. He hides the ball behind his body, pauses, and delivers. The better he hides it, the longer it takes the hitter to pick up the ball at Horton's release zone. This gives him a "sneaky fastball"; not that it's fast, but it's hard to read and react to.

I notice a fellow employed by the Mets using a radar gun to measure the velocity of Horton's pitches. The use of radar guns is standard practice throughout baseball. While radar guns are valuable as a tool for measurement and for reference, a team's evaluators are misguided if they use the readings as the definitive measurement of a pitcher. A radar gun can't tell whether a pitcher has mastered the art of pitching—the location of the pitches, their sequence, and their movement in the hitting zone.

Because Horton lacks an above-average fastball, he relies on location and changing speeds to get hitters out. That means he has to throw strikes and induce the hitters to swing at those strikes and hit the ball where he wants them to. If he falls behind in the count, he's in trouble, because he can't come back with his fastball to get the hitters out.

Horton is the type of pitcher who can drive hitters nuts. Since they are not intimidated by his fastball, they think they can crush any pitch they want, so Horton uses that to his advantage. With one out and a runner on first, Horton's first pitch to third baseman Howard Johnson is a fastball on the outside part of the hitting zone. Rather than waiting on the ball and hitting it to right field, Johnson tries to pull it. The result is a pop-up to shortstop for the second out.

Right fielder Darryl Strawberry steps up to the plate. Strawberry has the physical components to excel—speed, a good throwing arm, and the strength to hit the ball a long way—but this season he's been struggling, with his average near .220. I notice on Horton's first pitch that Strawberry brings his front foot high in the air—almost a leg kick—as the pitch is delivered, and brings it down as he starts his movements toward the ball. That, to me, is a problem. The more a hitter moves, the more he loses control of his body.

I also wonder whether Strawberry is landing too hard on his front foot, which can jar his head and interfere with his vision.

These are self-inflicted wounds. By losing control of his body, Strawberry is destroying the fine body control he already has.

Horton is eating Strawberry alive with breaking balls. With two strikes in the count, Strawberry has not changed his hitting approach one bit. He swings at another curveball for strike three, the same way he swung at the first two curveballs. Strawberry could have prevented this strikeout by using the "two-strike hitting approach," which I will describe later.

I enjoy watching Ron Darling pitch. He is a gifted athlete, and when he's on his game he has a real command of the strike zone. His pitch sequence to third baseman Terry Pendleton in the top of the second inning is brilliant. His first pitch is a fastball in on Pendleton's hands; the second pitch is a fastball on the outside corner. He throws his fastball up in the hitting zone and his split-fingered fastball low. Darling is using the entire strike zone to keep Pendleton off-balance. Darling jams Pendleton with an inside fastball and gets him to fly out to center field.

After right fielder Tom Brunansky walks, center fielder Milt Thompson steps in. I've always thought Thompson, who's played for the Atlanta Braves and Philadelphia Phillies, has been underrated. He has good speed and hits the ball hard; I know, because he killed us when I was with the Pirates. But for some reason baseball people had come to regard him as a reserve player. This season he's been indispensable as a replacement for Willie McGee, who's suffered one injury after another.

I remember calling Cardinals general manager Dal Maxvill after he acquired Thompson in December 1988. All I kept saying to Maxvill was, "How on earth did you get him? That deal is a steal."

With two outs and Brunansky on second, catcher Tony Pena comes to bat. Pena, who played for me in Pittsburgh, is one of the nicest and most dedicated players in the game. During his at-bat I recall our conversation before the game. Pena reminded me about the time in 1986, just before the All-Star break, when he was really struggling at the plate. At the time Pena had been holding his bat vertically rather than at a 45-degree angle, and swinging with his arms instead of using his hands and forearms. He'd had no luck working on his own or with the coaches, so he asked me for help. I immediately summoned Pablo Cruz, one of the Pirates scouts, to join me in Houston to work with Pena. Together, in the indoor batting cage under the stands in the Astrodome, we remade his stance.

With Cruz interpreting my suggestions in Spanish and adding his own insights, we taught Pena one thing at a time. That's the key to effective teaching: Identify and work on one thing at a time. First, we had the right-handed-hitting Pena put the bat flat on his right shoulder and bring it into hitting position as the pitch was released. We taught him to turn his body with his hands, and had him choke up for better bat control. By shortening his swing and getting him to use his wrists and hands more, we eliminated the extra movements in his swing. He took to it like a duck to water. Then, before each practice pitch arrived, I reminded him over and over, "Wait, and be quick. Wait, and be quick."

By season's end Pena had improved his batting average from .215 to .288.

Pena also told me that our subsequent conversations on a daily basis helped him sustain his success. "You'd come to me and talk about everything except baseball," Pena laughed. "But somehow, about five minutes later, one point you were making really hit me. You were trying to get me to relax and be patient, and that you did."

I don't redo a player's mechanics unless it's absolutely necessary. In fact, as an instructor I prefer to avoid the nitty-gritty of mechanics and instead use simple, positive suggestions. For example, when I was with the Pirates, Mike Diaz, a right-handed power-hitting first baseman/outfielder, got into a slump by trying to pull everything. Once during batting practice I went over to Diaz and said, "See that door along the outfield wall in right-center? I'll give you $100 if you can hit five balls against it." Before long I was $100 poorer.

I used a similar approach in 1989 with Jesse Barfield of the Yankees. Barfield was striking out a lot because he was trying to pull the ball. On a road trip in Detroit I told him, "Jesse, the ball you hit to right field last night was the prettiest hit you've had all year. I don't know of any other player who can hit the ball with power to the opposite field like you can. It's great to see you wait, then be quick." The more I reminded him of this, the more he hit to the opposite field and the less he struck out.

In the bottom of the second inning of the Cardinals-Mets game, left fielder Kevin McReynolds comes to the plate with a plan. He is going to wait until he sees a pitch he can pull. With the count 1-1, McReynolds gets one and hits a home run.

First baseman Keith Hernandez follows with a two-strike single to left-center. Hernandez has always been an outstanding two-strike hitter. As with McReynolds, Hernandez had formulated a plan of attack. Once Horton got ahead in the count, 0-2, Hernandez expected a curveball away; when that pitch arrived, Hernandez merely reached out and met it.

One out later Ozzie Smith robs shortstop Kevin Elster of a single by diving to his right and snatching Elster's line drive. That's another example of why Smith is the player scouts use as their standard for defensive comparisons against other shortstops. Smith can leave his feet, whether to catch a liner or turn a double play, and still be under control. The same goes for Pendleton at third. Three innings after Smith's catch, Darling hits a hard grounder down the third-base line. Pendleton reaches to his right, plucks the ball behind his body, straightens up, and makes an accurate throw to first for the out. National League scouts can't decide whether Pendleton or Tim Wallach of the Expos is the better-fielding third baseman. I'd take Pendleton, because of his range and quickness.

I've also been watching Hernandez at first, out of personal curiosity. See, during my season with the Yankees I came to realize that Don Mattingly has overtaken Hernandez as the best-fielding first baseman in the game. While Hernandez remains superior to most, I believe Mattingly has more range.

In the top of the third, Horton drives a 1-1 fastball down the pipe for a double to right-center. Herzog signals Coleman to bunt. What ensued irritated me. Twice, Coleman made poor attempts to bunt. He kept his bat behind him, in foul territory. I will later describe the correct bunting approach, but I must point out here that one essential step is to keep the bat in fair territory so you can bunt the ball fair. Coleman did manage to atone for his poor execution by chopping a ground ball to second base, advancing Horton to third.

Second baseman Gregg Jefferies leads off the bottom of the third with a single. Center fielder Juan Samuel flies out to right and fails to advance the runner, so a stolen-base attempt is in order with Howard Johnson at the plate. With the count 1-1, Horton has a mental lapse and doesn't pay attention to Jefferies. That will cost him, because Jefferies steals second easily and then Johnson singles to drive him home.

The Cards tie the game in the top of the sixth. Coleman singles and moves to second on a wild pitch. Two outs later first baseman Pedro Guerrero steps in. Seated next to me is Dom Scala, who at the time was the Pirates' advance scout. Scala says he thinks Darling should pitch around or walk Guerrero, the most consistent RBI man on the team. The

Mets decide to face him. On an 0-1 pitch, Guerrero hits a line drive down the left-field line for a double. Scala, a real animated guy, tugs at my arm and says, "I told you they should pitch around him. I told you."

I have a theory: When a hitter is swinging at every pitch the same way, without choking up or stepping closer to the plate, the only way he'll get a hit is if the pitcher hits his bat with the ball. Here, in the bottom of the sixth, Strawberry gets a belt-high fastball and hits a single to right. Watching Strawberry out of balance at the plate, I'd felt the only pitch he could hit was something belt-high. So, in effect, Horton put the ball on Strawberry's bat for him.

Before McReynolds steps in, Cardinals pitching coach Mike Roarke visits the mound, joined by the entire Cardinal infield. They review the situation and the pitches Horton will throw. This is an area where Herzog and his coaches excel. Roarke is telling the battery which sequence of pitches they'll use, and reminding each player of his defensive assignment. McReynolds singles, bringing Hernandez to the plate with runners on first and second and no outs. Scala wonders aloud whether Hernandez should try a sacrifice bunt in this situation. All I'm thinking is, Hernandez has to find some way to advance both runners into scoring position. On a 2-0 pitch, Hernandez grounds into a 4-6-3 double play.

Now Herzog, a believer in lefty-righty percentages, removes Horton and brings in right-hander John Costello to face the right-handed-hitting Carter. There was a time in Carter's career where he consistently drove in the runner from third base with two strikes. This time, Carter pops out to second base.

In the top of the seventh Brunansky and Thompson hit singles. Pendleton lays down a good bunt, but Darling springs off the mound, turns, and throws out Brunansky at third. No matter how good a pitcher's stuff is, if he can't field his position he is destined for mediocrity.

Herzog sends in Denny Walling to pinch-hit. I've known

Walling since he was in Double A ball, and even then, at an early age, he was an outstanding pinch hitter. The key to pinch-hitting success is mental preparation. Walling is always prepared coming off the bench late in the game to be tested by a fastball. Darling bears down and gets Walling and Coleman out to end the inning.

The Cardinals take advantage of an error by Jefferies on a ground ball hit by Ozzie Smith in the top of the eighth to take the lead for good. Oquendo singles, moving Smith to third. Here comes Guerrero. Because Guerrero has a quick swing, he can wait on pitches longer. With the count 2-2, Guerrero hits a grounder to second base, scoring Smith.

After the game I mentally replayed *my* highlights of the game. The Cardinals advanced base runners, while the Mets did not. I visualized the Cardinals' team speed; their superior defense; the communication among the players, manager, and coaches; and, most frequently, the clutch hitting of Pedro Guerrero, the player Dom Scala insisted the Mets should pitch around. Man, the way Guerrero punched that ground ball to second with two strikes in the eighth inning was beautiful. It was artistic. It was winning baseball.

3 DUCK HUNTING

Scouting reminds me of duck hunting. Some hunters can see the ducks way off on the horizon. I can see those ducks when they're little specks. As they get closer, some guys say, "I can't see them yet." Others don't see them until they come over the decoys. A few hunters don't see them until they're flying away.

You've *got* to be able to see them way over there, and you've got to be able to tell one of those ducks from a buzzard or a crow.

What separates a good baseball scout from a great one is vision: the ability to spot and evaluate players way before they reach their potential. By the time the player is "coming over the decoy," so to speak, he has been seen by rival scouts. Once he's "flying away," the scout is too late; the player has probably been signed or traded for by someone else.

What separates a good team from a great one is the quality of its scouting department. The information your scouting department provides on players from the major leagues all the way down to the rookie leagues and the college and high school levels has to be as accurate and thorough as possible. Without that information, a general manager cannot render good judgments.

Over the years I've heard some teams say that they wanted to invest in teachers rather than scouts. I say you've got to have the information before you set a curriculum of instruction. If a team lacks information, or its information is not consistent, how can it know which teacher is the best one for its program? I remember one spring training when a "teacher-oriented" major league team invited two well-known hitting instructors to help its major league instructor work with the organization's hitters. One of the instructors believed in swinging up at the ball, the other believed in a level swing, while the major league instructor taught the hitters to swing down at the ball. All that team had was a curriculum for confusion.

Major League Baseball has a scouting bureau that offers its information to every team in baseball. To me, that should only supplement the work of your scouts; there is no substitute for having your own personnel. A well-trained staff of your own will provide consistent, reliable information using the criteria the general manager and scouting director set.

Scouts who are responsible for amateur players have two ways to cover their territory: conducting tryout camps and scouting the player in game conditions.

Sometimes all a scout has is one game to make his evaluation. But a topflight evaluator will set up as many tryout camps as he can, since game situations often prevent the player from performing a variety of tasks. Tryout camps allow the evaluator to conduct a hands-on workout with each player under controlled conditions. Workouts are like auditions. In my workouts I'd have the player sing my notes.

When you observe a player, whether he's fielding, running, throwing, batting, or pitching, you start from the ground and move upward. Are his feet getting him off to a good running start? In which direction does he take his first step when pursuing a batted ball? Does he use his lower body in his batting stroke? On the mound, does he use his legs to drive off the pitching rubber?

You then observe the player's midsection, from the rib cage to the gluteus maximus to the thighs. The midsection is the player's center of gravity, where the greatest mass of muscles is located. The midsection is where you see the torque action—the coiling and twisting—that gives the hitter or pitcher his power.

For every action there is an equal and opposite reaction. At the start of a swing or a pitch the midsection coils, bringing the muscles of the midsection into play; the torque action generates the follow-through—the equal and opposite reaction—in the hitter's swing or pitcher's delivery.

Finally, you look at the player's use of his hands and upper body. In hitting, it's how the hitter holds his bat— flat, which makes him more likely to be a high-ball hitter; perpendicular, which makes him more of a low-ball hitter; or at a 45-degree angle, which allows him to handle pitches in both locations. Also, you observe how loosely he grips the bat handle. The best grip is one where someone could come up from behind and snatch the bat right out of the hitter's hands. A tight grip slows the hitter's swing because of the tension he's creating in his forearms, biceps, and triceps.

In pitching, you observe how he grips the ball for his different pitches; how his arms move in relation to his feet and midsection; his "release point," the moment he releases the ball from his hand; and how much arm extension he gets.

The great scouts don't stop there. They evaluate the *whole ballplayer*—his attributes as a person as well as a player. You can't make an accurate evaluation without going through the following checklist:

1. How great is the player's desire to excel?
2. How strong is his competitive spirit?
3. How aggressive is he?
4. How developed are his baseball instincts?
5. How does he react to adversity?
6. Can he make adjustments, physically and emotionally?
7. How great is his aptitude for baseball instruction?

From a business standpoint, why spend $60,000 to sign an amateur player or a draft choice who has great speed and a great arm if he lacks the intangibles—the qualities you can't see but can only discover? If he doesn't have the emotional makeup necessary to succeed in the big leagues, you've made a pretty bad investment. You've wasted the signing bonus plus the money and time spent on that player's development.

The scouts I train do a thorough background check of every single player—they speak with the player, visit his home, meet his family, and talk with his coaches and teachers—and submit a profile of his personality.

The most misleading thing a scout can do in evaluating the potential of an amateur player or a minor leaguer is to rely too much on statistics. As Mark Twain once said, "There are three kinds of lies: lies, damned lies, and statistics." Poor statistical totals may lead you to believe the player is failing, but they don't account for the circumstances that may have led to his low totals. A Double A pitcher may have a 2-12 record, but that could be caused by a poor supporting cast, or perhaps that pitcher was trying to master a new pitch or a different delivery.

The statistics of right-handed-hitting first baseman Randy Milligan, now with the Baltimore Orioles, provide an interesting twist on this point. As Milligan advanced professionally his statistics were always better the second year he'd played on a given level than the first. Check out these numbers: In the Single A Carolina League, Milligan batted .269 in 1982 and .292 in 1983; in the Double A Texas League, Milligan hit .275 in '84 and .309 in '85. Milligan began the 1986 season with Triple A Tidewater, but after getting only five hits in 60 at-bats (.083) was sent back to Double A. There, he batted .316. The next season, in Triple A, Milligan hit .326 and was named the International League's Most Valuable Player. When I was the Pirates' general manager, I acquired Milligan in 1988 in a trade with the New York Mets. In 40 games with the Pirates, Milligan batted .220, and in 63 games with the Pirates Triple A team in Buffalo he batted .276. After the '88 season the Pirates traded him to the Orioles. In 1989 Milligan won a job as the first baseman against left-handed pitchers, batting in the .260 range with 12 home runs.

In 1984, '86, and '88 Milligan's statistics would have made it seem that he was not capable of playing well in higher classifications, that he regressed after each promotion. The fact is, Milligan needed a full year to adjust to the new levels. Some players are like this. I can't explain it, but I've seen it enough times to know it can happen. One thing I saw during Milligan's season with the Pirates was that he seemed more comfortable hitting against right-handed pitchers than left-handers, but he played primarily against lefties. As I reflect on this, I now feel we may have used him incorrectly, putting him in a role that caused his low batting average.

I find statistics of some significance only in the evaluation of major league players who've established a positive level of consistency—like 20 home runs hit or 200 strikeouts thrown per season—over four or five years.

Since baseball is a game of comparative analysis, the simplest way to grade amateur and minor league players on their overall abilities is by comparing them with major league players you've set as your standard. When evaluating a shortstop, for example, a scout may compare him to Luis Aparicio. Another scout may use Ozzie Smith as his basis for comparison. The keys are that the scout's standards are consistent and that his organization knows what his standards are.

Let's look at the menu of player evaluation, beginning with the regular position player.

Speed

I've already mentioned the value of speed, both as a measurement of general athletic ability and in its effect on the outcome of a game. There are players, however, who possess sheer running speed but cannot put it to use on the field. A fast runner may not necessarily be able to cut and change directions, whether he's caught in a rundown play on the bases or has misjudged a fly ball in the outfield. Therefore, scouts time the player's "raw" speed in a 60-yard dash and evaluate his "usable" speed on the field.

What determines usable speed? A player's running form, his ability to cut, change directions, and accelerate, and his baseball instincts—knowing how and when to take the extra base and how to "read" the ball off the bat and anticipate where it will land.

Throwing Arm

Throwing arms are evaluated in two ways: the velocity of the throw, which is a measurement of arm strength, and the accuracy of the throw.

In a workout or a simulated game, measuring a player's velocity is easy. You station yourself behind first base

and, using a radar gun, time the throws of the infielders. Similarly, you can stand in front of second base or in
foul territory behind third and clock the throws of the outfielders.

During a game, when the use of a radar gun on regular
players is impractical, you can time the throws over particular distances by stopwatch.

As for accuracy, the scout observes the location of each
throw and records it in his report. If, for example, 15 of a
player's 30 throws were accurate, that ratio can be used as
a basis for comparison against his 30 throws the following
game.

An evaluator also measures the velocity and accuracy of
throws a player makes from different angles and within the
boundaries of his position, because in a game a player is
rarely stationary.

Take the shortstop position. A shortstop is called upon
in games to make throws from his traditional location on
the field, from the hole, moving toward second base, moving in on a slowly hit ball, making a relay throw from an
outfielder to the appropriate base, and making the throw
from second base to complete a double play. I want my
scouts to get a look at a shortstop's arm in all these cases.
Obviously, a controlled workout gives me the best chance
to see all this.

Fielding

Overall fielding ability is a function of body control and
coordination. The hands and feet must work in unison.

Baseball "hands" come in two varieties: soft hands, which
move softly and fluidly, able to adjust to an assortment of
bounces and catches; and hard hands, which jab at balls
and take throws rigidly, repelling instead of receiving.

The fielder's feet account for his range, his movement in four basic directions: to his left; to his right; going back on a ball; and moving in on, or charging, a ball.

The common denominator for all great fielders is balance. Proper balance and coordination allow him to move gracefully, gliding under a fly ball while running at full speed or fielding a ground ball and making a throw on the run. Players who lack body control will bounce as they run for a fly ball, which jars them and distorts their vision, or stumble as they go for a slowly hit grounder and not be able to make a throw.

I have used a simple test during workouts to measure the balance of infielders. I line every infielder up at shortstop, which is the toughest infield position to play, with the most area to cover. I have every player field a slow roller and make a throw to first base. Then in an intrasquad game I'll have them field slow rollers from their normal positions.

One of the more curious things I've observed about outfielders—but have never been able to explain—is that there are some who will show you a better arm from right field than from left field, and others who throw better from left than right. My only speculation is that they are more comfortable with the angle of the throws from the particular spot. Whatever the explanation, it is something for an evaluator to be aware of.

Hitting

There is a balance in hitting, too. To be a good hitter, your feet, midsection, and hands must work together and support one another.

The evaluation begins with the hitter's stride as he starts his hitting action. While there is no set way to stride into the ball, the stride must allow the hitter to use the full force generated by his midsection. If the hitter strides too early, chances are he will be way out in front of the pitch and pull the ball foul or miss it altogether. If his stride is late, he will prevent himself from generating line drives, since his midsection and hands have already committed to a swing. If he does make contact, he'll probably lift a soft fly ball or hit a weak grounder to the opposite field.

The hitter generates momentum from his back leg, the way a boxer gets punching power from his back leg. The most flagrant hitting problem is what we call the "back-leg breakdown." When the hitter's back leg collapses—when he bends it too much—as he swings, his power is lost. The back-leg breakdown causes his front shoulder to raise and open. He uppercuts at every pitch.

Sometimes that happens because the hitter sets up his waist in the batter's box before he sets his feet. You may notice this with some hitters: They step into the box, keep their waist still, then look down and dig their feet into the dirt. That's like erecting a building from the middle floor on down.

You then look at the position of the hitter's hands. The hands move like a pendulum—back as the body coils, forward as the body uncoils. Too much hand movement can throw the swing out of kilter.

Finally, you examine the torque—the turning, twisting force—generated by the abdominals and buttocks. The midsection is where line-drive and home-run power come from. With his body coiled—hands, front shoulder, front knee, and hip turned inward—the hitter's feet and hands, moving in symmetry with his midsection, explode forward.

How do you know when a hitter's coiling properly? You should be able to see from the mound the numbers on the back of his uniform. When Don Mattingly gets into a slump, a lot of times he raises up out of that coiled position during his swing.

A good hitter will move the middle of his body forward

only when his hands and feet are moving forward. If a hitter leads with his midsection, his arms cannot generate sufficient force to drive the ball solidly.

Now we come to the most misleading hitting phrase there is: "bat speed." You often hear television broadcasters, fans, even coaches on all levels describe a player whose swing was late as having a "slow bat," or a line-drive hitter as having great "bat speed."

First of all, unless you have a machine that can measure bat speed precisely, how can anyone know by observation alone what a fast swing or a slow swing is?

Second, the speed of the bat is actually the end result of the swing. If the hitter's action is out of balance, he is not going to swing correctly. So when you observe a "slow" bat, you have to go through each component of his swing—his feet, hands, and midsection. If he is in balance but is still not making good contact, he may have a problem seeing the ball, or his mental approach may be wrong, or he may not be visualizing properly (areas I will explore in later chapters).

When an evaluator looks at the hitter's bat, he is observing his hitting arc—the plane of the bat as it travels from the start of the swing through the hitting zone. There are different planes the bat can take, from a slight uppercut, probably the most common swing, to a downward stroke, where the bat is on a downward plane as it connects with the ball.

The evaluator charts the hitter's contact ratio—how often the ball hits the bat, where it hits the bat, and how much force is generated when the ball meets the bat—and notes the type of power the hitter has. He can be a line-drive hitter, have home-run power or power to the outfield gaps. He can have lofting power, meaning he hits the ball high in the air, or warning-track power, meaning he falls short of home runs.

All grades are projections of the hitter's future ability.

Pitching

When I scout pitchers, I think of the line actor Tom Cruise's character was so fond of in the movie *Top Gun*: "I feel the need for speed."

As a rule, the first thing I'm looking for in a pitcher is an above-average fastball. A pitcher with an above-average fastball has a better chance for success, because the hitter has precious little time to read, identify, and react to a pitch in the first place. And an above-average fastball is an innate gift. A pitcher's fastball, like a player's running speed, can be improved, as I'll tell you about in our tutorial chapter, but both players must have an above-average base for a teacher to build upon.

An evaluator observes the mechanics of a pitcher's delivery from the ground up—feet, midsection, hands, and front shoulder. As with a hitter, a pitcher strides back, coils his feet and hands (the numbers on the back of his uniform can be seen from home plate), then strides forward—driving off his back leg, unleashing the torquing power from his abdominals and buttocks—and follows through. If he leads in his forward motion with his front shoulder, he will decrease the force generated by his midsection.

There is no set way to deliver a pitch—some use a full windup, with their arms meeting at or above the head; others bring their hands only as high as their chest or waist; and a few pitch from the stretch position, even when there are runners on base. I give high marks to pitchers whose mechanics are smooth, fluid, and in balance.

When a fastball is thrown, an evaluator breaks it down into one of three categories: velocity, movement, and control.

The velocity is measured by a radar gun, which can be used by a scout standing behind the backstop during workouts, simulated games, and regulation games. By now, you've probably guessed that when I was the general manager of the Pirates I made sure that pitchers on every minor league level were timed in every game by radar guns.

When an evaluator views the movement, or "life," of a fastball in the hitting zone, he notes how much the fastball fell and whether it rode in on the pitcher's hands or veered toward the outside corner of home plate.

The definition of control, or "location," is where the ball passes through the hitting zone. An evaluator can divide the zone into five parts: inside and low, inside and high, outside and high, outside and low, and right down the pipe.

Evaluating curveballs is a little more difficult, because some young pitchers lack the dexterity to throw them. For example, a pitcher with a small hand may not be able to spread his fingers wide enough to release a curveball properly. Those pitchers may find it easier to throw a slider, which is thrown like a fastball. The slider is a quick-breaking pitch that depends on the amount of finger pressure a pitcher applies. The evaluator finds out which pitchers fall into this category by talking with the pitcher or his coaches during a workout.

During game conditions you are judging the tightness of the spin, or "rotation," of the curveball—the tighter the spin, the greater the break—and the angle at which it moves to the hitting zone. There are flat curveballs, known as roundhouse pitches, which break from side to side. There's the overhand curveball, which breaks straight down. And there are curves that break at about 45 degrees.

You also time the velocity of the curveball. Some pitchers throw a "power" curveball, which is almost as fast as their fastball. Others throw a big curve at a slower speed, in the 70- to 75-mile-per-hour range. The big, slow curve is a great pitch for a pitcher to have in his repertoire, since it throws off a hitter's timing.

One major league pitcher with an outstanding slow curve is hard-throwing Dwight Gooden of the Mets. Many years ago the curveball was nicknamed "Uncle Charley." Today's players have such respect for Gooden's big, slow curveball that they refer to it as "Lord Charles."

Attitude and Aptitude

I cannot stress enough how vital it is for an evaluator to learn firsthand about each player's attitudes—about baseball, schoolwork, his family, and himself—and aptitude—his willingness to learn and capacity to comprehend. These are the attributes that make or break even the most gifted players. I used to post a sign in clubhouses which read, "Attitude determines altitude."

Pirates left-hander John Smiley is an example of a player with the right attitude and aptitude. When we called him up to the major leagues in the fall of 1987, he had an outstanding fastball but needed to develop a curve. Ray Miller, the Pirates pitching coach, spent a few days tutoring Smiley, and he picked up the curveball as fast as you can say "Lord Charles." Other players may spend two or three years trying to learn to throw a good curveball.

There are ways for an evaluator to test the attitude and aptitude of high school and college players. Say you are scouting a high school pitcher who has never thrown a change-up. There are five or six different ways of throwing a change. You show him one, and ask him to try it for six pitches. If he can master it, you show him other grips. If he is eager to learn, and has the physical tools to go with it, you've got yourself a prospect.

What about a hitter? You explain to him some hitting concepts, such as the two-strike approach, and see if he understands them. If he does, you or your subscout pitch to him and see if can apply the techniques.

Here's another test: In a practice session, throw him pitches on the outside part of the plate and ask him to hit every one to the opposite field, and continue to do so until he becomes comfortable.

Then you throw pitches to the middle of the plate and again have him hit the ball to the opposite field. Finally, you pitch him inside and see if he can hit the pitch the other way.

Perhaps the hitter has done a lot of bunting in his high school career. Demonstrate the 45-degree angle bunt, which is used by many professional clubs, and see if he can handle it.

I'll give you an example of a personality test I've often used in workouts. Say you are working with an infielder. You hit ground ball after ground ball at him. The infielder boots one of the grounders. Since he's only human, an error is bound to happen. However, if he retrieves the ball slowly and acts disgusted, he probably gets easily discouraged; his frustration or anger will distract him from fielding the next ground ball cleanly. If he pounces on the ball, gets it right back to me and readies himself for another chance, he is exhibiting strength, confidence, and desire; this is the guy I'd rather have on my team.

You aren't teaching so much as you are testing the player's capacity to learn. Don't confound the player with techniques he may not comprehend fully, or make him feel like he's taking tests he must pass. Work with him slowly, in controlled conditions like a workout, keep your instructions and observations positive and supportive, and help him feel comfortable.

The evaluator should always watch for a player's level of aggressiveness. Is he willing to get his uniform dirty? Will he take a chance on making that diving catch? Will he slide hard into second base to break up a double play? Will he try to take an extra base when the grass is wet and the infield muddy? Is he willing to give that extra effort to get the job done?

Even with all this, it's helpful to see a player in game

conditions. Pirates general manager Larry Doughty, who served as the scouting director of the Cincinnati Reds from 1982 to 1987, has observed players who appear to go through the motions during workout sessions, then turn it on during games.

"I call them 'National Anthem players,' " Doughty laughs. "They don't show you anything until the stadium organist plays the National Anthem.

"Kal Daniels of the Dodgers is one of my favorite people," says Doughty, who recommended the Reds draft Daniels in June 1982. "But if you catch Kal Daniels before the game, you're not gonna see him do anything near what he does after they play that Anthem.

"I've seen great basketball players behave that way. Watch them warm up—nothing. Then when the game starts —boom, boom, boom. I think certain people mentally and physically prepare themselves in a different way than the majority."

It's also important to observe the player's baseball instincts. Does he know when to take the extra base? Can he anticipate situations? How quickly does he react in the field to a ground ball hit to the hole or a fly ball to the gap?

And, can the player adjust? Can he bounce back the day after striking out four times at the plate? Can he maintain his composure after allowing a home run? Can he adjust to living away from home, and enduring the long bus rides that await him in the minor leagues?

Rarely can an evaluator make these decisions in one afternoon. That's why the scout and his assistants must map out a plan in which they get to see the player as often as they can over the course of a season. If you are responsible for a territory in a cold climate, like the New England states, you may only get two or three chances to see the player. If that's the case, then you solicit the opinions of the coaches, teachers, teammates, and friends who know him well.

Let's examine those facets of a scout's job.

Organizing a Tryout Camp

An amateur scout combines the roles of recruiter, appraiser, and traveling salesman. You've got to see as many potential employees as possible in the territory you are assigned, and evaluate their potential to help your company years from now. If you believe they have what it takes, you have to sell them on the idea of signing with your firm.

The ideal is to see as many players as possible, as early in their careers as possible—usually in their sophomore year of high school—and continue to follow them for two or three years, or until they are signed. This way, the scout has a continuous flow of players to observe: those he's seen and those he is seeing for the first time.

I have to confess that when I was responsible for scouting amateur players I had a constant fear of not knowing about every player in my territory. I became so driven by that fear that I decided to turn it into something positive: I became determined that I would not miss a single one! Of course, I knew I would miss one or two, but the goal remained 100 percent.

The best way to reach that goal is by conducting tryout camps. If I had a territory that covered three states, I would schedule 15 tryout camps, made up of 100 players each, over an eight-week period.

To get a tryout camp off the ground you have to be well-organized; you have to manage your territory. Each tryout camp takes two to three weeks of preparation: getting the information to the local newspaper; notifying the high school coaches; sending out invitations; putting together your staff of part-time scouts, subscouts, and assistants.

The size of a scout's staff depends on the budget set by the team that employs him. Sometimes, working under budgetary constraints, all a scout has are his friends and contacts in that area.

I had a simple way of recruiting assistants. I used to go

into every town and ask one question: "Which person in this town knows and cares the most about baseball and young people?"

Those assistants must also be trained to recruit, evaluate, sell, and manage. Through proper, efficient management, the scout and his staff will be able to conduct hands-on workouts with 95 percent of the area's best high school players in their sophomore and junior years.

A well-planned schedule of tryout camps also frees the scout to attend games played by the minor league teams in that territory. I would conduct a tryout camp in, say, Gastonia, North Carolina, from 10 A.M. to 2 P.M. In the evening I'd go see the professional clubs in the Western Carolina League. If an American Legion team was playing, I'd see that game. I was able to see baseball players all day long; I was doing high-volume business. Safety in numbers, I always say.

A hidden value of scouting players on different levels is that you gain a wider frame of reference than you would by watching high school players only.

Organizing one tryout camp, let alone 15, is hard-assed work. But if you don't do what I've described, you can end up becoming what I call a "tournament scout." They are the scouts who gauge everything on the impressions they get watching players in season-ending, American Legion-type tournaments. You assume that the best players are participating in these tournaments, but that's not always the case. As I mentioned earlier, game situations sometimes mask a player's abilities.

And, frankly, the tournament is a little late in the game to do your scouting. Since I had already worked out every one of those players in tryout camps, I didn't have to go to those tournaments. My reports were completed and filed.

Keeping those reports organized is extremely important. I constructed player-information cards and work sheets. And I would put every player into an appropriate category: Definite Prospect, Chance, Marginal, and Follow. The players who were filed in the Follow category were the sophomores and juniors who we viewed as prospects for the following year, players we would continue to scout for two or three seasons.

I carried all these cards and work sheets in boxes. I stored them in the trunk of my car—my mobile office—and because I have a good wife and had a nice office in my basement, I was able to keep every record up-to-date. Today, I recommend each scout carry and use a laptop computer.

Let's compare the value of a tryout camp to game observations in terms of volume. Some high schools in the Northeast or in colder climates are limited to about 16 games in an eight-week period—two games per week. Say you see 20 players in each game. That's a total of 320 players in 56 days.

A tryout camp can be conducted in one day, but for the benefit of comparison, let's say that one tryout camp can last two days. So that comes to 30 days for 15 tryout camps. With 100 players at each tryout camp, you can see 1,500 players in one month under controlled conditions, compared to 320 players over eight weeks in game conditions.

I think back to the tryout camps we conducted in the first year of the Kansas City Royals Baseball Academy. We ran 144 tryout camps over an 11-week period (June, July, and the first two weeks of August) and looked at 10,000 players in order to pick the 40 best players we could develop. Our budget that year was $51,000. So, in effect, we spent a little over $5 for each player we saw.

You can't measure the success rate of tryout camps by the percentage of players you sign from them. It may be that in a given tryout camp of, say, 1,500 players, you may offer contracts to only 10 players, and of those 10 only one may succeed at the major league level. But if that one player can help your team win a championship, he makes the issue moot.

The Audition

At the beginning of a workout you have the players perform their regular routines. As the hitters take batting practice, you form impressions of every player's stroke. As the pitchers throw in the bullpen, you observe their deliveries and the movement of their pitches.

You, or your part-time scout, then talks with each player to get a sense of his emotional makeup.

Once you've made these initial observations, you can narrow the field of candidates you are going to work with to those who really meet your criteria. You divide the players into squads and have them play a simulated game.

The simulated game is like a theatrical audition, where the players sing and dance and react to your cues. You can play as many innings as you want, send as many batters to the plate as you choose—even eliminate bases on balls.

Whatever the construction, what you have is an opportunity to pit the best players in the region, of all different shapes and sizes, against each other. Sometimes a player has excelled in a league that has below-average competition. Another player may not have stood out in his league because his coach thought of him as a second-stringer. But in a tryout camp you have set a level of competition that should bring out the best in every player.

After conducting many tryout camps, I've learned that those players who came to the camps, who willingly put their talents on the line, and who eventually made it to the professional level never quit the game of their own volition. They never allowed themselves to be defeated. The only way they lost their jobs was when they were released by their organizations. That tells me a lot about the character and perseverance of those players.

The two players who impressed me most in all the workouts I've ever run were Rickey Henderson, because of his explosive speed, and Al Oliver, because of his usable speed.

I'll never forget Oliver's audition. He hit a line drive toward the gap and rounded first base running at full speed. The ball was cut off and thrown quickly to second base. Oliver stopped on a dime and returned to first. That may not sound like much, but few players have the body control to hit the brakes at full speed without falling down or lunging forward a few feet more.

The One-Game Evaluation

Sometimes the only opportunity a scout has to see a player is in an actual game. And, as I've said, the game may not showcase or tax the player's talents. So what a scout must do is get to the game early and see and learn as much as he can.

For example, if the team is going to have batting practice before the game, he must be there for it. I really like to see the batting-practice session, where I can watch a hitter from outside the batting cage.

During a game, a team's best hitter may be pitched around or walked four times. In batting practice I can see his hitting form, his action toward the ball, and the movement of his hands as he begins his swing.

I can also see in batting practice if a player who normally does not hit home runs during games has *latent* power. Perhaps under game conditions a particular hitter becomes tense, which hampers his ability to hit for distance. In batting practice, when he is relaxed, you might see him hit balls farther than he will during a game. (This is common among young players.)

I make sure to watch the starting pitchers warm up on the sidelines, observing how fluid their deliveries are, how their pitches move, and how serious they are about their work habits. I also watch the players take fielding practice.

And when I'm not observing players, I'm asking questions.

I listen to the opinions and observations of the player, his teammates, his coaches. If a parent or guidance counselor is on hand, I speak with that person, too.

This way, by the time the game is about to begin I already have a good composite sketch in my mind of what each player can do.

In all, the evaluator is a diagnostician. He conducts as many tests as he can and does as much research as possible before making his diagnosis. Only then can he and his organization's teachers begin to treat the patient.

4 THE
BOWDEN
BRAIN

The secret to building a winning franchise—
or any successful enterprise—is good information: gathering it, teaching it, and applying it properly. Without good information, you can't make good business decisions.

When I trained real estate agents, I could give all the motivational speeches I wanted on how to sell property, but if I didn't train them in the fundamentals—step one, step two, and so forth—and all the possibilities that arise in between, they were not going to get the job done. If my agents didn't understand finance, they weren't going to be able to sell or list. So I taught them finance, finance, finance, over and over and over again.

It's the same thing with baseball. The first thing a general manager must do when he joins a team is evaluate and upgrade its scouting department. The scouting department is your team's information center; your scouts and your front office staff must gather and process good information efficiently and uniformly, so it's readily available and can be digested and implemented easily by the players, the managers and coaches, and the general manager.

How do you upgrade your information center? The first thing I do is evaluate my evaluators. I need to know each evaluator's grading criteria, since an evaluator's grades generally reflect his subjective preferences. For example, one evaluator may issue higher grades to a power pitcher than a control pitcher. Or he may use Don Mattingly as his standard of comparison for other first basemen. If I don't know which current or retired players he uses as his standards, his grades won't make sense to me.

Comparison is the key element in evaluation, the same way it is in any type of appraisal business. Say you have a market-data approach and cost-reproduction appraisal in real estate. You look for comparable properties that have been sold, then grade them with pluses or minuses.

The general manager must conduct an annual meeting of his scouting department to establish what major league standards will be used. The grades issued for minor league players aren't based on their current performance, but on what they are capable of doing on the major league level. We call this a "projection evaluation." (When evaluators scout free-agent high school and college players, they grade them on current ability as well.)

My evaluators grade numerically every component of the player's performance. For a position player, we rate him in the following categories: throwing arm; throwing accuracy; hitting, which is graded as a whole and also broken into four subcategories—ability to pull the ball, hit it straight away, hit it to the opposite field, or spray the ball to all fields; running form; how he runs the bases; power; bunting; fielding; how soft his hands are in the field; how much range he has in the field; body control; baseball instincts (the ability to anticipate a situation); aptitude for learning baseball;

and attitude and aggressiveness. The evaluators also record the player's running times in a 60-yard dash and to first base.

For a pitcher, the evaluators grade in these categories: the angle of delivery; fastball; the life, or movement in the hitter's zone, of his fastball; curveball; slider; straight change-up, which should be five to 10 miles an hour slower than his fastball; change-up curveball; whether he has another pitch in his repertoire, such as a split-fingered fastball, and how effective that pitch is; control of the fastball and the curveball; fielding; body control; and attitude and aggressiveness. The evaluators also record their readings on the radar gun of the range of speeds his fastball travels, and whether he throws a four-seam or two-seam fastball.

The organization can use any grading scale it feels comfortable with—from 1 to 5, from 40 to 100, whatever—as long as it's consistent. Here's the way we graded each component with the Pirates: 60 was regarded as outstanding; 50 or higher was excellent; 40 or higher, very good; 30 compared to the average for a major league player; 20 was below the major league average; 10, poor; and zero was hopeless.

During a scouting department meeting we decide what attributes we want to see in a 60 player and which major league players are 60's (there are not many of those out there, you know). And we go through the grades all the way to zero.

When I was the general manager of the Pirates, I also instituted a simple numerical system of comparison, ranging from 1 to 4. A prospect who earned a rating of 1 was deemed to have superstar potential. For reference, we considered such players as Don Mattingly, Tony Gwynn, George Brett, and Will Clark in the 1 category.

Those evaluated as 2 prospects were judged above-average, every-day players. Andy Van Slyke and Barry Bonds of the Pirates and Joe Carter of the Padres come under the 2 category.

The 3 prospects were compared to average, every-day major league players. The 4 prospects were utility and fringe players. A player who was not considered a prospect was given an "NP," which stood for "no prospect."

Along with the categories mentioned above, a first-rate evaluator reports on general areas common to pitchers and hitters: stamina, durability, poise, and reflexive reactions. He also takes the time to discover the player's inner qualities, such as his personality, his relationship with his family, his level of consistency, maturity, confidence, and pride. When I rejoined the Pirates in 1985, I discovered that their evaluators were guided solely by a player's physical tools and his statistics, without checking his background and emotional makeup. That's like hiring someone by virtue of his resume, without conducting a personal interview.

During a scouting department meeting we nominate one player at a time and collectively evaluate him. We may have sent five or six scouts to see a particular player during the season, so each of those scouts discusses the grades he issued and his personal observations.

For the most part, the grades are pretty close. But when these gentlemen disagree, diplomacy goes right out the door. Evaluators can get excited and emotional in the way a crowd of bettors does watching a cockfight. If an outsider were to walk into one of these scouting department meetings, he'd hear these violent arguments about a particular player's abilities and think, These guys are ready to go for each other's throats, and they must despise the leader who's promoting the arguments.

In 1957, my first year as a Pirates scout, I was in a meeting run by farm director Branch Rickey, Jr. At the start of the meeting Rickey said, "I want every one of you to speak up. Don't be afraid of giving your honest opinions. And no one should be thin-skinned." When shortstop Dick Groat's name came up, one of the veteran scouts said he judged Groat's three seasons in the major leagues as below average and felt he would never be an above-average player. Rex Bowen challenged him, and within seconds they were screaming at each other at the top of their lungs. I was shocked; I thought either one of them was going to storm out of the room and quit his job on the spot. But when they stopped yelling, the meeting continued as if nothing had happened. I soon learned that this is standard operating procedure among baseball people. We speak our minds freely, with the sole purpose of getting to the heart of the matter. When these meetings are over, we calm down and go about our business. It's as simple as that. (The postscript to the Groat story, of course, is that in 1957 he hit .315 and three seasons later was named the National League's Most Valuable Player.)

In order for me to make good personnel decisions it is imperative that my evaluators track every player in base-ball—not just in the major leagues but in Triple A, Double A, Single A, college, and high school—from the first time he is seen until his career is over, whether the scouts like the player or not. I was shocked to learn that the Pirates stopped scouting players from the time they were drafted by another team until they reached the Double A level. They allowed these players to disappear from view for as many as three years, waiting instead until they *and every other club* knew which of these players had potential.

Most major league teams have a staff of around 25 full-time and part-time scouts deployed throughout the United States, in Canada, the Dominican Republic, Mexico, and Panama. Three or four are advance scouts, who scout major league teams and follow up on players our evaluators have already seen and reported on. Cross-checkers are busiest from February to June, getting us the comprehensive infor-mation we need for the June Amateur Draft. After the draft, the cross-checkers scout major league teams and provide us with the information we need to make trades. This improves the quality of our judgments. (If I owned a team I would not hesitate to double the size of the scouting department.)

We rotate evaluators using a scouting method known as "scouting by the weather." To give you an example, every February, when cold weather keeps amateur teams in the Northeast from playing baseball, Northeastern scouts migrate to the South to help Southern scouts with their evaluations. This gives a team more opinions on those players in the South.

My evaluators use specific forms for amateur players and free agents, for players with other organizations, and for our own players. On our free-agent report, the evaluator grades the player; describes his strengths, weaknesses, and any personal problems the player is having; and tells us whether he feels we can sign him, what the player is worth, and what dollar amount he believes we can sign him for.

When I use the term "evaluator," I include my managers and coaches. Their input is vital to the entire process. In Pittsburgh we instituted a system called the Minor League Daily Game Report, which made our minor league managers and pitching coaches active participants in the evaluation of the players in our minor league system.

The reports, sent to the major league office via a facsimile machine, give a daily, detailed account of how every player performs in practice and during the game. The reports help determine which players are ready for promotion and which need more instruction.

At the top of the report, the evaluator fills in the team name, date, the line score, and the team's won/lost record. Beneath that is the pitcher's statistics—his won/lost record, the number of innings he pitched, and the number of pitches he threw. The pitcher is graded, using the same numerical system our scouts use, on his fastball, his control of it, and its movement in the hitting zone; his curveball, slider, and change-up, and his control of each of those pitches; plus a fifth pitch, if he throws one.

Let's say the evaluator gives the pitcher a grade of 27 for his fastball and 35 for his control of the fastball. That means the pitcher's fastball is a little below the major league standard we compare it to, but his control of that pitch is better than average.

The evaluator enters the number of first-pitch strikes the pitcher threw and how many batters he faced; the percentage of four-seam fastballs he threw; and the speeds of his fastball. Our evaluators break down the radar-gun readings into three parts: the single fastest fastball the pitcher threw, the slowest fastball, and his comfort zone (the range in which most of his pitches were clocked).

The batters' performances are recorded in the middle of the page, beginning with his name, position, number of at-bats, and hits. Next to that is a wide column where the evaluator describes the at-bats. He'll write down whether a single was a line drive or a blooper, whether an out was a fly ball, a ground ball, a line drive, or a strikeout. In this column the evaluator can note any good fielding plays our players made. In the last column the evaluator describes any two-strike hits the batters made.

At the bottom of the page, the evaluator describes the pitcher's performance and tells us what drills our players worked on during batting and fielding practice, whether a player suffered an injury during the game, the status of other players who are injured and not able to play, and which of our pitchers is scheduled to start the next game.

All of our evaluators, from Single A to the major leagues, fill out a Club Report Form to evaluate opposing teams on every level. The categories on the Club Report Form are virtually the same as those on the Free Agent Report, but this form can accommodate as many as 16 regular players and 12 pitchers.

The Club Report Forms are submitted by our evaluators after every series; if the evaluator sees the same opponent twice within a two-week period, he submits his Club Report Form following the second series.

The major league manager and coaches can submit their forms following the season. I don't want the major league staff bogged down by paperwork, but at the same time I want them to maintain a habit of evaluating our opponents under the criteria we established.

Elmer Gray, my administrator of baseball operations with the Pirates, helped devise and name a system that immediately advised the front office about players on every level whom our evaluators believe should be acquired. It's called the "Gold Card" system. These Gold Cards—gold-colored, five-by-seven index cards—can't be used to charge goods and services worldwide, but the Pirates couldn't have left the cellar without them.

The evaluator grades the player the same way as I mentioned earlier, circles the appropriate prospect category, and adds his comments. At the top right corner, the evaluator checks off whether the player is "Ready Now," meaning ready to play in the major leagues. If not, the evaluator writes in the year he believes the player will be ready.

Imagine how valuable this information is to a general manager. When I talk trade with another GM, I know *exactly* which players our evaluators have the highest regard for. That's particularly helpful when I discuss Single A or Double A players, who are not as well known by other organizations. If I did acquire a Gold Card player, I'd have a good idea of how long it would take him to reach the major league team.

Back in 1988 we gave Gold Card status to such minor leaguers as pitchers Rob Dibble and Jack Armstrong from the Reds system; Kent Mercker and John Smoltz of the Atlanta Braves organization; catcher Craig Biggio from the Houston Astros; Dodgers pitchers John Wetteland, Tim Belcher, and Ramon Martinez; outfielder Bernie Williams of the Yankees; pitcher Willie Banks from the Minnesota Twins system; Chicago White Sox right-hander Melido Perez; Philadelphia Phillies pitcher Pat Combs; California

Angels pitcher Bryan Harvey; and Montreal Expos shortstop Delinio DeShields and outfielder Marquis Grissom. Grissom, by the way, had earned a 1 rating.

Only time, good health, and proper development will tell if these players fulfill the potential we felt they had at that time.

All the paperwork I've described becomes pointless if your staff doesn't process it efficiently. When I joined the Yankees they had plenty of reports, all stowed in their minor league headquarters in Tampa, Florida. When we needed to see those reports, we had to wait two days until they arrived in the mail. I remember asking for reports in preparation for trade talks before the August 31 deadline (a player traded after August 31 is not eligible for postseason play). I didn't see them until George Steinbrenner hand-delivered them from Tampa on August 21. That gave me 10 days to become a trading genius.

When I first sat behind my general manager's desk in Pittsburgh in November 1985, I noticed that the reports the scouting department submitted were not centralized in one office. We had little warehouses of paper in six different offices. I'd asked the scouting department to provide me with information on every player they liked in the Houston Astros organization. A few hours later one of my associates returned with a stack of papers and dumped them on my desk. Now what was I supposed to do with that? The baseball winter meetings were just a few weeks away, and I felt like I was going into that gunfight with a water pistol.

Jim Bowden had the answer. In 1986, Bowden, a bright young man of energy and vision who aspired to be a baseball executive and will one day be an excellent general manager, was an assistant in the Pirates public relations department. When he saw me swimming in a sea of paperwork—and loathing it—he volunteered to write a computer data-base program, load all of the reports into it, and turn out workable sheets for me to refer to during the meetings.

I was so impressed by Bowden's initiative. He spent an entire Thanksgiving weekend in our offices organizing and printing out the information on the one computer the Pirates owned, which was in the public relations office. I said to myself, I've got to get Bowden out of the PR department and onto my staff.

Malcolm Prine, who at that time was the Pirates' team president, also recognized Bowden's technological expertise. Prine made Bowden the manager of internal communications, responsible for developing a computer system for the entire front office—sales, marketing, finance, and the baseball operations—and upgrading the office telephone systems. True, we needed a new phone system—the most high-tech feature those phones had were hold buttons—but I desperately needed a customized, detailed information system in the baseball department. So, during his off-hours Bowden moonlighted in the baseball department, designing and building a data base that would grow to contain 72 million bytes of information. Once the new phones were installed and the glitches repaired, I was able to convince Prine to allow Bowden to join my staff as my assistant director of the minor leagues and scouting, a point man in our operation.

Bowden, whose philosophy is, "Computerize all good information you see," purchased more computers for our office and for the minor league department in Bradenton and linked them together using the Novell network. Our secretaries entered information into the computer system daily and printed out detailed sheets of information, which I carried with me in my time-management valise.

I got so spoiled by the immediacy of access to the information I needed for efficiency that one month after I joined the Yankees I was able to get the Pirates' permission to hire Bowden and have him work his magic in New York. Bowden designed a system for the Yankees tailored to the attributes their scouts evaluated and the forms their scouts submitted to the minor league office. Once Bowden installed the system in Tampa, he was going to computerize our offices at Yankee Stadium so we could have immediate access to the critical information we needed. Unfortunately, Steinbrenner, for reasons only he knows, decided we didn't need to link the New York offices into the system. That defeated an important part of the whole concept of this system.

Because there are still many of us who are not computer-literate (I confess that I don't even know how to turn one on), the concept of a computerized information system sounds exotic, like Big Brother is waging a counterintelligence espionage war. What Bowden did was to write a software program, a customized data base to organize and sort what people report.

As Bowden explains it, "The idea behind my system is to allow me to furnish Syd with the critical information he needs to make decisions, to brief him with pertinent files the way a legal researcher furnishes a lawyer with the information he needs to try a case."

Here are some examples of the applications of the program Bowden designed.

1. Org Lists: Bowden can print out a one-page, up-to-the-minute list of all the teams in our organization, showing every player we have, which team they play for, whether they throw left-handed or right-handed and whether they bat right-handed, left-handed or switch-hit, their running times, range of throwing speeds, and all the grades our evaluators gave them.

The expanded org lists for each minor league player gives his height, weight, date of birth, and social security number; the airport closest to his home (in case we need to go there or make arrangements for him to see us); the year he began playing pro ball; his hair color and eye color; whether he wears corrective lenses; the names of his parents, his wife, and his children; where he went to school and what subject he majored in; what his hobbies are; how we acquired him; which of our scouts signed him, and which of our scouting supervisors covers that territory; and the name of his agent.

Bowden also can call up organization listings of every other team in baseball. For every player in the major leagues, the data base tells the player's length of major league service; whether he has cleared waivers; every transaction move—trade, recall, option to the minors, signed as a free agent—in his career; his salary and the terms of his contract; and the name of his agent. For the players in other minor league systems, the data base adds the prospect category our scouts have ranked each player in and the name of the scout who signed him, which is important to me, since I'm familiar with the grading patterns of almost every scout in baseball.

Whenever a player is released by his organization, Bowden immediately runs his name through the computer and calls up every report the evaluators have filed on him. If the reports are good, we'll sign him.

2. Bio Hits: An in-depth biographical history of every player in baseball, including his career statistics; the dates our evaluators observed him; the grades they gave him; and their comments. I ask Bowden to print out a specific player's bio hit right before I'm ready to acquire him.

3. Club Hits: A listing of the type of players the other 25 major league organizations are looking for. This way, when I pick up the phone and call another general manager, I know exactly the type of players he'll want to hear about.

4. Gold Card Sheets: Lists of every Gold Card player in baseball. When talking trade I can scan these printouts to see if any player the other general manager mentions has been awarded Gold Card status by our evaluators.

5. Player Contract Terms: Obviously, financial information is important when I'm talking about a trade with

another club. Bowden can give me the salaries and contract terms of about 60 players on each club.

The system also allows us to enter our comments on the various salary negotiations we've had with the agents who represent our players, both on the major league and minor league levels. So we not only have a salary history of our players, but a negotiation history with each agent.

6. Scouting Assignments: Bowden's staff keeps track of the territories each of our team's scouts cover, and the teams that play in those areas. If I need a scout to give us an updated report on a particular player before I acquire him, I can find out in seconds which scout to contact.

Another file contains the name of every player each of our scouts has already signed and how he is doing in our farm system. This helps me measure my scouts' productivity.

7. Amateur Draft Lists: In preparation for the June Amateur Draft, Bowden calls up the names of every eligible player and sees which of our scouts has reported on him and how our scouts and cross-checkers rate him. He can print out a detailed report on those players we want to draft.

We can also follow the progress of every player we drafted and signed the year before: whether he played in our system or returned to school; if he returned to school, whether he received a scholarship; how he performed; how much we paid him; and how much commission our scout earned on the signing.

8. Minor League Pitcher Reports: The information our minor league evaluators provide us in their Minor League Daily Game Reports is sorted and assigned to a file for each pitcher. Bowden can call up on his computer screen the individual pitcher and see how he has performed in every outing this season and what his grades are. When we are deciding which minor league pitcher to call up, we'll first open his file and scan his grades.

9. Daily Injury Status Report: The trainers on each club in the organization turn in daily reports on every player they administer treatment to. Our staff enters these reports into the computer so we can be aware of any existing problems, recurrences of old injuries, any medication or treatment players are receiving, and how fit they are to play.

10. Weight Report: At regular intervals our trainers weigh every player and measure his body-fat content, girth, and musculature. This information comes in handy when a player encounters problems and you're trying to investigate every possible cause. If, for example, a player's weight gain has affected his performance, we can change his diet or add more aerobic exercises to his workout.

This information is valuable for injury prevention as well. We discovered that one of the outfielders in the Pirates' minor league system had a calf muscle that was half an inch smaller than the other. We relayed this information to Dr. Warren Sipp, the Pirates' conditioning coach, and he went right to work helping the player correct the imbalance.

11. Spring Training Running Times: Our coaches and running specialists record the times in the 30-yard and 60-yard dashes that each of our players are clocked at, and grade them on their running technique. This tells us which players need more instruction. During the season we time and grade our minor league players a second time to see if they have improved.

12. Current Visa Status: Every year there are players who arrive late to spring training because they could not arrange for a visa to leave their native land. We make sure all our players who do not reside in the United States are accounted for.

Each franchise in baseball is allocated by the Department of Immigration a set number of visas for those players who require them. (Teams can loan one or two visas to another team as a courtesy.) Visas come under two categories: H-1, a visa for a player signed to a major league contract; and H-2, for a player under a minor league contract.

13. Player Development Contracts: A major league franchise signs player-development contracts with all of its minor league affiliates that delineate the responsibilities and costs each party bears, from the staff to stadium maintenance to the baseballs they use. Bowden's system allows us to monitor our costs to the penny.

Doesn't Bowden's computer system sound simple? Nothing is simple. It only turns out to be simple if you've got all the goods.

5 A BASEBALL TUTORIAL

Baseball fans frequently debate whether the players of the past were as good as or better than today's players. If we teachers were doing our jobs properly, then, no question, today's players, who are bigger, faster, and stronger, would be clearly superior.

In my judgment, there is a great deficiency of baseball knowledge. A lot of people confuse strategy with baseball knowledge. Strategy is something separate, probably the most overrated part of the game. What we've done is create a generation of strategists instead of knowledgeable, attentive analysts, instructors, and teachers.

What holds teachers back? Too many embrace at face value baseball's supersaturation of meaningless, inaccurate phrases. You've heard such profound, dogmatic gems as *Get a good lead; There is no way to improve lateral range; Great hitters are born and not made; A fastball rises; There is no way to improve running speed.*

This is not to say that everything that was done in the

past was wrong. But many things from the past have been lost in the translation because so little on instruction was written down. What technique did Ty Cobb use to steal bases? How exactly did Babe Ruth hit for power? Did anyone diagnose and analyze their performances? We'll never know.

I always look for instructors who are skilled in their area of specialization, think on a higher level, and are flexible to new approaches. A young player's worst enemy is a closed-minded instructor who refuses to consider alternative teaching methods that have been tested and proven.

I believe every team needs specialized pitching, batting, fielding, and baserunning instructors throughout its minor league system and even on the major league level. If baserunning is the key to the treasure chest of your offensive baseball, why not have a person on your staff who teaches baserunning only?

An organization also needs a coordinator of instruction—a dean who will help establish and supervise the curriculum. He must ensure that there is uniform instruction on every level of the organization. A good coordinator conducts in-depth seminars with every manager, coach, and instructor in the organization during spring training and again during the Instructional Leagues to exchange ideas and lay the groundwork for the methods that will be used during the season. The last thing I'd want is for my major league pitching coach to have a different philosophy than my Triple A pitching coach, or a roving minor league hitting instructor clashing with a Double A manager over the value of the two-strike hitting approach.

Before you can teach a player the methods that can enhance and improve his performance, you must know *how* to teach, because there is a fine line between *in*struction and *de*struction.

See, a young player is anxious to succeed, easily discouraged, and fearful of failure. As he advances through the minor leagues to the major leagues, the pressure to perform before expectant fans and critical media increases his insecurities. Even a veteran player can succumb to those pressures. How do you eliminate the fear of failure? Arm him with good information. Make him the most prepared, most knowledgeable player on the field.

How do you teach effectively? By breaking every concept down into small parts. You're not a good teacher unless your pupil understands. Ray Miller has been a successful pitching coach with the Orioles and now with the Pirates because he maps a plan for every pitcher he works with, as detailed as any road map you've ever seen. And it works because he uses it each and every day.

In baseball, we're dealing with players' sensory and motor skills. You've got to work on one fundamental at a time, and you move to the next area only when the player has broken his old habit and mastered this new and better one. And you've got to teach at the rate of the learner, since every person is different. I told you earlier about how Pablo Cruz and I worked with Tony Pena; the only reason we were able to get him back to a groove of success was that he learned and implemented each step more quickly than we thought he would. We hit the right notes at the right time.

This chapter—this book—isn't a cookbook. You can't turn to page 79, find the recipe for chocolate-chip cookies, take out a cookie cutter, and whip up a batch. What I'm presenting here are guidelines for success. Everybody looks for *the* answer. There is no *the* answer here! If I told you that the best way to break from your baserunning lead to the next base is by first crossing your left foot over your right, I would be guilty of negligence. I've seen players who get a faster break extending their right foot first. The right foot may be dominant. Should I insist they use the crossover step? No. All I'd be doing is confounding them.

What I do insist on, however, is that when a player learns something he must practice it properly and to perfection.

Being an educator myself, I know that learners learn from each other. Students study for tests together. In baseball, players often turn to their teammates for help. That can make the player soliciting advice more confused, or it can be just what he needs. The better you educate each player, the more help players can offer each other.

You've got to make sure the player knows his welfare is your utmost concern. Jim Thrift, current manager of the Kingsport Mets (rookie league) team, says, "The best way to communicate with a player is to first tell him what baseball philosophies you believe in. Second, tell him you believe in *him.*"

Lou Piniella adds, "You've got to relate your confidence to them. You've got to pat them on the back. Even if they're swinging lousy, you've got to find something they're doing well. I'll say, 'We'll work again tomorrow, but, damn it, you're doing a good job. You've got a good swing going.'

"I may tell a hitter, 'I've told the manager to be patient with you because we're working on some changes that may set you back at first, until you feel comfortable with them.' That eases his mind. The next day you go out, work some more, and continue the positive reinforcement."

Conversely, if you expect failure to occur, it inevitably will happen. As people, we get into a habit of uttering negative things without realizing it. There is a saying: "Out of the mouth, the abundance of the heart speaketh." If you profess failure, I guarantee you will fail.

Some pitching coaches go to the mound and tell their pitcher, "Don't hang the curveball." So what does the pitcher do on the next pitch? He hangs the curveball, because he was told something negative. What the pitching coach should say is something like, "Keep the curveball down. Even if you throw it in the dirt, don't worry about it."

Dr. Bill Harrison's studies on the response to stimuli by our sensory systems and thought processes show that all comments or thoughts—positive or negative—prior to an act become self-fulfilling prophecies. I've recognized times, like with Mike Diaz and Jesse Barfield, when specific instruction—the movement of the hands in batting, for example—would only distract the player and confound his sensory systems.

The most effective instruction is repetitive, conducted at a slow, rhythmic pace, with every movement done precisely. That way, says Ray Miller, "when it does happen in a game, the player reacts at game speed and does all the little things exactly as he is supposed to.

"One thing I have my pitchers do at a slow pace is catch the ball on a grounder, bring their hands together and pull them to their belts, then make their throw to a base. This helps them regain their balance, and it is also the position they are used to throwing from.

"In the game, when the ball is hit very hard to the pitcher's left or right, he'll instinctively snatch it, pull it in, and snap the throw. And he's got balance. Even though he did all this rapidly, he did all the little things it takes to make a good throw."

A good teacher like Miller will combine drills when appropriate. While Miller's pitchers are getting in their running along the warning track before a game, Miller stands in center field near the foot of the track. As each pitcher nears, he flips a baseball to Miller; Miller tosses it back, leading him toward the gap.

Miller explains, "That simulates the one fielding play they have every game: covering first base. If the first baseman fields a grounder and flips the ball to the bag, the pitcher has to reach out and grab it.

"This also transforms the pitchers' running from a mindless thing into a comprehensive drill."

The evaluator's measurements I described in Chapter Three are great teaching aids as well. You can tell a pitcher about the four-seam fastball and it may go in one ear and out the other. But you can prove your theory by having him throw four-seamers and two-seamers and show him the time differential on a radar gun. The measurements can also help teach your teachers.

Every drill must have a constructive purpose. "If my players are not running the bases properly during a game," says Jim Thrift, "I have them put on their running shoes the following day in practice and run the bases. If they're not executing bunts correctly, they go out the next day and bunt during batting practice. If my outfielders aren't hitting the cutoff men, we practice relay throws.

"I don't believe in punishing players for lacking a certain skill. I've seen many basketball coaches, after a loss in which their team missed free throws down the stretch, run their players' guts out during the next practice, then have them shoot free throws over and over again. What does that accomplish?

"If I'm disappointed with the on-field behavior of my players, I'll have them run laps around the bases the next practice to drive a few points home: I don't want to see anymore equipment thrown. I don't want to see anymore getting on the umpires. I don't want to see you jogging to first base on a ground ball."

Let us now conduct a seminar of baseball instruction.

Batting

Batting is the most glamorous part of the game. Everybody wants to be a great hitter. Pitchers get positively giddy when they hit the ball over the fence in a game or during batting practice.

The key to batting form is body balance. "Being in balance, with your weight centrally distributed, allows you to cover the whole strike zone," says Piniella, who compiled a career batting average of .291 over 18 major league seasons.

Piniella breaks down the swing into the "takeaway," the coiling action, and the forward stride. "It sounds funny, but in hitting you're going back as you're going forward," says Piniella. "On the takeaway, you have to get an inward turn of your front shoulder, hip, and knee, all in unison, so that you can get your hands going. As you step out with your front foot, you want to land on the inside of the foot to hold your weight back. Avoid a hard landing, because it will jar your head and disrupt your vision.

"At the same time, you want your head going toward the baseball. For instance, if your front stride is six or eight inches long, your head should release six or eight inches on your approach. If you keep your head back, your body spins too much. The best way to shift your weight properly is to move your head laterally as you're approaching the ball. This way, as you turn, you'll be turning on your front side, and your head is turning with your body.

"Then, once the head releases, your hands start the swing. The important thing is, your hands should work together with the stomach, the hips, and your head. If you could draw an angle when you hit the ball, your head, hands, belly button, and hips are all on the same angle. They're all tied together.

"You want to make contact off your front side. Your bottom hand starts to extend, and as you make contact your top hand pronates and gets your hips through the ball.

"You don't want your top hand to dominate the swing, because if it does it makes you pull off the ball. If I get bottom hand extension, which generates power, the top hand, which acts as a rudder, brings your backside through. When you're hitting a baseball, you want to use all of your body weight. If that top hand comes over too early, it causes you to lose extension from your bottom hand and the force from your backside. You swing across the ball instead of through the ball."

Whatever the game situation is, the batter must always

bring a plan of attack to the plate. He should ask himself, What am I looking to accomplish in this at-bat? Hit the ball to the opposite field? Execute a hit-and-run? Sacrifice myself to advance the runner? Bunt for a base hit?

Jim Thrift has his players hone their mental approach by simulating game situations during batting practice. "We work on our fundamentals during our first round of BP every day," he says. "The hitter makes sure his feet, hands, and bat angle are in the proper positions. He visualizes a runner on first base and takes a few sacrifice bunts. He visualizes the hit-and-run play is on and looks for a ball he can hit to right field. Then he visualizes there's a runner on third base and practices squeeze bunts, or hitting fly balls deep enough for the runner to tag up and score. These are the fundamentals that, executed correctly, are going to win games."

I often wonder how many at-bats hitters waste—simply throw away—over the course of a season. How many times did they come to the plate with no plan of action? At the Academy we developed the two-strike hitting approach, a simple, effective plan that helps the batter be productive when he's behind in the count.

In the two-strike approach, a hitter with two strikes in the count chokes up one to two inches on the bat handle and, if necessary, moves closer to home plate. Choking up gives you better bat control; the closer your hands are to the trademark, the balanced part of the bat, the quicker your swing. You should also move closer to home plate to ensure maximum plate coverage. When the pitch arrives, you try to hit the ball straightaway or to the opposite field.

The two-strike approach may sound like the batter is taking a defensive posture, simply trying to punch the ball up the middle. Actually, it's more offensive than defensive. You are taking a more aggressive posture. You are going to eliminate the strikeout by making contact. The only thing you have to eliminate—and you do this through practice—is the fear of getting jammed.

What a player has to do using the two-strike approach is divide home plate in half. His aim is to protect the outside half of the plate. He focuses visually from the middle of the plate to the outside. If he's a right-handed batter, his visual foul lines are from the shortstop position to the first-base bag. If he's left-handed, his visual foul lines are from the third-base bag to the area where the second baseman normally positions himself.

To maintain this visual picture, the hitter must move his head and eyes farther back in the strike zone. He's still looking forward, but by having his head back he's going to hit the ball as it crosses home plate, not before. I learned this added dimension from former Cincinnati Reds and Kansas City Royals outfielder Hal McRae, who was one of the best two-strike hitters I ever saw.

This technique ensures that the hitter stays closed, so he can drive the ball to the opposite field, instead of opening up to pull the ball. And what happens if the pitch is inside? The hitter in the two-strike position can still pull the ball reflexively.

What kind of ball should the batter put in play with two strikes, less than two outs, and men in scoring position? A line drive or a ground ball, which will give his team a chance to get that run in. If you swing down through the ball, you've got a chance for a hard, fast, ground ball, especially on synthetic turf.

Piniella says, "I guarantee that if you can just make contact every time a runner is on third base with less than two outs, whether it's a fly ball or a ground ball, you can make a living off those RBIs alone."

Late in the 1988 season I had an interesting conversation with Mike Schmidt, who was then with the Phillies. We talked for an hour about hitting, and he told me some startling things that confirmed some of the points we have made in our search for excellence in hitting.

Schmidt said he was a productive, All-Star player for the

first five years of his big league career, but he knew he had one problem: With men on first and third and less than two outs, he was trying to hit fly balls and home runs, which made him an easy target for breaking pitches. So he scrapped that and decided on a new approach: He would visually move the left-field foul line to shortstop and try to hit everything from that new foul line to the right-field foul line, on the ground and as hard as he could, staying away from the fly ball. Even on low pitches, he swung down through the ball. If the ball was inside, he could still react to it.

Some hitters use a long, slow, timid swing and guide the ball to the opposite field. That's a waste of time. The hitter is developing a bad habit that will carry over when he's trying to pull the ball. When you're hitting to the opposite field, you need a short, inside-out swing, because your hands will be ahead of the barrel of the bat at the moment of contact.

To help a batter hit the ball to the opposite field, we use a drill called the "soft toss." The batter takes his stance at the plate. A coach, kneeling on the outside of the baseline, tosses a baseball to the outside of the hitter's zone. This permits the coach to watch the hitter's action toward the ball, and the hitter to practice at a slower pace.

I've talked to a lot of great hitters over the years, and they say that when you try to hit a home run, you don't. All you should do is wait on the pitch as long as you can and hit the ball as hard as you can.

If you're going to wait, your hands must be quick. Remember, if you hold the bat too tightly, the tension you build in your forearms and shoulders is going to slow the swing. Piniella urges hitters during batting practice to use the whole field. "Start working the ball from the shortstop area to the second-base area. Learn to use the middle of the field. It makes you wait on the ball longer than if you tried to pull it."

I believe the reason some right-handed batters have trouble hitting against left-handed pitchers is that they don't use this principle of looking away, with right-center field as their midpoint, and driving the ball to the opposite field. The wrong approach—on any part of the count—is going up there trying to pull the ball. Why? In most cases, a left-hander's fastball moves *away* from a right-handed hitter. If the pitch starts out toward the middle of the plate, it will wind up on the outside part of the plate. If the hitter is looking inside, he'll pull the breaking pitches foul and hit the outside fastball as a ground ball back to the pitcher or a routine hopper to the shortstop or third baseman.

There is no valid reason why the two-strike approach can't be used earlier in the count. Against certain pitchers or in situations where he had to move runners, Piniella sometimes went into the two-strike hitting mode with one strike or no strikes in the count.

If you're going up against a pitcher with the fastball of a Nolan Ryan, what's the point of slowing your swing by holding the bat at the bottom of the handle? Choke up. Move closer to the plate. Don't try to pull the ball; drive it up the middle or to the opposite field.

Why don't more players use it? Because they mistakenly believe that choking up will cut down on their power, that choking up is for singles hitters. I vividly remember a Pirates home game against the Padres in 1987. The Pirates had runners on first and third. Bobby Bonilla was at the plate, batting left-handed against right-hander Eric Show. With two strikes in the count, Bonilla choked up on the bat and moved closer to the plate. Bonilla's plan was twofold: If the pitch was outside, he'd drive it to the opposite field; if it was inside, he'd pull the ball on the ground into the hole between first and second, since the first baseman was holding the runner at first. Show threw him a breaking ball. Surprise! Bonilla hit it into the upper deck at Three Rivers Stadium, something only Willie Stargell had ever done.

In fact, eight of the 15 home runs Bonilla hit that year came when he used the two-strike hitting approach. Had he not used the two-strike approach in the at-bat I mentioned, he might not have hit a home run. If Bonilla was holding the bat at the bottom of the handle, the pitch might have jammed him and forced a pop-up.

When a hitter is not making contact, the last thing a teacher should do is remake his stance. Rather, he should go over each component—the starting action, the stride, hands, and midsection—and help the hitter make any necessary adjustments. If his swing is too long, for example, you review his starting position, the angle of his bat, and how far down on the handle he is holding it.

In my opinion, the best swing is down through the ball. It's almost like a golf swing, in that the head of the golf club goes down through the ball and then up. Since all pitches fall (which I'll explain in this chapter's section on pitching), if you swing down you're swinging at the ball. When you hit it, you give the ball backspin, which makes it carry farther.

Swinging down also keeps your mechanics in sync. If you swing up at the ball, your back leg buckles and your front shoulder flies up and out. That's why most hitters fail at all levels: They try to swing up at the ball and they hit the top third of the ball. That results in a routine ground ball.

A great device to help a hitter practice his downward swing through a ball is a batting tee. The hitter can raise or lower the tee to simulate different locations in the hitting zone. Don Mattingly spends hours hitting off the tee before almost every game.

Now let's talk about the most neglected, most poorly practiced offensive fundamental there is: the bunt. Few players bunt in batting practice, and of those who do many practice it incorrectly.

One of the best bunters and bunting teachers I ever saw was Joe Tanner, a former player who worked with us as our bunting instructor at the Academy. He wrote a bunting poem he recited to our players:

Front foot forward,
Back foot around,
Bend the knees deeply,
Slide the bat down.
Eyes and blade [bat] *tied,*
Let the body glide,
Heels in the ground,
Bunt the ball down.

To bunt the ball in fair territory, your front foot should be up in the corner of the batter's box, in line with the foul line, with your bat in fair territory. You should be on your heels, not your toes, for better body control. The last part of the equation is how you hold your bat.

Tanner had a technique where he held the bat *vertically* and was able to bunt every pitch precisely. I was concerned that our hitters might find this approach too intimidating, so Tanner and Buzzy Keller refined it into the 45-degree-angle bunt. Instead of holding the bat parallel to the ground when squaring to bunt, as most hitters do, players were instructed to hold their bats up at a 45-degree angle, with the end of the bat pointing forward slightly.

Why? If you're holding the bat parallel, you have a smaller plane. You have to make sure the ball hits the bottom half of the barrel; if the pitch hits the top half, the ball will pop into the air. At 45 degrees and slightly forward, you have a greater plane. Here, the ball can hit any part of the hitting surface; the worst you can do is bunt the ball into the ground foul.

A fundamental every player should learn is the slug bunt, which has also been called the "butcher boy" play. Say you have runners on first and second, with no outs, and are trailing by one run. Your opponent, expecting a bunt, puts on the "wheel play," where all five infielders are in motion. The first baseman and the third baseman charge toward the plate; the second baseman runs to cover first; the shortstop runs to cover third; the pitcher charges toward home plate. The defense is going all-out to get the force play at third. All the infielders are in motion, and the middle of the infield is open.

We are going to turn the wheel play to our advantage. Our batter takes his bunting position—his front foot open, toward the foul line; his hands in front of his body, in fair territory; and the bat held at a 45-degree angle, slightly forward. As the pitcher delivers, the hitter draws the bat back, slides his bottom hand up toward the bat's trademark, and swings down on the ball. The whole infield is wide open; all he has to do is put the ball in play. It may seem like you've left yourself with an awfully short bat, but consider this: By sliding up six to eight inches, you leave yourself with the sweet spot of the bat. Since your hands are near the trademark, the balanced part of the bat, your swing will be faster and you'll have better bat control.

The slug bunt is a good weapon for a team that plays on artificial turf, because the ball bounces higher, giving the runners more time to advance.

Baserunning

A baseball axiom we disproved at the Academy is, "You can't improve a player's running speed." How did we do it? We broke the 60-yard dash into two 30-yard segments. The first 30-yard segment is the "explosive" stage, in which the runner makes his initial burst; the second is the "endurance and conclusion" stage, in which the runner maintains his pace to the end of the distance.

We found that most players were strong in one stage, but not both. The average major league player covers 60 yards in seven seconds. Player A may post a time of 4.1 seconds in the first 30 yards and 2.9 in the second 30, and Player B may run 3.2 in the first stage and 3.8 in the second.

Why are the times different? I believe 95 percent of it stems from poor running form. In high school, the track season conflicts with the baseball season, so players don't have a chance to learn how to run properly. They don't know how to use their legs and pump their hands efficiently. They flail. I brought the great miler Wes Santee to the Royals Academy not only for his knowledge of proper running form, but because the counterclockwise ovals trackmen run are similar to the counterclockwise path around the bases.

Once our instructors analyzed every player's form in each stage, we were able to shave two- to three-tenths of a second off his time in the 60 by increasing his speed in his weakest 30-yard stage.

Let's move to the base paths. Timing is as important in baserunning as it is in hitting. To be a successful base runner you've got to know how to look before you run, how to use your feet to maximize your time, and how much time you have to take an extra base or steal a base.

During the traditional batting-practice routine, after a hitter takes his last cuts he runs to first base, then waits until the next hitter makes contact before going around the bases. What the runner should do while on first is visualize a situation where he will be required to run from, say, first to third. One component he must practice is his "quick look" at the plate, which comes a few steps after he's broken for second. He's got to be cognizant of whether the batter has made contact and where the ball's been hit. Too often I see runners during a game not making that quick look home. What happens? The batter hits a pop-up to a shallow part of the outfield. The shortstop makes the catch and throws to first for the double play. Meanwhile, that runner's still got his head down, going full steam for third. That's the most embarrassing mistake a runner can make.

Every player must learn how to take a lead off each base. What is a good starting lead? A lead in which the runner can get back to first base in two steps, or in one step and a dive, without getting picked off. From first base, that can be from 12 to 14 feet. From second base, where the runner isn't held on, that can be about 17 feet. From third base, it's about 15 feet. The distances will vary for each runner; one may have more spring in his legs, another may have better reactions.

You must take your lead *even* with the base to get to the next base in the shortest amount of time. Some runners leading off second base walk toward the shortstop, believing that will help shorten their turn around third. That's misguided thinking. The shortest distance between two points is still a straight line.

Once the player has his lead, he must determine whether the pitcher is a "one-looker," meaning once he brings his hands together and sets he looks at the runner once before delivering the ball home, or a "two-looker," a pitcher who looks twice before delivering.

After the pitcher looks over, the runner extends his lead by taking a few slide-steps toward the next base. When he takes those slide-steps—skips, not hops—his body must be centered over his feet and under control. If he hops, he loses control of his body. It takes more time for his feet to land.

You've got to exercise good judgment here. Some left-handed pitchers, like Jimmy Key of the Blue Jays and Frank Tanana of the Detroit Tigers, will nail you in your tracks. As they start their motion from the set position their right legs hang in the air for a second or two. Since they haven't committed themselves to throw home, they can fire the ball to first if the runner has broken.

Now here are the keys in the runner's footwork. First, his

feet should be shoulder-width apart for proper balance. Second, his right foot should be slightly behind his left foot, with the ball of his right foot even with the instep on his left foot. Why? Say the runner is going to break for the next base using the "crossover step," in which his left foot crosses over the right, increasing the thrust from his legs. If his feet are even, he may knock knees, trip, or throw himself off balance. With his right foot slightly behind, he pivots on the ball of his right foot, clears his left foot, and turns like a trackman.

Then, as the ball is thrown home, the runner must have his right foot in the air, and his right foot must land as soon as the ball hits the catcher's mitt. If the runner's right foot lands when the ball is in the hitting zone, before it hits the catcher's mitt, he has stopped himself too soon. He's going to be locked in his tracks for a split second, so he won't be able to take the extra base if the batter makes contact.

This running technique should be used at any base whenever the runner is not being held on, especially with two outs. Here's an example: Let's say Alvaro Espinoza, a shortstop of below-average running speed who knows how to run the bases correctly, is on second base, speedy outfielder Roberto Kelly is on first, and second baseman Steve Sax, an above-average runner, is at the plate with two outs. The pitcher looks once at Espinoza. As he starts his delivery home, Espinoza slide-steps another 10 to 13 feet toward third.

Sax hits a ground ball to the hole at shortstop. Because of Sax's speed, the shortstop knows he won't have a play at first. Because Espinoza had a big lead and took off at the proper time, the shortstop doesn't have a play at third. So he throws to second. Since the first baseman wasn't holding Kelly on, Kelly was able to take a larger lead and beat the throw to second. Instead of the inning being over, the bases are now loaded, the rally is alive, and the potential for a big inning remains.

If Espinoza's right foot doesn't land at the precise moment, the shortstop might have a play at third. The same goes for Kelly at first. And if Kelly doesn't take off and run all out, the inning is over. I say this because there are at least 10 or 12 times each season when, in this situation, the runner at first isn't doing all he can to get to second as fast as he can. He's watching for a possible play at third, just like the fans are. He breaks late, makes one of those pop-up slides at second, and is called out. Imagine how many more runs a team can score if that runner from first reaches second base safely just 10 more times?

How does a runner determine which lead is right for him? We quantified this at the Academy by developing *the timed, measured lead*.

In the first year of the Academy, Joe Tanner, who was a mathematics major, put horizontal chalk lines in the base paths and measured the leads of every player in game simulations. That showed the players exactly how far they could lead off the base and still get back in time. He also taught them the "spoke-in" slide back to the base, where the runner's left arm, resembling the turning of a spoke on a wagon wheel, pushes downward and toward right field. The spoke-in technique keeps you from diving on top of your arm, which will slow down your return to the bag or, worse, cause an injury to the hand or shoulder.

Tanner's aim was to eliminate the runner's fear of being picked off. An uneducated base runner is like a parakeet. What happens when you open a parakeet's cage? He flies out of the cage and heads right back for it. The cage is his security blanket. It's the same thing with a hard crab. If you knock a hard crab off a dock, he'll climb right back to the spot you've knocked him from.

By teaching the runner his proper lead, you instill a sense of awareness that all the best athletes have. Not only was Tanner giving players a road map to the next base, but he was marking the starting spot that said, "You are here."

While Tanner worked on the measured lead, Buzzy Keller timed every runner. During a think-tank session the following year, Steve Boros suggested we combine the measurements and the running times into a specific formula for each player. This was the birth of the timed, measured lead.

Keller says, "We clocked the amount of time it takes a pitcher to deliver the ball to home plate from his set position, and for the pitcher's pickoff throw from the set position to reach first base. We also timed the catcher's throw to second base, from the moment he caught it until it was received at second base. And we clocked both the time it took the runner to cover the 90 feet between first and second base and the time it took him to return to first from his leads off the base."

We came up with averages that helped determine the lead a player could take. An average pickoff throw reaches first base in one second; an average runner, taking a 12-foot lead, can make it back to first in one second. Then we had the runners increase their leads from 12 feet to 13 and 14 feet, as far from the base as they could go and still make it back in time. The longer the lead, the shorter the distance to second base.

The next part of the process was the runner's path to second. By adding the time it took the pitch to hit the catcher's mitt—say, 1.6 seconds—and the time for the catcher's throw to hit the mitt of the fielder covering second—say, 2.4—the runner would know he had four seconds to reach second.

We timed every pitcher and catcher we played against with stopwatches and radar guns, noting the times of each segment. When we faced that team again, our runners knew before the game started exactly how big a lead they would need in order to steal second base.

"The ability to steal second base is the crux of base stealing," says Boros. "Stealing second takes away the potential double play and puts the runner in scoring position. It also creates tension and concern on the part of the infielders, which causes them to shorten up or cheat toward the bag. In fact, you can get them to the point where perhaps they make some errors because they're so concerned about the runner at first."

A runner can take a larger lead from second base, because it takes more time for the pitcher to whirl around and throw to second, and more time for one of the middle infielders to get from his position to the base. Therefore, if the runner gets his maximum lead from second it is virtually impossible for him to be thrown out stealing third base. Say Espinoza took a starting lead of 17 feet, then slide-stepped another 13 feet. He's now a third of the way to third base and has only 60 feet to go.

Jim Thrift, whose Princeton team stole 170 bases in 70 Rookie League games in 1988 and whose Peninsula team stole 208 bases in the Carolina League in 1989, keeps track of the times of all the components of the timed, measured lead and has his players record them in notebooks, which they update after each series. "On my level, the players may not see the same pitcher that often," he explains. "But I want their note taking to become a habit. When they make it to the major leagues, whether the pitcher they're on base against has a great move or a terrible move, they already know what their step-back, dive-back, and stealing leads are.

"If I don't teach them how to run, speed or no speed, they become station-to-station ballplayers, advancing one base at a time when the batters get hits. I want them to know how to use their speed to create a three- or four-run inning."

The beauty of the timed, measured lead is that it not only demonstrates to a player how he runs, but *when* he should run. Initially, the player may have thought he would not have enough time to steal second base against Pitcher A, who throws a 95-mile-an-hour fastball. But if he knows he can make it to second in 3.4 seconds from his stealing lead, while it takes Pitcher A 1.2 seconds to deliver the ball from the stretch and 2.4 for the catcher to make his throw, he realizes he can do it.

Similarly, the player may have assumed he could steal second against Pitcher B, who has an 85-mile-an-hour fastball, by simply outrunning the ball. But if Pitcher B gets the ball to home in less than one second, the runner may not have enough time to steal.

However, pitchers do not always deliver every pitch from the stretch in the same amount of time. It may take Pitcher B 1.2 seconds to deliver his curveball. Aha! The runner may not be able to steal second against Pitcher B's fastball, but he *can* run on his curve.

Now the runner can think on a higher level. He can ask himself, How does Pitcher B like to pitch to the hitter behind me? When in the count is he most likely to throw a curveball?

You don't always need above-average speed to steal bases. "The delayed steal," says Boros, "is a useful technique for runners who only possess average speed. There are a few ways to teach it. One method we used is where the runner takes two skips as the pitcher is delivering the ball to the plate. The two skips are ordinary, so as not to draw the attention of the infielders to the fact that you may be delay-stealing.

"In the course of those two skips you get anywhere from 10 to 12 feet closer to second base. About that time the infielder, who has been glancing to see if you're breaking, believes you're not, so he turns his attention to the plate and focuses on the hitting zone. The runner breaks for second when the pitched ball is about 10 feet in front of the hitting zone. You will surprise the catcher and beat the infielder to the base."

Another technique Boros used frequently during San Jose's minor league record-setting 372 team steals in 1974 was the double steal.

"Here's one of the double-steal techniques we used when we had runners on first and third and a left-hander was pitching. Remember, when a left-hander is on the mound his back is toward the runner at third base.

"Either runner can start this play. The runner at third can start it by breaking for home, while the runner on first purposely stumbles or falls down. As soon as the left-hander makes his first move to first base, the runner at third breaks for home and scores.

"Or, the runner on first can break for second and then fall down. When the pitcher throws to first, the runner at third breaks for home.

"The point is to draw the throw from the left-handed pitcher to the first baseman; when he does, the runner at third scores."

Pitching

A winning pitcher is not the one who merely throws the best pitches. He must also be well schooled in the art of pitching —how, when, and where to throw a pitch—and in fielding fundamentals.

If your pitcher doesn't know how to hold a runner close to first base or pick him off, chances are the runner will wind up on second before the next batter does anything. If the pitcher keeps the runner close to first, he may advance only one base should the next batter hit a single; if the runner is already on second, he may score on that single.

I had a pitcher in the Pirates' minor league system who knew how to pitch, but I held him back from the major league level because he couldn't field his position properly. What if that pitcher had allowed only one run going into the seventh inning of a game and the other team decided to bunt on him? They could start a rally and disrupt his concentration. The fielders behind him sense this and start to dwell on negatives. Now your entire team starts thinking about their reactions instead of thinking about the game situation and reacting instinctively.

Practice sessions are when a pitcher should be thinking about his physical reactions and his execution.

Whenever Ray Miller teaches his pitchers or conducts a drill—even when they are running sprints—he has them hold a baseball in their hands. "When he has a ball in his hand, he thinks," says Miller. "For example, he may hold it differently one day and discover a new grip."

Miller likes to drill his pitchers collectively, as a unit. "We can talk together about pitches or plays we might need to work on, or I can ask one of my pitchers who has a great change-up to show it to another pitcher. You create a team-within-a-team attitude. The guys work real hard, and when things happen they talk about them. By spending time discussing areas that are going to help them and their team win ball games, they feel better about themselves."

The drill in which the pitchers toss the ball to and receive it from Miller while running on the warning track is one part of what we call "PFP," an acronym for pitchers' fielding practice. During spring training Miller's pitchers spend two to four hours each day on PFP drills. He labels every topic—Class 101 or Class 102, and so forth.

During one class, a pitcher takes his position on the mound, with Miller standing behind him. Miller flips a baseball where the pitcher can't see it—the ball may touch his body or fall before him. The pitcher runs toward it, picks it up, brings his hands to his belt, takes a step, and throws to a base.

In another class, Miller implements what he calls a "scramble drill."

"In almost every game there's a ball hit off the pitcher's leg or a ball he must knock down. When that happens, he loses sight for a moment of where the ball is. I train them to fundamentally pick it up and get it to the base quickly."

He'll conduct a "stop bunt" drill, where he leaves a ball sitting on the ground at a spot in fair territory, a third of the way up the baseline, where a bunted ball may rest. The pitcher runs to that spot, leading with his right foot, and picks up the ball and throws in one motion. "Invariably, there's one play where the pitcher has to field a ball that's just lying there. The pitcher can't simply bend over. He has to get his rear end down, pick up the ball, and throw without straightening up. If you do this drill over and over, he'll be able to pick it up and throw in one fell swoop, without taking a long step."

"When you first start these drills, the pitchers fall all over themselves," Miller laughs. "The drills take a lot of concentration and coordination. But each day the pitchers get better and better at them. Then, when the situation comes up during a game, the pitchers on the bench will yell, 'PFP,' or, 'There's Class 102.' It's something they've worked on and feel good about."

As the pitchers progress, the teacher adds more elements to each drill, approximating every game situation they will encounter. For instance, on the scramble drill we may start by telling the pitcher, "There's a runner on first base." When he knocks the ball down and picks it up, he makes his throw to second base to start a double play.

We'll have a coach hit fungoes to the first baseman, who starts the double play by throwing the ball to the shortstop; the pitcher runs to first and receives the throw for the second out.

Before a workout or a game, Miller has his pitchers stand about 40 feet apart and play catch with each other for 15 minutes. "While they're loosening up their arms," he explains, "they talk and think about little things that can help them during a game.

"During the last two minutes of that drill, they move close together and go through pickoff moves, at game speed, to get the feel of throwing to first base."

Let's move to the mound. Before a pitcher throws a single pitch, he needs to understand and visualize the hitter's zone. The hitting zone is different from the strike zone, because hitters will swing at—and can get hits off of—pitches that are out of the strike zone.

If you were to stack baseballs into a rectangular box as long as the distance between a hitter's shins and his shoulders and as wide as the plate, the box would contain from 63 to 70 baseballs.

You can then divide the rectangle into the five specific locations I discussed in the previous chapter—the center, inside and low, inside and high, outside and low, and outside and high. What made Jim "Catfish" Hunter a Hall of Fame pitcher is that he knew exactly where to throw every pitch. He threw every pitch to perfection.

Before you throw a pitch, it's incredibly helpful to understand how pitches move aerodynamically. At the Academy we conducted time-motion studies of the pitched baseball in flight. Two people who played important roles in these studies were John Garver, a physicist and inventor from Youngstown, Ohio, who had brought to the Academy a bazooka-shaped pitching machine he invented, and Dr. John Nash Ott, a retired banker from Chicago who had worked as a time-lapse photographer on movies for Walt Disney.

Garver was fascinated by the rotation of a pitched baseball. In the course of building his pitching machine, he came up with formulas showing the number of times the baseball rotated from the moment it leaves a pitcher's hand until it crosses the plate. We took his studies a step further by photographing pitched baseballs, using 16-millimeter cameras.

Against a background screen on which we marked off the distance from the mound to home plate in four 15-foot segments, Ott photographed the movement of the baseballs Garver's machine hurled. At first, we could not distinguish the rotations. Then Buzzy Keller suggested painting half of the baseball black. Presto! We could count the seams rotating 14 to 16 times.

We then studied and measured the movement of a variety of pitches, using different grips. The photographs proved that *all pitches fall*. Despite what you've heard, there is no such thing as a "rising" fastball. A fastball doesn't rise; it simply is affected less by gravity than slower pitches. The faster you throw it, the less time it spends in the air and the less it falls.

In our tests of the fastball, our pitchers used two different grips: the conventional "two-seam" grip, which is held along the baseball's stitched seams; and a "four-seam" grip, in which the baseball is held across the widest spread between the seams. We consistently saw that, no matter who the pitcher was, *the four-seam fastball traveled three to four miles an hour faster than the two-seamer*. Those four seams cause a molecular mass underneath the ball that sustains it a little longer in flight, with less turbulence.

The slower, two-seam fastball falls three inches or more before it reaches the plate; *those three inches are equivalent to the diameter of the baseball*.

How does this help a pitcher? Since pitching and hitting are interrelated, to know one you have to know the other.

A batter has 42-hundredths of a second to react to a 90-mile-an-hour fastball. We found that the best hitters read, identify, and begin their stride from zero to eight feet from the point of the pitcher's release. The very best hitters can tell from the time the ball leaves the pitcher's hand whether it's a fastball, slider, or curveball by identifying the angle of the pitcher's hand and the rotation of the ball. To them, the ball looks twice its normal size. But the average hitter can't differentiate between pitches as quickly.

Most hitters hit all balls the same way. They simply don't have the time to adjust to different pitches. In effect, the batter is not hitting the pitch with his bat; the pitcher is hitting the batter's bat with his pitch.

Let me explain. Say there is a right-handed pitcher on the mound and a left-handed batter at the plate. The pitcher throws two four-seam fastballs that are 91 and 92 miles an hour. The batter fouls them off or misses them. His swing is late.

The next pitch is a two-seam fastball that travels 87 miles per hour. The batter hits that pitch over the right fielder's head for a triple.

Why? Because he was swinging at the two-seam fastball the same way he did at the four-seam. He employed the same stance, the same start action, and the same swing as he did on the first two pitches, only this one went for a triple. The third pitch fell three inches more than the first two. Therefore, on the third pitch, the pitcher did the batter a favor: He hit the hitter's bat. Had he stayed with the four-seamer, he might have struck out the hitter.

To the naked eye, a four-seam fastball looks as if it's rising, but the reason for this optical illusion is that the average hitter, who swings the same way at every pitch, is missing the four-seamer, which falls less than other pitches, by an average of three inches.

So a pitching coach is mistaken if he tells his pitchers to keep the ball down in the strike zone on every pitch. The hitter has less time to react to a pitch up in the strike zone. In fact, there are some major league pitchers, like Jim Deshaies of the Houston Astros, who are successful throwing 85-mile-an-hour four-seam fastballs up in the strike zone.

Only the best hitters can compensate for this. I once asked Ted Williams if he hit all balls the same way. He said, "No. If a guy throws across the seams I hit at the middle of the ball. If a guy throws a sinker I hit at the bottom of the ball. If I hit two ground balls in a row off that sinking-fastball pitcher, I'd place an imaginary ball under the ball."

I now ask you to put a baseball in your hand so I can begin a class on the five different grips that can be used to throw a fastball with the same arm movement, beginning with the four-seamer. (For the sake of convenience, we will assume you are a right-handed pitcher.)

To employ a basic four-seam grip, find the part of the ball that is stamped, "Official Ball, American (or National) League," and hold the ball so you can read the stamp horizontally between your fingers. Now turn it one-quarter to the left. The seams will be in the shape of a horseshoe, with the top of the horseshoe to the left.

Put the closed end of the horseshoe above the ring finger of your hand. Spread your fingers a pencil's width apart. Now put your thumb on the seam on the underside of the ball and the joint of your ring finger underneath the ball on the slick part (the horsehide). Notice your fingers and joints are evenly distributed on the ball. This grip will make your fastball rotate more and fall less, so you'd use it to pitch to the higher locations of the hitting zone.

If you want your four-seam fastball to have a "cutting" action—boring in on or away from the hitter—simply turn the ball slightly off-center. (Keep your index and middle fingers a pencil's width part.) The closed end of the horseshoe is now outside your index finger. This gives you a different point of release because of the seam construction.

Now let's use the two-seam grip. Center the ball and turn it one-quarter to the right. Your index and middle fingers will overlap the seams. (If you turn your hand toward you for just a moment, you'll see the stamp of the ball horizontally above your thumb.)

You can place your thumb anywhere along the underside of the ball. If your thumb is on the horsehide, you'll get a true two-seam flight, in which the ball sinks more. Therefore, if you're going to throw the two-seamer, you want its location to be in the lower portions of the hitting zone. A well-placed two-seamer will fall below the hitter's reach. If the pitcher threw a two-seamer to the upper parts of the hitting zone, by the time it reached home plate it would fall into the middle of the hitter's zone. A professional hitter will hit that fastball for a home run.

For a variation on the two-seam grip, turn the ball one-eighth to the right (away from you). Now your index finger will be on the horsehide to the left of the left seam and your middle finger will overlap the seam on the right.

With one finger overlapping a seam, the ball will sink more. With two fingers overlapping the seams, the ball will ride more. Why? Because having both fingers on the seams gives you more traction; the more the traction, the greater the ball's action in the strike zone.

How do you control the side-to-side, cutting movement of a fastball? By finger and thumb pressure. If you apply more pressure to the right, outside half of the ball, it will slide like a slider. If you apply more pressure to the left, inside half of the ball, it will bore in and sink like a screwball.

I can tell from behind home plate or from a few rows back in the stands whether the pitcher is throwing a four-seam fastball or two-seamer. How? The four-seamer appears smaller and more blurred, while the two-seamer looks larger and whiter.

If you use the four-seam grip for an overhand curve, it will result in a sharp, downward break, because all four seams are meeting the wind. This was discovered by Igor Sikorsky, the inventor of the helicopter. During the fifties, Sikorsky, a baseball hobbyist, conducted tests in a wind tunnel to determine whether a curveball actually curved. According to Sikorsky's tests, if a pitcher threw a four-seam curveball of over 80 miles an hour, the curve would break as much as 19 inches. With the same speed and rotation but only two seams meeting the wind, the curve would drop about seven and a half inches.

By changing the release of the ball, positioning the baseball deeper into the palm of your hand, the pitch will travel slower. This is a change-up.

Ray Miller teaches a succinct philosophy about the art of pitching: "Work fast, change speeds, throw strikes."

"My approach teaches the pitchers to relax and let their defense do the work for them," says Miller, "as opposed to trying to overpower every batter on every pitch and burning himself out.

"I don't mean that you don't try to strike hitters out. Rather, the success in pitching is not allowing the hitter to be comfortable in timing the speed you're going to throw the ball. If the pitcher works fast, the hitter doesn't have a lot of time to think and adjust."

If you throw a curveball and the batter is way out in front of it, you can tell he is timing his swing to your fastball. If you can throw him the same curveball within 10 seconds of the last one, I guarantee you he won't hit it. Studies show that images and thoughts remain in muscle memory for 10 to 11 seconds. If you've ever driven through a stop sign, it takes more than 10 seconds for that realization to clear from your mind. It's the same thing with this hitter at the plate; he won't have a chance to correct his brain and make the adjustment.

Now, if you throw him a fastball on the next pitch he might hit it out of the park because you have played into his timing, since his mind is still set from the last pitch.

If he fouls off your curve, you should not throw him another one on the next pitch, because he already has it timed. You change speeds instead.

Using the different grips I described, a pitcher can throw four pitches using the same arm speed: a four-seam fastball at 92 to 95 miles an hour, a two-seamer at 88 to 91, a curveball at 78 to 79, and a change-up at 72 to 73.

"There's also such a thing as a 'batting-practice fastball,'" adds Miller. "The normal fastball is thrown with a nice, smooth delivery, with your arm moving like a bullwhip—it makes a tremendous arc and snaps at the release. That's what propels the ball at 90-plus miles an hour. The batting-practice fastball is thrown with the same starting motion as your normal fastball, but you don't finish it off with that snap. You throw it lazily, with less velocity, away from the batter where he can't pull it.

"This doesn't work for Little League or high school pitchers, because they may not throw hard fastballs to begin with. But it's a good pitch on the college or pro levels in a particular point in the count where the batter is expecting a fastball.

"Let's say John Smiley of the Pirates is facing Andres Galarraga of the Montreal Expos in a close ball game. In the course of the at-bat Smiley might have thrown two 96-mile-an-hour fastballs, a change-up, and a couple of curveballs. Now the count is 3-1. Galarraga knows Smiley can't afford to walk him, so he commits himself 100 percent to a fastball.

"With the same motion Smiley threw his earlier fastballs, he throws Galarraga a batting-practice fastball at 87 miles an hour, 10 less than his four-seam pitch. Galarraga sees the fastball, charges for it—but it's not there. He has to slow down his swing to put the ball in play, so he pops the ball up or hits a weak ground ball."

The third part of Miller's philosophy—"throw strikes"—seems obvious. When Miller talks about throwing strikes, he emphasizes the first strike. The higher a pitcher's ratio of first-pitch strikes, the more batters he is going to get out.

"The name of the game is 'strike one,' " says Miller, "simply because if the hitter doesn't swing at another pitch you need only two more strikes out of the next five possible pitches to the plate to get him out.

"Most young pitchers start out with a fastball and a second pitch. They use their fastball to get ahead of the hitter in the count. When they get to a higher baseball echelon, they need to develop other pitches they can throw for strike one. If a pitcher learns to throw something slower for strike one, the hitter automatically becomes defensive. He now has to worry whether the pitcher's going to throw the next pitch real hard or even slower.

"If the pitcher has the ability to change speeds, the batter is going to swing at his fastball more often, whether it's a strike or not, because he is fooled by the other pitches. Consequently, he'll swing at a fastball a couple of inches out of the strike zone."

Miller's plan for his pitchers includes copious diaries of each outing, which he uses in preparation for his pregame meetings.

"I conduct my meetings in steps," says Miller. "Before the first game of each series we play, I have a general meeting with all the pitchers and catchers. We talk about the characteristics of the different hitters on that team, as a way to familiarize everyone.

"On the day of the game the first thing I do is sit down with the catcher. We'll go over the other team's lineup, what good things our pitcher can do against each hitter and which hitters he should pitch carefully to. Then while the other team is taking batting practice I'll sit down with the catcher and our starting pitcher. We'll go briefly through the lineup and talk about specific pitches to use against certain hitters. The pitcher sees which six or seven guys he can get out and which two or three he needs to be careful with.

"The day after he's pitched I put in his locker a list of every hitter he faced. The list has the game's line score at the top and all the hitters he faced. I provide spaces for the pitcher to write down anything he wants to remember about those hitters. The reason we do it the next day instead of immediately following the game is that he is more reflective and not as emotional.

"And I keep that list on file, so whenever he is scheduled to pitch against that team in the future, we review his written comments. They come back to him positively, helping to reinforce my suggestions."

What does Miller see when he watches a game? "I never take my eyes off the pitcher, except to look for pickoff plays," he says. "I know in my mind what his good, smooth delivery is. I keep watching him to make sure he doesn't slow down or speed up his delivery. I know what he's going to do with each hitter, so I watch the pitch selection.

"Between innings I talk to the pitcher, always trying to say something positive. There are times when a pitcher will have thrown an off-speed pitch to a weak hitter. His teammates come back to the dugout angry and jump all over him, not knowing there were other times when he did the same thing and got away with it. That's where my job comes in. I tell the pitcher, 'You've gotten that hitter out in the past with a change-up, but I wouldn't keep throwing it all day. He's a weak hitter, so give him a pitch he can put in play.'"

Miller shares my belief in keeping every critique positive. "When I go to the mound during a game, I want to talk with the pitcher about the game situation. My voice and my demeanor must be calm, my comments simple and objective. If he needs one out to get out of the inning, I may tell him, 'You've got a good change-up. Stay back and don't worry about the base runners, and throw it. This guy will hit a ground ball to second base.'

"That situation came up two times early in the 1988 season, once when Smiley was pitching and another time when Doug Drabek was pitching. And in both instances the batter hit a ground ball to second base and they got out of a bases-loaded situation and went on to win.

"If I've spotted a flaw in his mechanics—maybe his body is a little too quick to the plate and his arm is late—I can't tell him directly. I do it in a roundabout but simple way.

"I'll say, 'You've pitched a great game. You've got the

right guy at the plate for a ground ball if you get the ball down, so what I want you to do is slow your body down so that you have time to get your arm out there. Let your arm work with you. If you throw him a sinker, he'll hit the ground ball for you.' "

A pitching coach can also enlist his catcher to help a pitcher follow the game plan or correct a flaw in his mechanics. "You can be more direct with your catcher," says Miller. "You can tell him which pitchers he may need to be stern with, and which pitchers need a pat on the back.

"You can even have signs to tell your catcher what he should say when he goes to the mound. If the catcher has been told before the game that his pitcher has been opening his front shoulder too soon, you can work out a sign with him where, if I touch my left shoulder, he should go to the mound and tell the pitcher, 'Your shoulder is opening up too soon. Stay back and everything will be fine.' "

Miller sets his base for comparison by studying the pitcher when he's pitching well—but not talking with the pitcher about it.

"I look at his cadence. I look at types of pitches he uses. With some pitchers I look at the percentage of fastballs, curveballs, or change-ups he throws in those games. Then I file those impressions.

"A good pitcher should be successful three out of four times. Maybe on that fourth time he just didn't have it, or the other team swung the bat particularly well. I just throw that one out. But if the pitcher's had three or four bad outings in a row, if you've done your homework the solutions should jump right out at you."

He also believes in leaving a pitcher alone on the day of a start. "I have a deal with the starting pitchers: 'The day you pitch is yours. We'll have a pregame meeting, but once you go out to warm up use your intelligence and prepare accordingly. If you want to ask me something, I'll be there.

Otherwise, I won't. If I see things I want to work with you on, we'll talk about them the next day or before your next start.'

"I don't talk to the pitchers when they warm up. I always hated that when I was a pitcher. I would be trying to build a positive attitude, and after five warm-up pitches some pitching coach would be standing there telling me, 'Get your arm up. Stay back a little bit longer. Make sure you don't hang that curveball'—so many negatives.

"I think the greatest tribute I ever got from any pitcher was from Mike Flanagan, who won the Cy Young Award when we were with the Orioles. He was on a tremendous roll in August and September. A reporter asked him about my work with him. Flanagan told the reporter, 'One thing about Ray—he's always there when I need him, and I always know when he thinks I'm pitching well.' 'How do you know that?' the reporter asked. Flanagan replied, 'Because he leaves me alone.' "

Defense

What's the number one method of improving your defensive ability? Playing catch with a teammate. This simple routine helps you perfect the basic task of fielding.

During your catch, visualize how you will catch the ball, bring your hands together, and make your throw. When you throw, point your front foot toward your target (a straight line would be ideal). Your hand, at the release point, should also be in the direction of your target.

Say you throw right-handed. If your feet are squared, you decrease your velocity, because you are depending solely on your arm and not using the rest of your body. If your left (front) foot is to the right of your right foot, you will be throwing across your body, which decreases your accuracy.

Your throws will be either too high or too low. Remember, the ball always goes where the hand goes.

These instructions may sound simplistic, but if you execute them properly you can turn an erratic arm into an accurate arm.

Another basic way to improve fielding, particularly for infielders, is to practice without a glove. During this drill the players pair up in two rows, eight or 10 feet apart, and toss soft one-hoppers to each other, varying the hop with each throw. This helps the player get a better feel for the ball than he would wearing a glove.

Here's a drill to use with a glove: Keep your throwing arm behind your body as ground balls are being hit or thrown to you. This trains you to keep your glove hand open and facing the ball, instead of bringing your glove from behind your body and turning your wrist over.

In a balanced fielding stance, your knees should be bent slightly and your weight evenly distributed. Your hands should be in front of you, in catching position. If you stand upright with your arms dangling at your sides, you are not going to be able to reach down quickly enough.

Let's examine the fundamentals of each fielding position and the drills we use to improve them, beginning with the infielders.

Proper footwork is imperative for a first baseman. When a ground ball is hit to one of the other infielders, he's got to get to the bag quickly, plant the heel of his back foot at either of the corners of the base facing the infield, and be in position to take the throw.

There are a variety of drills he can use to improve his footwork. One is to field ground balls while receiving throws. The instructor hits a ground ball to him; he fields it, tosses it back, gets to the bag, takes a throw from one of the infielders, and gets into fielding position for the next ground ball. The point is to make the first baseman so comfortable with these movements that in a game he doesn't watch the play and then scramble to get to the base in time.

During a workout an instructor can chalk three lines along the field, five feet apart. The first baseman stands over the middle line in his fielding crouch. In a controlled amount of time—say, 30 seconds—the first baseman slide-steps to the line at his left, back to the middle line, over to the right line, and repeats. This "line drill" helps the first baseman improve his first step without relying on a crossover step.

When the workout is over, or as part of an exercise regimen, the first baseman should skip rope to quicken his feet.

The first baseman must also work on receiving throws. During practice one first baseman stands by first, another by second base. They then take turns throwing short hops to each other. In an expanded form of this drill, the first baseman takes his stance near the base. The instructor hollers, "Go!" The first baseman runs to the bag, sets up, and receives the throw from the other first baseman.

The first baseman and third baseman are closer to the batter than the middle infielders, so they've got to quicken their reactions to the batted ball. During practice the corner man stands in fielding position on the lip of the infield grass (which is softer to dive on than the infield dirt). The instructor, standing 30 feet or less before him, throws ground balls to him. Being this close means the corner man has to react more quickly.

We use a similar drill for middle infielders—the instructor, standing behind the pitching mound, throws ground balls in all directions—because in games they have to field the ball and make quick throws on the run.

I like to use the pitching machine to improve the lateral range and footwork of the infielders, an idea we first came up with at the Academy. Since a pitching machine can be set to shoot out each baseball at the exact same spot, the instructor can turn it around and point it at the fielder, shooting out a series of ground balls. The fielder moves closer or farther away, helping him develop the dexterity in his glove hand for short hops, and to the left or right, which allows him to practice and improve his lateral movement.

The pitching machines produce uniform bounces, so we can also measure and compare the fielders' reactions. And since ground balls hit during a game do not bounce uniformly, we supplement the drills by using a curveball-pitching machine, which produces trickier bounces. This simulates the spin of a ball hit off the end of the bat that goes down the line to the opposite field.

All infielders should keep their hands low to the ground. This way, if the ball stays low the hands are ready; if the ball bounces up, you can bring your hands up or block the ball with your chest. If you don't keep your hands low, when you reach down for a grounder you will jab at it and likely knock it in another direction. And when you bend for a grounder, bring your buttocks down. If you hunch over, you're not going to reach a low hop.

There are three types of hops a ball can take: a big, high hop, a short hop, and an in-between hop. The fielder's goal is to avoid the in-between hop whenever possible.

The best way to avoid an in-between hop is to turn it into a short hop or a high hop. To turn it into a short hop, when you approach the ball bring your glove hand in a downward plane and take it through the ball. Shortstop Rafael Belliard and second baseman Jose Lind of the Pirates execute this to perfection.

Never bring your glove hand backward when shortening the hop; that gives the ball more time to bounce upward, increasing the short hop to an in-between hop.

On a hard-hit ball that must be caught behind your body—which often occurs at first base and third base—you can let your glove flow where the ball is going and catch it at a higher level.

When the ball is hit hard to either side of the first baseman or third baseman, or to the holes at second or short, the infielder's got to move back slightly at a 45-degree angle toward the outfield to give himself more time. Say the batter lines a shot down the third-base line. The third baseman should dive at a 45-degree angle, facing the seats along the left-field side. This gives him one more hop to snag the ball. Former Yankee Graig Nettles was exceptional at this, and Wade Boggs of the Boston Red Sox has greatly improved his range because of this technique.

Say the infielder has to dive for the ball. Again, he moves at an angle slightly away from it. The most efficient way to get to his feet is to pull his knees to his chest, spring up, and make the throw. If he has to crawl to his feet, valuable time is lost.

Because the third baseman is involved in so many bang-bang plays, he's got to be relaxed and ready before the ball is hit. Some third basemen, like Carney Lansford of the A's, get set in the fielding stance and wait as the pitcher starts his windup. Others, like Bobby Bonilla, walk toward home plate, then set as the pitcher releases. When we work with third basemen, we suggest they emulate the side-to-side movements tennis players use while waiting to receive a serve.

The third baseman should then focus on the hitting zone and not the hitter. Otherwise, he gives away a precious split second.

Another thing the third baseman has to work on is handling bunts. In a sacrifice situation, the third baseman has a little more time, because he's come in on the grass before the pitch. His challenge is when he's back on the infield dirt and the batter bunts for a hit. Traditionally, the third baseman charges, fields the ball bare-handed, and throws sidearm or in a submarine style to first. Know why that's been described as the "do-or-die" play? Because the third baseman has little control on a ball thrown from those angles; if his throw isn't perfect it's going to sail up the line and pull the first baseman off the bag.

Here's a better way, one that takes a lot of practice to master: When the third baseman bare-hands the ball, he throws his left side open to square his shoulders and makes an overhand throw. This may take him a half-step longer to release the ball, but he'll make up for that time with a stronger, more accurate overhand throw.

The key for middle infielders is to execute the double play, so during practice we work in stages on their footwork at the front end of the double play, the throw to the base, the angle of the throw, and the footwork on the back end.

We'll start the drill by hitting, throwing, or using a pitching machine to shoot a ground ball to the second baseman. If the ball's to his left, he's got to field it, pivot, and make a sidearm throw to second; to his right, he shovels the ball as he moves toward second. Through repetition, he learns which throw is best on a ball hit straight at him—sidearm or shovel—relative to his location.

The shortstop, on a ball to his right, plants if he has enough time, and throws overhand to second. If he doesn't have enough time he's got to throw the ball from whatever angle he receives it. To his left, he can throw sidearm or shovel the ball.

Whenever a corner or middle infielder shovels the ball, he's got to get his glove hand out of the way so his teammate can see the ball clearly. Don't hide the ball from the recipient.

A throw that takes a good deal of practice is the backhanded flip from behind second. That throw has to be as straight as possible. If the shortstop is upright, or if his legs are tired from running toward the bag, the flip may hang in the air too long.

When the middle infielder covers second, he's got to step away from the base to avoid the sliding base runner after taking the throw from his partner and making the throw to first. Whenever possible, the middle infielder should step toward first base. This way, he can make an 89-foot throw. Former Pirates second baseman Bill Mazeroski was expert at approaching the bag at such an angle that he was stepping toward first as he made his throw.

The instructor times the middle infielders turning the double play so they learn to turn a double play in, say, 4.1 seconds against a batter running in 4.2 seconds to first.

It's important that your middle infielders drill together to get a better sense of where each of them likes to receive the throws. Every now and then we flip-flop the second baseman and shortstop so they get a feel for the footwork from the other side of the base. This also makes them more versatile; you never know when they may be called upon in a game to fill that position.

Outfielders should work as hard on fielding ground balls as infielders. Sure, when a ball's hit right at them, they usually have enough time to step down on one knee and block a bad hop with their torsos. But with runners on base a good outfielder must be able to field a ground ball, whether it's hit right at him or to either side, and make a strong throw to the right base.

When we work with outfielders on grounders we hit fungoes or use the pitching machine, because a thrown ball can't match the speed of a batted ball hit during a game. The curveballs from a machine simulate ground balls and line drives that tail away from the outfielder and roll to the gaps or the corners. For fly balls, we use a fungo bat.

Then we go over the outfielder's footwork. On all plays, an outfielder has to run on the balls of his feet. If he lands on his heels, the force will jar his head and cause him to lose track of the ball.

On a high fly ball hit with runners on base, the outfielder should take a few steps back, then a few steps forward. This way, when he catches the ball his momentum takes him toward the infield, which allows him to use the full force of his body for the throw. When he catches the ball, he leads with his right foot; as he transfers the ball from his glove to his throwing hand, he steps forward with his left foot and throws.

The next time you see a Pirates game, watch center fielder Andy Van Slyke make this play. His body control and co-ordination are so exceptional that it looks as if his legs flick only one step.

The outfielder's got to take a 45-degree angle toward the fence on balls hit to his sides and then, as he's about to field the ball, circle forward to keep the ball in front of him, like a shepherd circling his flock. Why? If he takes a direct path to the ball, he's not giving himself enough time to reach it; a single or double becomes a potential triple or inside-the-park home run. If he does cut the ball off, it will take as many as five steps before he can stop his momentum and make the throw. And if the ball's to the left of a right-handed thrower or to the right of a lefty, he's got to whirl around and make an out-of-control throw. By corralling the ball, he's in position to throw.

You asked, "But isn't he giving up time by circling instead of running straight?" Theoretically, yes, but the total time elapsed by making your throw sooner is less. Think of it this way: Every tenth of a second you have the ball in your hand allows the runner to run three feet farther on the bases.

On a low liner, the outfielder has three options: Make a shoestring catch; slide toward the ball legs first, as if you are sliding into a base; or dive headfirst. The shoestring catch, which requires body control, is preferable, because you remain on your feet, ready to throw. Jesse Barfield likes to slide, because it keeps his head still, allowing him to watch the ball longer.

Diving seems like the easiest route, but when done incorrectly it guarantees injury. When you dive for a ball, you should extend your body. As you catch the ball and land, turn the wrist of your glove hand toward your body; your throwing arm can either be extended straight out or down to the side of your body; slide on the front of your chest and on the latissimus dorsi on your glove side, two areas of the body protected by muscles. Then, when the catch is made, bring your knees to your chest, spring up, plant your feet, and throw.

If you keep the wrist of your glove hand extended, your hand will jab against the ground and injure your fingers or wrist. If your throwing hand is bent or underneath your body, you can injure your elbow or shoulder.

We use a "touchdown drill" to help outfielders go back on a ball hit over their heads. When we yell "Go!" the outfielder takes off and we throw bombs over his head. He takes a look at the ball to judge its flight, runs on his toes to the spot where he thinks the ball will land, looks up again, extends both hands, and attempts the catch. This develops proper form and concentration.

The instructor then takes a fungo bat and works with the outfielder on the "home-run drill," or, as Jim Thrift likes to call it, "The 'CNN Play of the Day' drill." When the ball is hit, the outfielder goes to the warning track as quickly as possible to give himself enough time to make a nice, easy, running jump off the foot opposite his glove hand for a ball hit over or high against the wall. Through repetition and body control, and outfielder can learn to "climb" the wall—make the first jump off the foot on the side of his throwing hand, and take a second step against the wall off the foot opposite his glove hand, propelling himself even higher. Dave Winfield of the Yankees, who has superb body control, is a sight to behold when he climbs the padded outfield walls in Yankee Stadium and turns potential home runs into high-lights for CNN.

Most fans judge catchers by their effectiveness in throwing out base runners attempting to steal. What physical asset most accounts for a catcher's success rate? No, not his arm—his *legs*. After he receives the ball, he's got to spring up, stride forward with his left foot, shift his weight from his back foot forward, and throw. The quicker he is, the less time he gives the base runner.

Bob Boone of the Royals is so good at this that, when he's really on his game, he shifts his weight to his right, takes a small step toward second base, and throws.

As with first basemen, catchers should jump rope to im-prove their footwork.

Catchers also need to quicken their reactions to handle pitches outside the strike zone. At the Yankees' Instructional School in 1950, Bill Dickey stood 15 to 20 feet in front of the catcher and threw balls in every direction. Again, being closer forces the catcher to react faster. You supplement these drills by using the pitching machine. Shoot balls right at him, to his left, to his right; short hops, curveballs, any-thing he'll encounter in a game. You teach the catcher to block pitches he can't catch by having him drop his knees to the ground, keeping his head down and his hands by his sides. The catcher doesn't want to leave any gaps between his arms, body, or legs and the ground for the ball to squirt through. When he drops down, his shoulders should be squared, so if the ball hits him it will bounce in front of him. When the catcher becomes proficient at this, he can learn to angle his shoulders just a bit—his left shoulder slightly in front when a left-hander's pitching, his right shoulder slightly in front when a right-hander's on the mound—to compensate for the direction from which the pitch is coming toward him.

Whatever your position, there are two ways to tell that you have arrived as a fielder. First, you really want the ball to be hit to you, regardless of the situation. Second, you have your fundamentals down cold, so you are able to anticipate and react. Before the ball is hit, you ask yourself, What type of pitch is my pitcher going to throw? Where is the batter likely to hit it? What do I do if it's hit to me? Do I throw home? If it's hit a certain speed, do I go to second base instead?

If you are mentally prepared, you will eliminate the doubt and indecision that result in errors.

Good team defense can control the speed of an offense. If your pitcher works fast, he is increasing the efficiency of your defense, because your fielders have to be alert at all times.

If there are runners on base, your pitcher can throw off their timing by using a slide-step, which cuts down his delivery time to the plate. In the slide-step, the pitcher, about to deliver the ball from the set position, slides his front foot forward as he throws, instead of bringing it up toward his body.

If the runner can't time your pitcher to steal second base successfully, the next batter may have to bunt him over. But your defense, proficient at catching and throwing and mentally ready, fields the bunt and throws out the lead runner.

Now the batter is on first. Let's say he's the fastest runner in the league. The next hitter lines a ball to the right-field gap. This situation pits the runner's time running the bases against your time handling the ball.

Your right fielder moves at an angle away from the ball, which gives him a little more time to cut it off. Since he has already visualized this situation, he throws to the cut off man, who relays the ball to third base. If the runner takes too wide a turn rounding second base, your defense will throw him out, no matter how fast he may be. Or, if he or his third-base coach knows your defense can handle the ball, they may decide to hold up at second base.

"Because my teams are aware of the impact of speed on offense," says Jim Thrift, "they understand what they need to do when they run across an opponent of equal or better speed. They know that if they can handle the ball, are lined up in the right position, and hit the cutoff man, they will eliminate the runner.

"When we play catch, we sometimes envision two speedy runners on the bases. Our first priority is to throw out speed merchant number one. But if they can't, for lack of time, they immediately focus on throwing out speed merchant number two."

The Winning Baseball Player

I define a winning baseball player as one who is prepared, can execute plays, gets the most from his abilities—and knows when to disregard the conventional statistics.

Giants second baseman Robby Thompson is such a player. Maybe his statistics aren't particularly striking, but he does everything he's called upon to do and does it well, without a lot of fanfare. On the very last play of the 1989 National League Championship Series, Thompson turned a tough ground ball that would have handcuffed other second basemen into a routine play by backing up at an angle to give himself more time and ensure proper footwork.

In an appearance on Roy Firestone's TV show, "Sportslook," Hall of Fame center fielder Duke Snider of the Brooklyn Dodgers was asked if he felt he hadn't gotten the recognition he deserved because he had to share New York's spotlight with Mickey Mantle and Willie Mays. Snider replied, "I never thought about that, because Mr. Rickey always said that if you play unselfish, winning baseball, your numbers will be greater than you ever dreamed."

It's true. When Robby Thompson gets on base by knowing how to work out a walk, Will Clark and Kevin Mitchell get more RBIs. When setup relievers Ken Dayley and John Costello of the Cardinals hold the opposition, closer Todd Worrell gets more saves. The better-paid players are judged by RBIs and saves, but how would their stats look without the unheralded winning players? And would those winning players be winners if they focused on their numbers?

I recall a period during the 1988 season in which Bobby Bonilla had collected two hits in 22 at-bats. The newspapers were quick to point out this "slump," and pretty soon Bonilla started thinking negatively.

Our staff had been keeping track of every one of those 22 at-bats. I told Bonilla, "Look what you've done. On five of the balls you hit that became outs, the center fielder crashed into the fence and caught them. And twice the runners on third base tagged up and scored. On another four of those outs, the fielders robbed you. Had any of those balls become hits, you would have 11 hits in those 22 at-bats. You did your job. You did not fail!"

Bonilla realized he was not in a batting slump, but had he dwelled on that two-for-22 statistic he would have succumbed to a mental slump. He would begin to press. Then he might not have hit any balls hard. And mental slumps are contagious. His teammates start pressing to make up for his lack of production.

Too many players live and die by the traditional box score, which measures only a fraction of a player's success. The box score ignores so many of the things that win ball games, such as moving the runner into scoring position on a ground-out, scoring a run without a base hit, or making an important relay throw. As in Bonilla's case, it also can't describe the type of outs a player makes.

We didn't use the traditional baseball statistics at the

Academy. For example, we did not keep players apprised of their batting averages. Had we done so, we would have given them tunnel vision. Instead, we posted rating charts in the hallway of the main dorm. Some of the categories we compiled were: sacrifice flies; swinging to aid a player in a steal; aiding the runner while in the on-deck circle; and signs and pickoffs. We wanted to encourage team spirit. We wanted each ballplayer to be well rounded, to know how to execute the types of plays needed for winning baseball, because those kind of "winning" players have long careers.

Jim Thrift created for his players an enlightening statistical device he calls the "Quality Performance Rating System," which records, measures, and awards points for each aspect of every player's performance. As an added inducement to the players, he takes the money collected from fines and at the end of the season distributes it proportionately to the players who've earned rating points.

The Quality Performance Rating System is critical for beginning players, because it allows them to maintain their confidence no matter how low their batting average or how high their earned run average may be.

"A manager has to stress to his players the smaller things that win games, and redefine and expand on the conventional baseball terminology," Jim Thrift says. "I try to find at least one reassuring fact for each player that I can build on.

"For right-handed hitters, a successful hit-and-run has been defined as hitting the ball to the right side of the field. That's a pretty difficult task for an 18-year-old player just out of high school, unless he has God-given talents and superior bat control. A successful hit-and-run can be a triple to left-center field, or even a high chopper in front of home plate where the batter reaches base successfully and has advanced the runner. To me, both of those are quality at-bats.

"Perhaps the batter lined a smash to right, but the right

fielder has an arm like Andre Dawson and throws out the lead runner. Still, the batter has reached base, which keeps open our possibilities of scoring. That's also a quality at-bat.

"In my rating system, I list every possible fundamental skill. I keep organized, up-to-date charts and graphs of the things that we do successfully, no matter how small.

"Under the offensive category 'Bat,' I have a section for 'at-bat,' where I put down everything the player did in that at-bat, from the types of pitches he got, whether he hit with the count in his favor, how he executed a sacrifice bunt or a suicide squeeze, whether he moved the runner up, what he does with two strikes on him, and what type of hit he got. And I continue to monitor his progress.

"A hitter may not be aware he's a good two-strike hitter. He could be thinking, I'm always hitting with two strikes on me. But I show him that, in fact, he's a pretty tough out. I'm giving him something positive without being unrealistic.

"My report may list a hitter as going oh-for-four on a given day. I also describe the type of outs: two ground-ball RBIs, a two-strike line-drive out, a fly ball which allowed the runner to tag from second. Whenever a hitter moves a runner into scoring position he earns more quality points."

He measures pitching and defense together as a means of reinforcing to his players that good pitching depends on good defense. "Our goal defensively is to set the pace of the game. We want to speed things up so that the offense has even less time to react. We're trying to negate their offense, defensively, the way a basketball coach uses a half-court or full-court press.

"When we take the field, we do everything crisply. The players sprint to their positions. The pitcher and the fielders finish their warm-up throws and wait on the batter to get into the batter's box. I give them team points for maintaining a brisk pace defensively, as well as offensively.

"I award the pitcher points for throwing strikes and keeping us in the game. We want our pitcher to throw strikes, particularly in the first two innings, because constantly having to come from behind after two innings makes the players stale. They whisper to each other, 'Old meathead is pitching. It's going to be three-to-nothing after the second. We've got to battle back again.'

"Say our opponent has a man on second with no outs. If the pitcher induces the batter to pull the ball to shortstop, which keeps the runner from advancing, he gets a higher-quality rating because he made the right pitch in that situation. That's what will make him a winner in the big leagues.

"If a reliever comes into a game and completes the inning leaving runners on base in scoring position, he gets points per runner.

"If a pitcher retires the side in order, he gets a high rating. If he strikes out the side, he gets the highest possible rating, because he minimized the chance of a batted ball being put into play. Striking out the side may be a rarity, but I want them to be aware that it can be done.

"Conventional fielding statistics may say a player is making too many errors. On my chart I describe the error. My second baseman may have gone to the shortstop side of second base to reach a grounder and made an errant throw to first. The official scorer gives him an error. The way I look at it, how many other second basemen are going to get to that ball in the first place? Joe Average may have fewer errors because he doesn't get to as many balls as my second baseman does, so which player would you consider to be the better fielder?

"Here's another scenario: One of my outfielders makes an unbelievably strong throw to the plate and the catcher mishandles it. An error is registered. But, again, something positive came out of a negative. If the catcher had held on to the ball, the runner would have been out by 20 feet. So I make sure to award points to the outfielder."

All this "small" talk has a big payoff. You have not only developed every player as an individual, but you've taught them all the ways they can contribute to their team. You have increased their net worth, and converted them from prospects into winning players.

A winning player can play in the major leagues for 12 or 15 years—even if his statistics are not impressive—because teams will appreciate his knowledge and execution of the components needed for winning baseball. Everybody loves a winner.

6 TRAINING THE BRAIN

The eyes are the gateway to the brain. The optic nerve is an outgrowth of the brain and comprises an actual brain tract.

A regular player's visual systems account for roughly 80 percent of his total performance. By visual systems I mean his ability to see clearly, recognize what he sees, track a moving object, and relay that information to his brain, which signals his body to react.

You often hear a good hitter say the pitches he sees look as big as grapefruits. A struggling hitter will tell you he has trouble picking up the ball. In both instances, it's not what they're seeing—it's how they are *using* their eyes.

Dr. Bill Harrison, one of the first optometrists to work with athletes, says, "So many coaches in different sports stress the importance of hand-eye coordination. But it's the eye-mind-body coordination that makes things click.

"In football, when a receiver makes a great catch the coaches and fans say he has 'good hands.' Actually, he's got good eyes—a good visual awareness of what he needs to do."

In baseball, a hitter becomes visually aware of a pitch within the first eight feet of its release. Now, that sounds impossible at first blush, but it works out mathematically when you analyze it in a time-space approach.

John Garver demonstrated this graphically to our players and staff at the Pirates' 1988 spring training camp by conducting what he calls "The Curtain Test." Garver divided the 60-foot, six-inch distance from the pitcher's mound to home plate into four 15-foot segments. Then he strung a seven-foot-high curtain from home plate to a point eight feet from the pitcher's mound. He set the curtain at such an angle that the hitter in the batting cage could see the pitched ball travel the first eight feet and disappear behind the curtain, while my staff and I, standing on the side of the cage, could view the complete path of the ball, all the way to home plate.

The hitter was asked to point with his bat or his hand to the location he thought each pitch landed in the hitting zone—knee level, waist level, inside, outside, and so forth. Time and again, our hitters were correct, even though they had only seen the ball travel the first eight feet.

A player can have great eyesight but not focus on the ball. From the time a hitter or a fielder initially sees the ball until he reacts to it, a variety of learned skills come into play. For example, he can see the ball as part of a big picture that includes everything in its background. That is called "soft centering." Or he can see the ball and cut out all the background objects. That's "hard centering." The harder he centers, the more clearly he sees the ball. Likewise, a pitcher can pitch with greater control by hard-centering on a specific target—whether it's the

catcher's mitt or one of the strike zone's four locations—as
he throws.

The player may also have difficulty following the ball as
it moves in different paths. Steve Boros says, "We in baseball
are just beginning to realize that the ability to track a ball
is extremely important for a hitter. There are a number of
organizations who now give vision tests to their drafted
players before they attempt to sign them.

"The old notion that you can get an idea of a player's
visual ability by putting up an eye chart on the wall and
having him read it is way off base. I'm particularly attuned
to this, because when I was a young player coming up in
the fifties and sixties I could read any eye chart on a wall.
But during the course of my career I was hit on the head
four times by pitches, and all four times I never moved.

"While I was at the Royals Baseball Academy as a minor
league manager, Dr. Harrison discovered I had a lazy left
eye. The eye muscle was weak and couldn't move the eye
into the proper position to track the ball in its new path.
Harrison asked me, 'How in the world did you hit a slider?'
I laughed. 'Not very well, if you look at my lifetime average.'

"If I was playing today with a team that administers comprehensive vision tests, the problem could have been corrected."

"Injuries aside," says Dr. Harrison, "I really do feel that
a lot of players are forced out of baseball prematurely because they have some visual difficulties that were never
identified and never solved."

There are many roadblocks to good vision, and they've
got to be removed so the brain can process information
effectively. Some of the roadblocks come from the eyes and
eye muscles, others from the brain itself. However, vision
is a learned response, so with proper testing and training
you can improve what you see and how quickly you react
reflexively.

Corrective Measures

Every player should undergo thorough eye examinations at regular intervals. Over the years I've had Dr. Harrison visit every one of my major and minor league teams and administer tests with his portable equipment.

"The tests involve all the basic vision testing that would be done in an optometrist's office," Dr. Harrison explains. "I test their visual acuity, the clarity of sight.

"I determine their contrast sensitivity, their ability to recognize what they see and its gradation of colors, like gray on white. Contrast sensitivity was first researched by the Air Force. They had discovered that some pilots who had 20-15 vision still had difficulty recognizing enemy aircraft. Those pilots with better contrast sensitivity recognized the aircraft more quickly.

"I check their eye alignment, to see if their eyes turn up or turn down. I measure their depth perception, the ability to judge objects at different distances. I use an instrument called a refractor to measure their refractive error, which essentially determines whether the person is nearsighted, farsighted, or has astigmatism. Then I decide whether the player needs glasses or contact lenses.

"We also have a variety of equipment that tests the coordination of the muscles of the eye. There are 14 muscles that control how our eyes operate. Twelve of them are about an inch and a half long and about a half-inch wide, and there is a circular muscle on the inside of each eye. If those muscles work well together, players have better tracking skills."

Once any flaws in the player's vision have been diagnosed, Dr. Harrison teaches him skills to correct and improve on them.

While working at the Academy, Dr. Harrison was asked to examine an 18-year-old player in the Royals' organization named George Brett.

"George had hit well in Rookie League ball," says Harrison, "but he had a serious handicap. Every time he blinked, that slight visual disruption caused him to have blurred or double vision for a split second afterward. He tried to compensate by staring, and he walked around with his eyes opened as wide as possible. Of course, it was impossible for him to do this during a game.

"I had him wear polarized glasses and use a Polaroid vectogram, a device with two polarized pictures that you view at arm's length. George had to separate the pictures manually in various directions, while making his eyes and brain fuse them into one perfect, three-dimensional picture.

"After only two weeks of daily half-hour drills, his eyes worked so well together that blinking no longer impaired his vision." And, as radio personality Paul Harvey might say, you know the rest of Brett's story.

Later on, Ewing Kauffman asked Dr. Harrison to evaluate Lou Piniella, who began his major league career with the Royals. Dr. Harrison discovered that, although Piniella had perfect eyesight in each eye, his brain was paying attention to one eye at a time. This had caused Piniella poor depth perception, so he had trouble reacting to changes of speed. Dr. Harrison had Piniella train his eyes with a vectogram and other apparatuses to help him redevelop this skill, and soon afterward his eyes learned to work together.

In one of the drills Harrison uses to improve tracking, numbers are projected onto a wall, moving rapidly from left to right. "We ask you to track every number. After 20 numbers, we ask you to recall, for instance, how many number eights you saw, how many number twos.

"You have to be locked in visually to do this. It's easy to lock in if you have no other task to do. So we simultaneously involve them in some kind of coordination drill, like a jumping jack. We also may ask them other questions or have machines emitting sounds at the same time.

"We call this 'stress therapy.' The player learns to focus on his primary task despite the bombardment of distractions."

Vision and the Mind

If your brain is clouded with thoughts, you will not be able to execute your primary task with full and undivided concentration. You lose your visual awareness. The visual images drop out.

Dr. Harrison offers an example. "Driving down the highway, you have a tendency to daydream. Suddenly you realize you've missed a turnoff. Or, you've driven a long distance and it suddenly dawns on you that you have no idea how you got there.

"If someone was watching you drive, they'd think you had great concentration, because you were looking straight ahead. And yet nothing registered, because your mind was on the radio, a conversation in the car, or other thoughts.

"That same thing can happen to a hitter, even on the major league level. He steps into the batter's box with great determination, but he doesn't see the ball well until the last 15 or 20 feet. That happens for a variety of reasons. Sometimes, when a hitter's on automatic pilot, his visual systems get tangled up in the pitcher's motion. He sees the pitcher's arms and legs, and the ball just flies out of there. But more often than not, the hitter is thinking about too many things. He hasn't prioritized his thoughts.

"We teach the hitter to identify the pitcher's release zone, which is really challenging because of the different pitches that are thrown. Once he can identify the release point, we teach him to look at some other place on the pitcher's body. It could be his belt buckle, or his hat, or the team insignia on his arm.

"So, while the pitcher is going through his basic motion, they stay fixated on that spot on the body. Then, at a precise time, they shift the eyes over into the release zone. The eye shift serves several purposes, but the most important one is it clears the mind, wiping out those other thoughts. At the moment that the ball is released, their concentration is focused. As a result, they see better. This is a technique George Brett has used for years.

"Likewise, a good driver shifts his eyes away from the road to the rear-view and side-view mirrors, or to the left and right, then ahead once more. When you do that, you are aware of everything that is going on."

That technique is part of a system known as visualization, which helps make a person aware of success by finding the weak link in his concentration and putting his thoughts into perspective. "My emphasis," he explains, "is on the ability to tune in visually—to have good visual concentration despite distractions, stress, and changes in circumstances."

Dr. Harrison, a pioneer in the field of visualization, began to explore this subject while in optometry school. "Being a baseball fanatic, I became curious about what it was that made Ted Williams such a great hitter. I had heard that he supposedly had 20-12 eyesight and could see the spin, speed, and trajectory of the ball in flight. But there are thousands of people—perhaps millions—who have that kind of eyesight and can't hit a baseball.

"Following optometry school I studied the development and influence of the visual systems of people with learning disabilities. From that, I started to get some insights on how to teach hitters in baseball to see and track the ball better.

"I also continued to read more and more about Williams. I discovered he had exceptional depth perception, which I learned in optometry school was a trainable skill. One of the things Williams did that really caught my attention was to spend a lot of time studying and seeing the opposing pitchers. Therefore, when he stepped into the batter's box he was aware of how they were going to pitch to him. He had great anticipation, which triggered his eyes to work effectively."

During his years at the Academy, Dr. Harrison learned that when athletes are performing well, they're not fully aware of what they're doing; they react automatically. Nor can they articulate their reactions. The description they commonly offer is being "in a groove." And when they aren't performing well, they tend to be very aware of something being wrong mechanically. They re-create in their minds poor performances over and over and over.

Dr. Harrison says, "I found that the players who performed well and were aware of their bodies had a heightened visual awareness—they could see the ball earlier and for a longer period of time. And the ball would look bigger, as if it was traveling in slow motion.

"So I have developed a variety of training drills that emphasize visualization, which enhances visual awareness and lets the body react. The philosophy behind visualization is based on how we use our sensory and motor skills together. I'm referring to our systems of smell, taste, hearing, touch, vision, coordination, balance, thought, and what we call the 'energy system'—the degree of tension and relaxation. For good athletic performance, each of those systems have to work well together."

George Brett was one of the first players to use Dr. Harrison's visualization techniques, and he continues to use them to this day. In the on-deck circle, Brett visualizes the pitcher, what pitches he's likely to see, and how he will react to those pitches. If he strikes out in that at-bat, he may analyze that performance in the dugout, but when he goes to the on-deck circle for his next at-bat he has already erased that strikeout from his mind. Instead, he visualizes his most recent successful at-bat.

If Brett gets into a slump, he'll go back in time as far as he has to and visualize a successful at-bat from the past.

There are times when he'll go as far back as the 1980 American League playoffs and visualize his ninth-inning, series-winning home run against Goose Gossage of the Yankees. He remembers that form. He *feels* the goose bumps he got while rounding the bases. It's as if Brett has a VCR in his mind and can replay success.

Brett has so mastered his concentration and visual awareness that during a pause in the game—like a pitching change—he lets his mind wander. He relaxes. When the game resumes, he flips on his concentration the way you'd flip on a light switch. "The mind," says Brett, "can destroy you, or it can be the greatest asset you have."

I recall a comment pitcher Orel Hershiser of the Dodgers made in 1988. He said that when he threw 120 pitches in a ball game, it was as if he threw 240—the 120 pitches he visualized before he threw them and the 120 he actually threw.

Ray Miller is a great believer in having his pitchers use visualization techniques to enhance concentration. When you have a fine visual focus, Miller tells his pitchers, it's as if you're looking down a funnel.

Some players can visualize naturally, without training. Dr. Harrison says visualization came so easily to Rod Carew that Carew assumed everyone could do it.

Dr. Harrison taught reliever Jim Gott, now with the Dodgers, visualization techniques that he now uses in the bullpen and on the mound to snap out of any lapses in concentration.

"In the bullpen, Jim vividly visualizes the exact game situation he's going to enter, the pitching motion he will use, and the pitches he's going to throw," says Dr. Harrison. "If he needs a strikeout, he will imagine himself throwing a good, high fastball to a precise target. He visualizes to such an extent that he feels the ball coming out of his hand.

"On the mound, it's important for him to take a little extra time between pitches. If he doesn't, he tends to get pumped up and loses his focus. So he takes a moment to visualize the spin and trajectory of his pitch in its last 20 feet."

One of the most damaging emotions to the visual systems is anger. A player misleads himself by thinking anger helps him focus. You've heard the phrase, "I was so mad I couldn't see straight." That's literally true, since the eyes are an extension of the brain. Anger causes your eyes to dance and dart the way the eyes of a wild animal do. It can take as long as a third of a second for your eyes to refocus on a target.

The Pirates' Bob Walk would lose his temper after making a bad pitch, which made him lose his picture of the strike zone when pitching to the next hitters. Once he learned to let go of his anger and focus on positive visual images, he became one of the club's most consistent starters and was named to the 1988 National League All-Star team.

Advanced Technology

My association with Bill Harrison, which had begun at the Academy, continued when I went to work for the Oakland A's. Since we had a lean budget, Dr. Harrison worked with some of our minor league players for free. When I returned to the Pirates organization, I put him on the payroll and gave him a title I coined: "director of visualization."

In that capacity, Dr. Harrison not only tested and trained our players, but brought to our attention any new technologies that could improve vision and reflexive reactions. We would then buy them and have them installed in a room specifically used for vision training, next to our indoor batting cage. A bright young man named Al Kasprowicz, a psychology major from the University of Pittsburgh, was available to operate the machines and monitor each player's progress.

Let me explain the benefits of machines that can train your visual systems. When you demonstrate something to a player, he absorbs the information cognitively, involving his central nervous system. To give you an example, reading this book is cognitive learning.

When he undertakes the task and experiences all the sensations, that is noncognitive learning, which involves his autonomic nervous system. An example of noncognitive learning is riding a bicycle. You probably didn't study the biomechanics of bicycle riding before you first climbed on a bike; you simply got on, pedaled, teeter-tottered, and felt your way. You learned by doing.

The machines we have used train and teach a player to improve the control and speed of his involuntary reactions without him being cognizant of these reactions.

I am now going to share with you a secret weapon Dr. Harrison introduced to us: a $25,000 machine that taps into the autonomic nervous system by the use of sounds to improve vision, depth perception, peripheral vision, and contrast sensitivity in a matter of minutes. In fact, after six months of weekly sessions, the machine can in many cases eliminate the need for corrective glasses.

The machine is called the Accommotrac Vision Tester, and it was invented by Dr. Joseph Trachtman, a brilliant optometrist from Brooklyn Heights, New York. Among Dr. Trachtman's customers are the U.S. Olympic Shooting Team and the Israeli Air Force, the most efficient air force in the world today.

Dr. Trachtman has earned degrees in optometry, education, and experimental psychology, and has a graduate fellowship in computers and medicine. One of the subjects he studied in optometry school was myopia, or nearsightedness, one of the most common human afflictions. Myopia can be caused by an elongation of the eyeball, which can sometimes be corrected surgically or by environmental factors. When a person reads, for example, his eye muscles contract, allowing the crystalline lens to expand and focus on a close object. When a person reads for an extended period, sometimes his eye muscles are unable to relax. The muscles may even spasm, which keeps the lens in an almost constant state of elongation. This decreases his visual acuity. In an effort to compensate, he squints.

As a graduate student at Johns Hopkins University in 1970, Dr. Trachtman studied biofeedback techniques, which allow you to exert control over your involuntary, noncognitive bodily processes. Merging his background in optometry and psychology, Dr. Trachtman visualized a machine that could train a person to control his eye muscles by biofeedback of accommodation. (Accommodation is the process in which the eye adjusts to objects at different distances by changing the crystalline lens.) This way, if a doctor wanted to test a person for myopia or even hyperopia (farsightedness), he could bypass the eyes per se and go right to the nervous system.

Dr. Trachtman began his research in 1975, and his first Accommotracs were trademarked and ready for market in July 1984. Dr. Harrison ordered an Accommotrac for use with his own patients six months later. Dr. Harrison found that the Accommotrac could also help a person improve his contrast sensitivity. Some of his patients reported that objects appeared brighter after the training than before.

How does the Accommotrac eliminate the need for glasses? As the patients gradually learn to control their eye muscles and focus more easily, the doctor can weaken their prescription until they no longer need glasses. Dr. Trachtman was able to help one of his patients, a candidate for the New York City Fire Department, pass the required eye examination by improving his vision from 20/400 to 20/40 in just 20 sessions.

"When people are nearsighted," Dr. Trachtman explains,

"the brain makes the eye muscles focus too much. When people are farsighted, the brain does not make the eye muscles focus enough.

"The ciliary muscle, which is the focusing muscle, is controlled by the autonomic nervous system. The autonomic nervous system also controls all the other automatic processes: heart rate, blood pressure, body temperature and regulation of body fluids, emotions, hunger, and thirst.

"The Accommotrac uses sound to help people focus, rather than having them use their eyes. With the feedback we teach you something new, which is much easier than breaking a habit. We teach you to train your focusing muscle."

The patient sits in a darkened room, his chin and forehead resting on padded surfaces and his forearms and elbows resting along the table. When he looks into the Accommotrac, he sees a whitish circle, as if he's staring at the moon. The optical part, which can be raised or lowered or moved forward or back, is connected to a sound machine. The machine emits sounds that can be adjusted to the patient's preference. (If he desires he can listen to a sound resembling a video game.) The sound machine has two windows, one measuring the sound waves and the other giving a digital reading of the sounds. Dr. Trachtman holds a stopwatch to time your session, having you pause at certain intervals to rest your eyes. All you do is look at the circle and listen to the sounds. Your goal is not to detect anything visually, but to simply make the sound go faster.

"The instrument," says Dr. Trachtman, "measures the clarity of an infrared image on the back of the eye 40 times a second and immediately converts that into two sounds that change.

"There's a little nerve center inside the spinal column between the shoulders and the head. In order to make the sound go faster, that little nervous center has to get turned on. It has to start generating more signals to get the focusing muscle to open and relax. As the muscles relax, the signal on the retina gets clearer, the back of the eye gets clearer, and the sound goes faster.

"The interesting thing about that particular nerve center is that it will simultaneously signal other parts of the body, from the brain to the internal organs. So what we have is a strong connection between what you're seeing, what you're thinking, and how you're feeling. In essence, we're training concentration.

"What happens with baseball players is they learn how to concentrate on the sound, and as they concentrate on the sound, parts of the brain get stimulated, so that their attention and awareness become increased.

"One part of the brain they stimulate is the reticular activating system, which is responsible for awareness and alertness. The reticular activating system is the same part of the nervous system that can be stimulated by amphetamines and cocaine and give people an altered perception. Here, we're heightening awareness and attention naturally.

"People can have control over functions pretty readily if you get into the right state. Some of the players we worked with were able to make the sound go as fast as it could. As a result, they were able to develop a visual field that's bigger, so whatever they see appears slower. A batter will be able to see the rotation of the ball as it leaves the pitcher's fingers.

"We started to learn about this when I was working with black-belt karate masters several years ago. I'd have them come into my office and do kung fu or akido, in the same state of concentration they used in competition. The lesser athletes were inconsistent, but the martial-arts masters were able to attain an altered space perception. They saw things in slow motion and their field was very wide.

"Their level and consistency of concentration is what separates these athletes from the average person. That was what led me to think this would be helpful for other athletes."

The altered state Dr. Trachtman has described is the

"groove" baseball players talk about when they're playing well.

Not long ago, Dr. Trachtman put himself into an altered state in order to complete a task he had not been prepared for. "I was about to move into a new house on a Friday," he recalls. "The ground floor was to be used as my new office. We had arranged for a cleaning service to come in at 7 P.M. the night before. A half-hour before the cleaning service was to arrive, they called my office and canceled the appointment.

"My wife went crazy. I simply went upstairs, put on my work clothes, and cleaned all night, without any sleep. I put myself into an altered state, so I was able to work at my full capacity without feeling fatigued.

"Some of the elite athletes have learned to generalize their level of concentration to other tasks. They can just turn it on. They end up being successful in business and in their personal lives."

If you've ever had the misfortune of being behind the wheel of a car that's about to crash, you may remember how the seconds before impact felt like hours. Everything appeared in slow motion. That, too, is an altered state. You had an adrenaline reaction, what doctors call the "fight-or-flight mechanism."

"What the patient is doing with the Accommotrac," says Dr. Trachtman, "is pumping adrenaline to the reticular activating system almost selectively."

Some patients make the sound go faster by simply telling themselves to do so. "All I tell my patients is, 'Here's the sound. Make it go faster.' About 95 percent of my patients devise some strategy. One of the karate masters was able to make the sounds go fast by visualizing himself facing an opponent in competition. Other patients can't verbalize that strategy until they've used the machine five or 10 times."

We invited Dr. Trachtman to bring the Accommotrac to

the Pirates' spring training camp in 1988. Before we used the Accommotrac, Dr. Harrison checked our medical charts as a routine precaution to make sure no one had any existing condition that might prohibit us from using it on him.

We then had a number of players and front office staff try a session. Most of the players showed a substantial improvement in their visual field. Even Larry Doughty and Jim Bowden, my assistant director of the minor leagues and scouting, had immediate, noticeable improvements. The only side effect a few of them experienced was an aroused, pleasurable sensation, which was probably caused by the stimulation of their reticular activating systems.

Mike Diaz, who played for the Pirates from 1986 to 1988, was so adept at the Accommotrac that he drove the sound as fast as it could go. The white circle he was initially looking at disappeared from his view, like a moon in a total eclipse. When Diaz came to the plate in a game, he was able to pick up the baseball as it was leaving the pitcher's hand and see its rotation and movement in slow motion.

With this widened visual field, a fielder can visually slow down the movement of a hard-hit ball, which gives his brain more time to digest the visual information. This helps him react more quickly. And with increased contrast sensitivity, an outfielder can look into a bright sky for a fly ball and locate it more readily.

A pitcher can visually expand his target in order to make better pitches. Jim Gott, who had already mastered the four-seam fastball, combined his visualization techniques and the widened visual field the Accommotrac helped him develop to register 34 saves for the Pirates in 1988.

Bob Walk also benefited from the Accommotrac. He improved his concentration to such a degree that he could lock in on the catcher's mitt and block out all other sights and sounds.

Bill Harrison and I believe the Accommotrac is not only a valuable tool for baseball teams. Imagine the impact the

Accommotrac would have if it was introduced to students on the elementary school level. The children could correct or prevent any environmental influences and improve their concentration skills. Needless to say, the Accommotrac also could put children's eyeglass manufacturers out of business.

Other Hand-Eye-Mind Drills

Dr. Harrison also purchased for the Pirates a machine called the Wayne Saccadic tester, a hand-eye coordination device that has become popular in recent years on the college and pro level.

Saccades are the rapid, jerky movements your eyes make as they jump from one point to another. As you read this sentence, your eyes are jumping from one word to the next. The Wayne Saccadic uses flashing lights to train your eyes to pick up a stimulus and your hands to react to it.

The Wayne Saccadic, three feet tall by three feet wide, is mounted on a wall. In a 30-second drill, a player is asked to touch each light as it flashes. Each light stays on until the player punches it out. As he becomes better at this, the machine's operator makes the lights flash faster. He also instructs the players to use one hand at a time.

The Wayne Saccadic also comes with a balance board you control with your feet. The player rocks forward or back, to the left or right, depending on where the light flashes. Again, the operator adjusts the speed and frequency of the flashing lights to test your reactions over a period of 30 seconds.

"If you're going to have quick hands," says Dr. Harrison, "you've got to have quick feet. I've done a lot of work in this area with John Scolinos, the longtime baseball coach at California State Polytechnic University in Pomona. He firmly believes a major requirement for being a good infielder is having quick feet."

A Videotape Library

Videotape is a great form of cognitive learning. It allows the player to see and compare his current and past performances. Not only can he and his coach diagnose problems, but the player can absorb the video images of his proper form at each stage of execution and visualize successful performances before he takes the field.

When a pitcher is having problems with his mechanics, for example, Pirates pitching coach Ray Miller will sit down with the pitcher in front of a TV set and review his motion, frame by frame. The pitcher can also study the pitch selection he used against the opposition.

Videotape offers so many benefits. Unfortunately, when I arrived in Pittsburgh the Pirates were one of the few major league teams that did not have a videotaping department. I quickly recruited the services on a part-time basis of Richard Sutphin, who works for television station KDKA, and Brad Hines, who free-lanced for a few TV stations. They taped players on our major league club, as designated by the manager and his coaches. In January 1988, I hired Hines full-time, to set up and run a video department.

During spring training and in the Instructional League, Hines roams the various playing fields, taping every player in the organization. He tapes batting practice, all the hitting, fielding, running, and pitching drills, and the exhibition games. If an instructor has detected a problem with one of his players, or wants to reinforce a procedure, he takes the player immediately after practice to a room that has a television and videocassette recorder. Together, they review his performance while it's fresh in the player's mind.

Also during spring training, Hines puts together instructional tapes for our players and coaches to view at their leisure. In these tapes, instructors demonstrate the proper techniques in such skills as bunting, pickoff moves, and stealing leads.

Hines travels with the major league team during the season. He positions himself along the first-base line or the third-base line, depending on whether the opposing pitcher is left-handed or right-handed. He wants to get a full view of the front of the hitter's body. He also tapes the Pirates' pitchers from that same angle. "The coaches feel that's the best angle to see what the player's doing right or wrong," says Hines.

He doesn't follow the ball after it's hit, because his camera would be whirling too fast to get a good picture. Instead, he uses the audio to indicate the result. For example, he'll say into the microphone, "Flyout to left field," or "Single up the middle."

If the need arises, Hines will isolate on a fielder during a game. "I did that when Bobby Bonilla was moved to third base from the outfield," says Hines. "I would then tape other third basemen in the league, like Mike Schmidt, and show that to Bobby. It's not necessary for Bonilla to imitate Schmidt. But maybe he can pick up something Schmidt does that could help him, too."

During a home stand Hines programs his videocassette recorders to tape other games that are being shown on cable TV or by satellite. The footage is filed in his video library, from which players and coaches can borrow the tapes and watch opposing players. We in the front office used those tapes for what we called "satellite scouting," a measure that enhanced the reports from our advanced scouts of a future opponent.

While Hines is on the road, he has the Pirates games taped as well. When he returns to Pittsburgh, he edits the tapes, putting each player's performance—as filmed by the TV station's center-field camera, and as he taped it—onto a single tape. "That way," says Hines, "a hitter can see the pitcher, the pitch, its location, and how I taped him swinging at it."

Before every game a pitcher or hitter can pop his personalized videocassette into a portable machine in the clubhouse and observe his last performance against that day's opponent. Or he can watch a customized tape of the opposing pitcher. He can rewind, fast-forward, or freeze the picture to his heart's content, creating mental images of every situation to sharpen his concentration.

I'm really excited about the work of Dr. Tony Stellar and Alan Blitzblau. They've developed a system where they can transfer video images into computer graphics that pinpoint each component of the player's performance.

All of the machines, tests, and techniques we have described in this chapter serve important purposes. They allow us to measure, diagnose, and help correct any visual problems. They give us more insights into a person's physiological ability to use his eyes, mind, and body. They help us teach more effectively. And they allow the player to increase his field of vision, his awareness, his concentration, the amount of time he has to react, and his productivity.

After all, time is a person's most precious resource, and knowledge is his most valuable asset.

7 THE EMPLOYEE BENEFITS PACKAGE

When you interview for a job, I'm sure one of the questions you ask your prospective employer is, "What types of benefits does your company offer?"

It's a valid question. The more opportunities your job offers—such as a comprehensive medical plan, career counseling, education programs—the more you can increase your net worth as a professional and as a person. From the company's perspective, job benefits improve employees' morale, make them more productive, and cut down on their time missed because of illness. The employee who feels his company cares for him gives that much more effort in his job. He trusts you.

I believe baseball teams should feel a responsibility for helping every player improve his net worth. While I was with Pittsburgh I was a member of four Major League Baseball committees. One of the committees dealt with the players' lives outside of baseball during and after their careers. Now I don't want this to sound demeaning, but a majority of players don't spend time during their careers planning for the second career that inevitably follows, nor do they take the time—or have the opportunity—to learn more about the many things that affect their professional lives today. I'm talking about such things as learning how to handle their finances, how to take care of their bodies, and how to deal with personal problems.

Educating a player about his life off the field is every bit as important as teaching him on the field. To that end, my staff and I instituted programs aimed at educating the player and improving the total team environment.

For example, just because the Major League Baseball Players Association provides its membership with medical and dental insurance doesn't mean a player is actually going to see his doctor or dentist. (Do *you* run to see your doctor or dentist?) Therefore, it must be the club's responsibility to see that every player is given complete physical and dental examinations during spring training and, if warranted, during and after the regular season.

There are times when players suffer from headaches. A headache can be caused by a multitude of things. We've seen cases where a player was suffering from headaches caused by a decayed tooth that became impacted. What does the player do? Sometimes a younger player is afraid of doctors and will doctor himself. He'll take Tylenols every few hours and hope the pain disappears. Sometimes his manager, unaware that there's a true physical reason for the headaches, may think the player has an attitude problem. A proper examination can head off the trouble.

A franchise needs a nutritionist to advise the organization on the right foods to serve and how to supplement the players' diets. There was a time in baseball not long ago where the postgame buffet consisted of fried chicken, cold cuts, potato salad, and soda. That's not a good meal after a day of physical exertion. That's a barbecue.

You need people on staff who can train the players in

public speaking and counsel them on media relations. See, the baseball player works in an entertainment industry. Part of his job is to meet with the fans and community groups who support his team, so you want him to be prepared.

During my years with the Pirates, Buzzy Keller arranged for teachers to conduct English classes during spring training for our players from Latin America. In a classroom setting, the players were taught the basic skills of reading, writing, and conversing in English. I think it's a good idea to set up Spanish classes for the English-speaking players and coaches, too, as a way to break down communication and cultural barriers.

Perhaps your franchise can't afford to sponsor a year-round instructional program along the lines of the Kansas City Royals Baseball Academy. That doesn't mean you can't have one that lasts one month or two months. When I became the Pirates general manager, I invited our best minor league prospects to an early spring training program called STEP—Specialized Early Training Program—patterned after the Academy. Each player received individual instruction geared at speeding up his climb to the major leagues. And in the fall we had *two* Instructional League teams, where as many as 70 players could receive individual instruction.

How about a student-exchange program? We had that, too. We signed a working agreement with the Mexico City Reds, who play on a level comparable to our Triple A, whereby we sent a few of our Double A players to play on their team. It gave the Pirates a "second" Triple A team, and it gave our players a chance to experience the culture that so many future major leaguers are growing up in.

A franchise must have an effective program to rehabilitate players in the organization who suffer from drug or alcohol abuse. If you don't know how to establish one, there are many qualified people to call upon. Sam McDowell, a former major league pitcher who is a recovering alcoholic, has been invited by many teams to speak with their players about the dangers of these addictions and to help educate their staffs about the warning signs to look for.

When my managers and coaches submit personnel reports, I ask them to note and chart any player exhibiting behavioral problems. If the problems are drug- or alcohol-related, we immediately arrange for his treatment. And you've got to keep this in the *strictest* of confidence; the fewer who know—even within your organization—the better, or else the program won't work.

A person suffering from such a disease gets into a vicious cycle. He gives up on himself, so those around him give up on him. Mike York, a right-handed pitcher of enormous potential, had been released by three organizations because of his drinking problem. York's career, for all intents and purposes, was over before it really began. I made a deal with him: I would sign him if he promised to spend as much time in a rehabilitation facility as he needed to lick his problem. If he failed, the contract would become null and void.

I am proud to tell you that York lived up to his end of the agreement and his baseball career is on a promising course. The Pirates put him on their 40-man roster at the close of the 1989 season.

Another program we instituted with the Pirates that I'm proud of is child care. We had babysitters at Three Rivers Stadium who took care of the players' children. Their wives could watch the game from the stands, or on a television set in our child care facility.

Believe me, these kinds of employee benefits cost relatively little. Many outstanding consultants are willing to donate their time or to charge a reduced fee to play a role in a major league organization.

Here are four types of employee benefits that improve a player's net worth.

Individualized Conditioning

Players are funny when it comes to physical conditioning. They work diligently on their conditioning to get to the major leagues, but when they reach that plateau, they stop doing what got them there. They pace themselves. It stays that way until they get to the twilight of their careers. Then they become born-again believers in conditioning.

A player is grossly mistaken if he assumes he gets a full workout from a game. Playing baseball works the agonistic muscles—the thighs and quadriceps by hitting and running, the pectorals, chest, and latissimus dorsi in the front of the shoulder by pitching—and ignores the antagonistic muscles—the hamstrings in the back of the legs and the muscles in the back of the shoulder.

There are some players who work out religiously and still get hurt, because they do the wrong exercises. In today's parlance, players say they like to get "buffed"—build bulky chests and biceps. All they're doing is creating muscle imbalances. They bulk up their torsos but ignore the legs. Or they develop the quadricep muscles but ignore the hamstrings. Left to their own devices, these players do themselves more harm than good.

Often, the worst culprits in fostering poor conditioning techniques are the teams themselves, who rely on the same conditioning methods baseball has used for 50 years. If you visit a spring-training camp, you'll see the players run and throw, with some stretching mixed in. All they're doing is working on already-developed muscles. And when spring training ends, so does the conditioning.

When injuries become widespread during the season, as they routinely have the last few years, fans are flooded by so-called experts with theories and opinions: It's the tough schedule; it's because players aren't eating enough red meat; it's because young pitchers are working too many innings before age 25. This is nonsense!

The answers are simple. First, you have to test the muscular flexibility and strength levels of every player—which can be done with a Cybex machine—to establish their base levels. You measure their girth and body-fat percentages. Then your conditioning coach or consultant designs a specific workout for each player to use all year long.

Baseball players need to work consistently on their antagonistic muscles as well as their agonistic muscles, and work those muscles through a full range of motion. And they must use exercises that improve one area of performance without weakening another.

"Specificity of training is the key to success in all sports," says Mackie Shilstone, the director of the Human Performance Institute at AMI St. Jude Hospital in New Orleans, Louisiana, who is a conditioning consultant for the Giants and the Yankees.

Shilstone says that hamstring muscles must be developed to no less than a 60 percent strength capacity of the quadriceps. To achieve that, Shilstone has the players do single leg curls with weights, hip extensions to keep the legs flexible, and a variety of stretches to ensure a full range of motion.

Pitchers, he says, must maintain a ratio of 3-2 between the strength of the internal muscles in the front of the shoulder and the external muscles behind it; if the ratio becomes 4-2 or 5-2, the pitcher risks serious injury.

Traditionally, pitchers throw about 125 pitches during a game and as many as 400 on the side between starts. "They're moving their shoulders forward over and over again without doing anything in the reverse mode," says Shilstone. "They need a strong shoulder capsule to withstand the torque." So between starts Shilstone has pitchers take a small weight or rubber cable and, simulating their pitching movements, work in the reverse—decelerating— direction, from their release points to their starting points. In all the exercises the hands are kept at or below shoulder level to prevent injury.

Pitchers must also develop their legs, says Shilstone, "because 40 percent of the pitching motion comes from the legs. Pitchers dissipate force through their legs." Well-conditioned legs, combined with a strong shoulder capsule, are the reasons Nolan Ryan has pitched so well for so long.

Muscular imbalances also impede a player's performance. At the start of the 1989 season Shilstone discovered that outfielder Kevin Mitchell's buttock muscles and hips were so tight that they prevented him from rotating fully at the plate. So Shilstone put Mitchell on a program that helped him loosen those muscles and the oblique muscles (where we say the "love handles" are) on his sides. Mitchell put small weights in his hands and slowly rotated his trunk to the left and the right, on an x-axis, to loosen his buttocks and strengthen his obliques for more torque.

At the start of the 1989 season Giants third baseman Matt Williams's back muscles were so tight that he couldn't rotate his midsection fully. This caused him to slap at outside pitches. Shilstone designed a program that, done regularly, unlocked Williams's midsection. During the 1989 season Williams, who split time between the major league level and Triple A, and Mitchell hit a combined 91 home runs.

In his role as the Pirates' strength and conditioning coach, Dr. Warren Sipp sets up and supervises individualized physical conditioning programs to suit the needs of every player in the organization. Dr. Sipp, who earned his Ph.D. from the University of Pittsburgh in 1983, was on the school's faculty for 17 years as an assistant professor, and served as the strength and conditioning coach for all sports except football. He also is nationally recognized for his coaching of handicapped athletes.

Dr. Sipp, who's studied the work of G.V. Bourette, incorporated into his program the use of rubber tubing for resistance training, which develops all the muscles around a joint.

He also devised an interesting stretching program for the

position players who are not in the starting lineup. "We have them do a 10-minute stretch in the clubhouse during the sixth inning of every home game and the fifth inning of every road game, under my supervision or the supervision of the trainer.

"This routine is unique to us," says Dr. Sipp. "The stretching gets them mentally and physically ready to enter the game. We implemented this late in the 1986 season because one of our key men off the bench, R. J. Reynolds, was prone to hamstring pulls when he was called upon to pinch-hit or pinch-run late in the games. After sitting on the bench for most of the game, he jumped into the action without stretching. We decided it would be worthwhile for all the reserve players to stretch at the midpoint of every game."

Cardiovascular fitness is important because it helps keep your weight in line, improves your heart's efficiency, and helps rid the body of lactic acid, which makes joints stiff. But running laps around the field is not necessarily the best way—nor is it the only way—to improve oxygen intake and blood flow. Players who have knee problems should ride a stationary bicycle because it develops the muscles without putting stress on the joints. Auburn University coach Hal Baird has his pitchers go through a plyometric routine in which they jump rope with a heavy, rubber rope. The arm movements increase the aerobic impact.

For an effective conditioning program, there must be consistency in the approach of the entire medical staff. When I hired Shilstone to work with the Yankees, I had the team doctor call him and discuss how they would coordinate all phases of the Yankees' conditioning program.

When I was with the Pirates I used to bring Dr. Sipp, Kent Biggerstaff, the team's trainer, and Dr. Jack Failla, the team's orthopedist, to the baseball winter meetings. They would spend hours together in conversation, talking about ways to refine and improve the players' medical care.

"We have a continuum of conditioning," says Dr. Sipp.

"For instance, when Barry Bonds underwent knee surgery following the 1988 season, Kent Biggerstaff sat in on the operation. He helped communicate to Barry exactly what was going on during and after the surgery.

"When the operation was completed, Kent informed me of the results and we went to work on a plan for Barry's rehabilitation program. We planned the length of the program, what he needed to do during the off-season, how we could monitor his progress, and what goals should be established to have Barry at full strength by spring training."

Shilstone says the missing link in conditioning is nutrition. You might assume an athlete can get all the nutrition he needs by eating foods from the four basic food groups. But circumstances make that difficult. Here are a few scenarios:

If a player is trying to gain weight and build muscle, he may need to consume 5,500 calories a day. Eating that many calories in solid form will put a tremendous strain on his digestive system. Or a player might be allergic to certain foods. Perhaps he can't consume dairy products because of a lactose intolerance. Or say the player has a night game followed by a day game. Since he doesn't have enough time, or is simply too tired, he'll grab a cup of coffee the morning after the night game and head to the ballpark.

Muscles need the right fuel to repair, recover, and heal after physical exertion. Shilstone, who has a master's degree in nutrition, analyzes each player's needs and recommends liquid supplements that provide the player with the proteins, carbohydrates, and amino acids he needs to reach his fitness goals. Because they're liquids, they're easier on the system than solid foods. And they're convenient. During the 1989 season, Shilstone made sure that supplements were shipped to the visiting clubhouses before every Giants road game. All the players had to do was drink it.

How do you judge a conditioning and nutrition program? Not by the way the athlete looks. It's how he performs. The first athlete Shilstone worked with was boxer Michael Spinks in 1982. At the time Spinks was the light-heavyweight champion of the world. Spinks was having trouble making the 175-pound weight limit, so Shilstone set up a plan that helped Spinks lose fat and not muscle. A few years later Spinks decided to move up to the heavyweight division, so Shilstone put him on a regimen that helped Spinks gain 25 pounds, increase his punching power, but not lose his hand and foot speed. Spinks then defeated Larry Holmes for the heavyweight championship.

Ozzie Smith, Shilstone's first baseball client, was a great-fielding, slap-hitting shortstop who decided he wanted to increase his line-drive and home-run power. Under Shilstone's supervision, Smith, who weighed 144 pounds, added 23 pounds of muscle, improved his batting average and power, but lost none of the quickness that makes him the best defensive shortstop in baseball.

Shilstone worked with Will Clark following Clark's off-season elbow surgery in 1986. Together they improved Clark's overall condition and reduced his percentage of body fat. The next year they worked to increase Clark's lean body mass; the year after, to enhance his skills. Because Clark's body allows him to put all his talents to use, he's become one of the game's best hitters. "I don't make Will Clark hit better," reminds Shilstone. "I just keep him at the plate."

Psychological Therapy

There are occasions when a well-trained, physically fit player is still not performing to his capabilities. Once you've ruled out the physical factors, you consider the mental aspect.

In specific cases I have recruited the assistance of Dr. Eric Margenau, a sports psychologist in New York who happens to be co-owner of one of the Pirates' minor league teams.

Dr. Margenau, the executive director of the Center for Sports Psychology, has worked with world-class amateur athletes, golfers, tennis players, and basketball and hockey teams to help them identify and treat psychological obstacles that negatively affect athletic performance.

In 1987 I asked Dr. Margenau to work with a second baseman in the Pirates' minor league system who was having trouble making accurate throws to first base.

"After the first couple of errors," Dr. Margenau explains, "he started to develop a real phobia about throwing the ball to first base, and it got progressively worse. Syd asked me if I could meet with him for several sessions over the course of a week or so. We arranged a schedule, and the Pirates sent him to see me in New York.

"When we identified the problem, we began using a combination of hypnosis and self-hypnosis techniques, and imagery and visualization exercises. We wanted to get him back to a point where he discharged the fear of making the mistake, relaxed, focused, and concentrated on what he had to do. To help him achieve and maintain this state after our sessions, I created for him a relaxation tape, which put him into progressive relaxation and gave him certain suggestions. He then made remarkable progress."

How does self-hypnosis work? "Assuming the subjects are able to be hypnotized," answers Dr. Margenau, "I teach them how to put themselves under and give themselves certain suggestions to relax and concentrate, and do what we call a 'rehearsal exercise' while they're in this base hypnotic state. They create an image of completing the task successfully. In the case of that particular player, he imagined himself fielding the ball and making an accurate throw for an out."

Dr. Margenau feels that certain players, depending on their personalities, are susceptible to what doctors call performance anxiety. "There are different forms of it," he says. "Some people have a generalized performance anxiety, the fear of not doing well in general in a performance situation. Others develop it around a very specific aspect of the performance.

"There are certain personalities that are more susceptible to it, such as those who are insecure about how other people think and feel about them. They measure themselves against the standards of other people."

Dr. Margenau uses a test called TAIS, which is an acronym for the Test of Attention and Interpersonal Skills. "The TAIS wasn't developed only for athletes, but it does give us a picture of how the athlete responds to stress. The TAIS defines certain components which deal well or poorly with stress. It tests two different categories of skills.

"For the attention skills, the test tells us what the person does with information. Is his focus narrow or broad, objective or subjective? Can he integrate a lot of information, or must the information be kept simple?

"The other aspect, the interpersonal skill, tells us whether the person is introverted or extroverted. Does he talk about his problems? Does he form relationships? Does he respond to an authority figure? Can he take coaching?"

Toward the end of the 1988 season we asked Dr. Margenau to see a player who played extremely well in the first half of the season and then began to press himself to maintain it. I suspected the player was thinking about his contract, which was to expire following the season.

"I studied his background, did some testing to get a fix on his problem, and did some hypnosis with him," says Dr. Margenau. "I later spent some time with him when the team came into New York. When we understood his problem, I gave him a relaxation cassette tape and instructed him to play it on a daily basis."

Soon after, the player stopped focusing on things beyond his control and showed a distinct improvement in his play.

The treatment of performance anxiety is just one facet of the work Dr. Margenau does with professional teams in other sports. "I help those teams evaluate their talent, and in some cases choose their talent, based on the players' personality profiles. Whether it's before a player draft or after the team has chosen the players, there are certain things you can do to optimize their performance. For example, we can match certain players with certain coaches to make a better fit. We can group players in certain kinds of training regimens that will work best for them."

Before I left the Pirates, I had planned for Dr. Margenau to visit our Instructional League teams in the fall and test every player's emotional makeup. Had he been able to do that, the Pirates' managers, coaches, and, especially, scouts could have gained great insights into the one area of a ballplayer we cannot always see so readily—his *emotional* performance—but can still measure and help improve.

Financial Counseling

In the best possible circumstances, a good major league baseball player can make a lot of money over a short period of time. Sounds nice, doesn't it? In reality, instant wealth is one of the things a player thinks about most but is least prepared for.

Since the player is playing baseball from February to October—and, perhaps, winter baseball from November to January—he doesn't have the time or inclination to deal with his finances. So he delegates his financial matters to an agent and/or spouse. He *thinks* he's rid himself of the stress.

What can happen—and believe me, it does—is that his agent, acting on his own, may invest his money poorly. The player's wife, who has to pay the household bills, becomes frantic. Now money becomes the player's major cause of stress in both his career and his marriage. Since his baseball salary has become the only source of income within his control, he asks his team to renegotiate his contract. If the team turns him down, *he* becomes frantic and his performance suffers. And if he hasn't planned for his future, let alone the present, he is essentially forced to hang on to his playing career beyond his productive years.

The point is, whether or not the player has the time to work on a budget, write out checks, and invest in his future, he must know how that works, how to monitor his agent's decisions, and how to find reputable financial counselors.

I asked Tom Martin, my personal financial consultant, to work as the Pirates' roving financial instructor for the players throughout the organization. In 1974, Martin, a certified financial planner, cofounded the Washington, D.C., chapter of the International Association for Financial Planning, which now has 600 members. He conducts 50 seminars a year with government, civic, and corporate groups on such subjects as investment, budgeting, business management, taxes, and estate planning.

Every season Martin conducted seminars on such topics as goal setting, budgeting, and consumer purchases. "We structured different seminars each year," he explains, "but they all had the same theme: personal management control.

"We addressed the typical mistakes that young men will make with money," he recalls. "We covered such topics as how to buy a car, how to negotiate with a car dealer. What is a checking account? What is a savings account? What are investments? How does the tax system work? And what are your goals for your next career?

"The common psychology is that we want things that are simple and certain. A financial person or a salesperson may tell you, 'This is an easy decision. You're gonna make a lot of money on this, buddy. Now, write your check to so-and-so.'

"A decision is never that simple. We tell the players, as

we do all our clients, 'Don't put all your money in one investment, and don't sign anything until you know what it means. If you don't understand it, tell us so.'

"That admission is hard for a sports or entertainment person to make, because he has an ego which is fed by the system. That ego makes him feel like he's capable of anything. 'I make two million dollars a year! I can make a decision about buying a $100,000 house.'

"But can he make the *right* decision? Does he know how to get a competitive loan and pay less points? He'll reply, 'Well, it's only another two or three thousand dollars. I'm not going to worry about it.' Unfortunately, with that mentality a few thousand here and a few thousand there adds up before he knows it.

"I've also heard such comments as, 'I've got enough money. I can just hire a CPA. He'll take care of that.' We counter, 'Fine, but who watches that CPA if you don't know how to?'

"This is the first time many of the players think about the realities of the financial world. When you're addressing a group of 40 players, some pay attention, others tune it out. What I found rewarding was when those who found it helpful the first year came back two and three years later with follow-up questions. They asked me to sit down with them privately. That's when I could explain things in a little more detail and introduce them to some new concepts."

In 1988 Martin held workshops at which a group of players started a mock company. Here's a sample session.

"I ask the players to suggest a business we'd like to start," says Martin. "One of them volunteers, 'Let's open a television retail store.' I ask the players, 'Do the rest of you agree that's a reasonable goal?' If they do, we pick a start-up date, say, seven years from now.

"Then we talk about the components of making a business work: capitalization, site, product, and management. We agree on a figure of $100,000.

"Where will we get the money? That leads to a discussion of the kind of investments that would produce a sufficient rate of return. How does inflation erode that rate of return? If we're looking seven years ahead, and the inflation rate is 10 percent a year, that means we have to earn $200,000 instead of $100,000. So our real goal is $200,000.

"What can you earn on your money after inflation and after tax? What is your yield? That leads to a discussion of types of investments in general, what their historical yields are, and how inflation affects those investments.

"I use financial tables to show them our time frame and the rate of return. When they see how much they need to save each month, the figure looks like a horribly impossible accomplishment, particularly to a minor leaguer making $14,000. So I show them a chart of the average earnings of major league baseball players at various positions. *USA Today* does a real nice job of that each year.

"Say you're a first baseman. A major league first baseman earns several hundred thousand dollars a year. If you play that position in the major leagues for five years, you will make up for the money you weren't able to invest the first couple of years. Now the investment goal becomes plausible.

"Through this, the players get an understanding that a dollar five years from now may be worth half of what it is today. When they learn that they are what we call 'individual businesses,' they begin to take control of their income. They come to realize they're in baseball for a short period of time and then have 30 years in the business world to deal with afterwards."

Martin also led financial classes for the Latin-American players, using a Spanish-speaking coach or player to translate simultaneously. "We had special sessions on how the United States' economic system functions. We discussed checking and savings accounts, borrowing money, cash flow, and the tax system."

Players were free to contact Martin for counseling on an

individual basis. "It wasn't unusual for me to spend several hours with them one-on-one when they had a problem that needed to be solved," he says. "Perhaps they needed help planning. Maybe a tax problem came up. They may have needed advice on buying a house. I helped prepare their income taxes. I helped Latin players with their 1040-NRs, the nonresident alien tax they must pay. I provided that as a courtesy to Syd.

"If they became a client of mine, it was at their cost, though I gave them a preferred rate. Many of them couldn't afford to pay my normal fee, but the key was to have them pay something. Then the service has a value. If it's free, it doesn't have a lot of value.

"At spring training I gave every player in the organization my regular telephone number and a number for a 24-hour message service, so whenever they had a problem all they had to do was call."

Environmental Improvements

Think about how invigorated sunlight makes you feel. Whenever I'm in a restaurant or a hotel room, I sit near a window. And when I go outdoors I wear gray-tinted sunglasses, which allow my eyes to take in a fuller spectrum of the sun's rays.

Why is sunlight important to humans? According to Dr. John Nash Ott, the founder and retired director of the Environmental Health and Light Research Institute in Sarasota, Florida, your eyes and your skin take in the sunlight's energy and convert it to chemical energy, the same way a flower does. He says that light energy influences a variety of internal factors, such as your blood pressure and cholesterol level.

"When I went to grade school," says Dr. Ott, "my teachers explained the importance of photosynthesis in plants, how it converts sunlight into food energy. They pointed out that you could trace the human respiratory system back to the way the plants actually breathe through the pores in their leaves, and our digestive system back to the way the plants utilize the food energy. They added that this carries over from plants to animals, but the basic principle of photosynthesis doesn't.

"That's still considered the explanation today. In my tests I'm trying to show that light through the eyes influences the endocrine system. There seems to be a basic carryover of the importance of the light energy. I refer to it as biological combustion, comparing it to an automobile engine. You have to have food or nutrition for your fuel, and you have to have air. And we recognize that an automobile engine has to have ignition. In my research, I've discovered that light, the electromagnetic spectrum, interacts through the wavelength absorption of different chemicals with the food and minerals we take into our system. Light triggers it off and makes it work."

I found two of Dr. Ott's many discoveries relevant to the performance of a baseball player. First, his tests have shown that an increase in ultraviolet light—which, doctors warn, can be harmful under prolonged, excessive exposure—gives the body more energy. Second, he learned that certain colors, such as green, red, yellow, and orange, inhibit the eyes from taking in light energy and can weaken a person's muscles, while gray and blue do not.

In all his research Dr. Ott has yet to find direct answers to these biological mysteries. However, he has recorded the same results consistently over the years in hundreds of tests.

When I became the general manger of the Pirates, I asked Dr. Ott to suggest ways to improve our working environment at Three Rivers Stadium. We changed the color of the outfield walls from green to blue. We changed the underside of the bills of the players' caps from green to gray. We had the yellow clubhouse walls repainted white. And we replaced the existing fluorescent bulbs with Ott-Lites, a fluorescent bulb manufactured in Bradenton, Florida, by Electrodex, Inc., and sold by a company in Tampa called Environmental Lighting Concept. Dr. Ott helped develop these lights, designed to duplicate outdoor daylight as closely as possible.

How Dr. Ott, a banker from Chicago, arrived at his discoveries is a remarkable story.

"In 1927, during my school days, I started taking time-lapse pictures as a hobby," says Dr. Ott. "Primarily, I shot flowers and plants as they grew every few minutes. The effect was to see them bloom on a screen in a matter of seconds. This hobby led to a job with Walt Disney in the early forties. Disney contacted a lot of advanced amateurs like myself, accumulated all of our film, and wrote scripts around them. Among those films were *Nature's Half Acre* and *Secrets of Life.*

"Then his studio gave me a script that called for taking pictures of the growth of a pumpkin, from the emergence of the first shoot to maturity.

"I planted some pumpkins in boxes down in the basement under a small skylight—more or less a window light that depicted the natural daylight—and I put up some fluorescent fixtures on the ceiling to supplement the restricted daylight. The pumpkin vine grew, but it didn't produce any pumpkins. The pumpkin is a monoecious plant, meaning it produces the stamen and pistil—the male and female blossoms—separately on the same vine. I was getting only the stamen, the male blossom, and I couldn't figure out why.

"I told Walt Disney, 'I can't get the pumpkins to grow in my basement, but I've got a more spectacular picture of a tomato turning a nice, bright red color.' He said he couldn't use it because he needed to tie the pumpkin to the story of Cinderella's carriage. He asked me to try again.

"I went back to the hardware store and bought more fluorescent tubes. I knew some of the fluorescent tubes gave off slightly different colors, but I didn't pay too much attention to that.

"The second year I got all female flowers and none of the male flowers. I discovered that the first year, when I was using lights that had more energy in the yellow, I got the male blossoms. When I used daylight white, which has more energy in the blue, in shorter wavelengths, I found I could get 100 percent control. I got all the male blossoms using daylight, and with a little more blue in the spectrum I got the female.

"Not long after, the University of Loyola's department of biology asked me if I would help them take time-lapse pictures of fish egg embryos. After we got started I suggested putting different lights in the laboratory. They thought it was a crazy idea, but they went along with it.

"Since we knew that with plants the principle growth mechanism, if you want to call it that, is the process of photosynthesis, it seemed reasonable that if you change the characteristics of the light it's going to affect the end result. So through the process of photosynthesis, depending on where the peak of energy was in the whole spectrum, we could get males or females. What we found was we could influence the offspring of fish—getting 100 percent male or female—by the type of light we used.

"The chinchilla breeders were just getting started at that time. They were trying to put their animals outdoors in the cold to make them develop a heavier fur. Outdoors, they reproduced at about fifty-fifty, male and female.

"However, the chinchillas couldn't stand the cold weather, so the breeders brought them indoors. They put them in garages, basements, wherever they could put them. When they did that, they began getting ninety-eight percent males. They couldn't keep up the breeding. So we changed the lighting and it worked. Chinchilla breeders all over the world now are using lights that I recommended in their breeding rooms.

"It's known that light received through the eyes of animals influences the pituitary gland. The pituitary gland controls the entire endocrine system, which governs the production and release of body hormones which control body chemistry. So we saw in plants, fish, and animals the effect of light through the eyes influencing chemistry."

Dr. Ott then began to explore the effects of light energy on people. I had read of Dr. Ott's work and invited him to the Kansas City Royals Baseball Academy.

We asked him to examine a student who was hyperactive, hostile, and sometimes uncooperative. It so happened the player loved to wear pink-tinted sunglasses, which were in vogue in the "mod" era of the late sixties and early seventies. Dr. Ott made a simple recommendation: Have the player stop wearing pink sunglasses and use a medium-gray tint instead. In no time, the student transformed into a relaxed, confident person, and his performance improved. I was amazed.

He then studied the environment of another student who had displayed similar behavior. That student had adorned his room with psychedelic red lighting. Once we removed it, he regained his usual good performance.

Dr. Ott explained to us that both players were suffering from "malillumination." Dr. Ott believes that just as in malnutrition, when people become ill because they are lacking something in their diet, certain colors deprive the eyes of the light energy it takes into the body, which turns into chemical energy.

"You and a friend can demonstrate this using pieces of colored paper or thin cardboard you buy from an ordinary art store," says Dr. Ott. "Cut a piece of pink paper, oh, two and a half feet long by maybe a foot and a half high, hold it up in front of your friend so that it fills his full field of vision, and have him hold his arms straight forward. Your friend's muscles will feel so completely weakened that it's unbelievable.

"The same thing will happen if you use orange paper. But if you try blue paper, he will be at his full strength.

"This was once demonstrated by a weight lifter on the television program 'You Asked for It,' " says Dr. Ott. "First, he lifted a heavy weight. Then the host held a pink card in front of his eyes and he couldn't budge it."

I told my dear friend Rex Bowen, who was a scout for the Reds, about Dr. Ott's work. Bowen contacted Dr. Ott, and during their conversation he mentioned that the underside of the bills of the Reds' team caps were a yellowish green. Dr. Ott told him that player performance would improve if the Reds' management changed it to gray. "Light is reflected off the underside of the visor," Dr. Ott told him. "There's a natural reflection of light bouncing off the ground. If a batter holds his head up, or if a fielder looks up to catch a fly ball, the light will reflect off the underside of the visor." And when the light reflects off the visor, the green inhibits its energy.

The Reds made the switch to gray and went on to win the pennant. Coincidence? Perhaps, but since that time virtually every team in baseball has switched to gray on the underside of the bills.

The idea of increasing the ultraviolet phosphors in fluorescent lights first came to Dr. Ott in 1969. That year he was using fluorescent lights that contained some ultraviolet phosphors to take time-lapse photos of flower growth for the movie *On a Clear Day You Can See Forever*. Seeing how quickly the plants grew under this light, he conducted tests using these lights in Sarasota classrooms. The doctors in charge found that the lights calmed hyperactive students, and that students with learning disabilities showed improved reading abilities.

We made these lights available to our front office staff. Jim Bowden and I had them installed in our offices. Bowden, who spends a great deal of time behind a computer, says he actually feels better, with more energy, under those lights.

Why Do Smart Players Fail?

We have scouted, trained, and taught the player. We have expanded his vision and have created an environment for success. And yet, the player may fail. Why?

Reason One: The player abandons the things that made him successful. By nature, people face problems when they are forced to. When the problems are corrected and things are going well, we tend to put the problems out of our minds. We say to ourselves, It's all behind me now. If you don't keep in mind the methods that brought you success, slowly but surely you will repeat the behavior that led to the problems in the first place.

Managers, coaches, and instructors will tell you this happens with ballplayers all the time. The player gets into a hot streak and thinks he's invincible. A few weeks later he tells himself, I don't need that other stuff anymore. When the streak ends, as it inevitably does, he's at a loss for an explanation.

Reason Two: The player expects a technique to pay immediate dividends. Say you haven't been watching your diet. Two months later, you get on the scale and see you've put on 15 pounds. So you lower your caloric intake, start an exercise program, and will yourself into losing that weight. After one week of this regimen, you hop on the scale, eager to see the results. But the scale says you've lost only one pound. You say to yourself, This diet is stupid. What's the use of killing myself if all I'm going to lose is one pound!

If a player has been struggling for months because of a problem in his mechanics, any changes he and his coach put into effect are going to be uncomfortable, because he has already settled into an ineffective rhythm. If the new approach does not yield instant success, he may decide to scrap it, figuring, Let me go back to what I was doing; at least it felt more comfortable.

If the problem is stress, he may expect Dr. Margenau to make him well in one session. He'll listen to the relaxation tapes, visualize himself succeeding—then strike out four times the next game. Then he'll tell himself, I didn't like those tapes anyway.

Reason Three: Stress. The player becomes so anxious that he tries everything under the sun, only to overload his senses.

Reason Four: Disagreement among his coaches. The pitching coach instructs his pitcher to work high in the strike zone. The next game, the pitcher gives up a game-winning home run on a high fastball. After the game, his manager yells, "Don't ever throw a fastball high in the strike zone!"

Reason Five: The coach doesn't believe the player. I recall a situation in the 1989 season where a player told the media he thought he was performing poorly because of a mental block. When the media asked his manager about that, the manager replied that what the player needed was a smack on the head.

Reason Six: The coach refuses to allow the player to work with a specialist the general manager has brought in. The coach, set in his tried-and-true ways, thinks a conditioning coach or a visual expert will merely confuse the player with newfangled methods. The coach says to the player, "Don't listen to that guy. He might know something about his field, but *I* know baseball, and you don't need that stuff for baseball. Did Babe Ruth need it?"

Reason Seven: The manager, general manager, or owner berates him publicly after a subpar performance. Beating people over the head, putting negative pressure on them, isn't motivation. It's demoralization.

These reasons demonstrate the necessity of a coordinated, consistent, positive, and open-minded approach throughout an organization. If the player knows his organization cares about his needs, shows faith in him, and is willing to be patient, he will take advantage of every available opportunity to achieve success and increase his net worth.

8 THE MANAGING GENERAL

Whenever I take over a team people ask me, "What's your plan?" My plan, I reply, is to win championships.

How do you win championships? I think it's obvious by now: by having a well-trained scouting department; an efficient front office staff; managers, coaches and specialized instructors who are excellent teachers and motivators; and, last but not least, players of great athleticism who have been properly trained in the art of winning baseball.

What is my biggest challenge? Time. You try telling an owner or the media or the fans to wait and be patient because our team will be better any year now. In baseball today, the executive who talks about a five-year rebuilding plan will be shown the door in five minutes.

Besides, I don't think it makes sense to wait until tomorrow to improve something when it can be improved right now. Time wasted is time forever lost! As General George

Patton once said, "A good plan violently executed right now is far better than a perfect plan executed next week."

Another question I'm asked is, "Do you focus on improving the major league club first, or the farm system first?" I do both at the same time. That's what the owner wants and that's what I expect of myself. The last thing I'd want is to work night and day seven days a week improving the farm system alone, because by the time those players were ready the franchise might be sold to a new owner and moved to a different city. Then we who developed those players would wind up out of work, sitting at home during the playoffs watching those players we developed and listening to the television announcers say what a smart guy the new general manager is.

If I decided to focus only on the major league club, I would have to live and die by my trades, with no other resources to summon. And if I didn't have a deep minor league system of players ready to step up to the major leagues, my trading power would be severely limited. (I'll have a lot more to say about this in the next chapter.)

Even if a team shows marked improvement, becomes a contender, or wins a championship, that doesn't translate into job security for the general manager. I know, because I've been there. See, in the book of baseball fairy tales, the number one fairy tale is, "Hire good people and let them do their jobs." I wonder how owners define "good people." Are today's good people the ones who know how to lie low and do or say whatever's necessary to keep their jobs?

I embrace many of the policies used by successful corporations, but I'm not what you'd call a "corporate type." I pour all my energies into every task, and I expect my staff to do the same. If you've got initiative, you're on my team. If you're worried about what time your lunch break is, or how soon you're going to get your Christmas bonus, step aside. If you have an open mind, I will encourage you to follow your instincts and gain as much knowledge as you can. Don't tell me, "Yes, but . . . " or "We've always done things *this* way, and this way is the only way." The classic line I've heard thousands of times is, "We've tried it before and it didn't work." It probably didn't work the first time because you didn't pay enough attention to the details that make it work.

I like direct, honest communication. I don't like my staff obsessed with writing memos. I choose to spend my time productively. I don't clear my schedule for cozy golf outings with the higher-ups. And I refuse to sit around someone else's office and talk about the employees who are not in the room.

When I see something a player is doing incorrectly, I report it to the coach responsible for that area. For example, during the Pirates' 1988 spring training camp I observed that one of the minor league pitchers had what I call a "wandering foot." Every time he threw a pitch, his front foot landed in a different spot, which made control difficult. After watching him from a distance for a few minutes, I sought Ray Miller and asked him to observe the pitcher with me. I told him what I saw and asked, "Do you see this, too?" He did, and began working with the pitcher. I walked away. My responsibility is to see but not to interfere. If I were to stand alongside the coach and interject my observations, I would only confuse the player and make the problem worse.

The timing of teaching is as important as the technical knowledge you convey. You have to pick the right time, in the right environment, and what you say must be plain and simple. There are times when I'll spend a week thinking about something I've seen performed incorrectly, waiting for the right time to discuss it with the coach or the player.

And I'd have plenty of opportunities, because in addition

to attending every home game, I believe the general manager ought to travel with the team on the road. I love going to games. Every time I walk onto a baseball field I feel a surge of energy, an electricity, watching the players and interacting with people in the baseball world.

When I'm with them on the road, I have more time to communicate with the major league manager and his coaches. I'll talk with the manager about the things he sees and the moves he feels I should make to improve the club. I'll ask the pitching coach which pitchers he's working with, and how much progress they're making. I'll ask the batting instructor how his hitters are adjusting to the various pitches thrown by different pitchers.

Being on the road with the team allows me to see firsthand how our players comport themselves in the clubhouse, in batting practice, during the game, and away from the ballpark. The road is the best place to be with the players, because when the team is at home the players spend most of their time in their homes. The only contact I have with them when the team is home is at the ballpark.

During the course of a road trip I can sit with a player in the hotel lobby, ask him to come by my room, or share a taxi ride to the ballpark. We'll talk about anything, from baseball in general to his playing performance to his hobbies to his personal life.

I used to do this with Glenn Wilson when he played for the Pirates. Wilson, whom we acquired from the Seattle Mariners, went through a difficult time. The previous winter a doctor had diagnosed Wilson as having a heart problem and prescribed medication. The medication made Wilson so weak that in spring training he couldn't hit a ball to the fence. Since it was his first season with the Mariners, at first he didn't tell the organization about his condition, so baseball people assumed Wilson was simply losing his skills. His career seemed in jeopardy. When the Mariners discovered what was affecting Wilson, they sent him to a cardiologist.

That doctor discovered that Wilson didn't need the medication after all.

When we acquired Wilson we knew it would take him about a half-season to recover his strength. I tried to alleviate his fears, reminding him that we in the organization really cared about him.

I think every player in my organization, from Class A to the major league level, should know and believe that we in the team's management care about them as people more than anything else. And the general manager should know them, because if he can't remember details about the careers and lives of 180 players, he's in the wrong business.

I didn't adopt this philosophy because it is an effective management tool. I've always behaved this way. My parents trained me to care about the welfare of others and speak with them honestly and sincerely. You can't fool people with phony talk. Once I know my players as people, I can serve them better. If I can't convey and establish a trust, I can't accomplish anything.

By speaking directly and openly with the players, we can break down the traditional fears an employee has toward his boss, where he's afraid to speak because he worries his boss will hold it against him. He begins to realize, This man is not my "employer," he's my friend. He's giving me straight answers because he's interested in my welfare.

If a player feels comfortable enough with me to discuss a particular problem, whether the problem is physical or emotional, I can help by arranging for him to meet with qualified professionals, in or out of baseball. And I keep the conversations that are of a personal nature in the strictest confidence.

Jim Gott says, "It's important for me, as an employee, to have the general manager take some time to understand who I am. We are individuals and the game is not our whole life. By understanding the other side of the player, he helps us become better players."

By traveling with the team, I get to observe every one of our opponents' players, so there's never a lost moment for me at a baseball stadium. Also, being on the road gives me the option of renting a car and taking side trips to see our minor league clubs. For instance, when the Yankees were in Cleveland for a three-game series, I drove to Canton, Ohio, to watch our Double A Albany (New York) team, then drove back to Cleveland. After the game the next day I drove 140 miles to Columbus to visit with and observe our Triple A club play against Rochester, Baltimore's Triple A team.

During the Columbus game I got a chance to see left-hander Chuck Cary pitch one inning. Cary really impressed me with his 90-mile-an-hour fastball, his good breaking ball, and his screwball. He had three major-league-caliber pitches he could get strikeouts with. After the game, I met with Columbus manager Bucky Dent and his coaches to discuss the team. I told them one thing I'd concluded was that Cary was ready to pitch in the majors, and I was going to bring him up right away.

I've always been aware that my constant presence takes some getting used to. Few baseball executives travel with their team on a regular basis, so when one shows up on the road or at a minor league park, the managers, coaches, and players start thinking, He must be ready to make a trade, or release somebody, or fire somebody. I remember a Saturday morning in September 1988 when the Pirates were in Philadelphia for a three-game series against the Phillies. I was waiting for an elevator in the team's hotel. When the doors opened, there was Ken Oberkfell, a 10-year veteran whom I'd traded for a week earlier. As we rode to our floors I asked him, "How are you today?" He said, "Okay," but he looked uneasy. While I talked about things I'd seen during the previous evening's game, he fidgeted, as if he thought I was about to reprimand him for something. When he got off the elevator on his floor, I smiled. He just hadn't had a chance to get to know me yet.

Whenever I join a team I assemble all of my managers and coaches and tell them the following:

"There are no territories and no boundaries on this team. You will see me on the field. You will see me in the dugout. You will see me in the clubhouse. You will see me talking to players and working with them. And get used to that, because I am not only an office general—I'm a field general, too.

"And while you may have specific responsibilities, whether you work with hitters or pitchers or base runners, for you to be most beneficial to your manager I implore you to tell your manager and fellow coaches what you see about our other players and how you think they can improve. Share your teaching philosophies with your manager and fellow coaches, so their teaching methods can improve. Support each other. Be synergistic."

After I preached my philosophy to the Pirates staff in 1986, some of them still didn't know what to make of me. I heard them whispering about what they perceived as interference. One of them came over to me and cracked, "You're the first general manager that I've ever seen on a field talking about this and explaining that."

I answered, "A lot of those other guys you're talking about may be busy with extracurricular activities. I don't have time for anything other than this team, because the ox is in the mire. That's spelled M-I-R-E. And it says in the Bible that when the ox is stuck in the mire you have to work seven days, including the Sabbath, to get him out. That's what we're doing here. I'm working all the time, and I expect that of you, too."

The players get used to my presence a lot faster than the coaches do. The players feel comfortable with me, because they know I'm a veteran baseball man, a diagnostician who's been down the road they're now traveling along. Someone'll ask me, "What did you see in yesterday's game?" After I share my insights with him, I pass my observations on to the particular coach who works with him. This lets the coaches know what I'm seeing and *saying*.

At the start of the 1989 season I read a book called *A Passion for Excellence*, by Tom Peters and Nancy Austin, which describes methods for improving your capacities for leadership. Peters and Austin coined a term that describes my style to a tee: "Managing by Wandering Around." The authors, who run hundreds of intensive management-development seminars, believe that there are two ways to achieve excellence in business: take care of your customers through superior service and quality, and constantly innovate. The person in charge can reach those goals by listening to his customers and his employees and building their trust in him. When the leader wanders around among his clients and his staff, he is getting in touch with every phase of the operation and all the newest developments and preparing himself to adapt to any changes.

See, the general manager must be involved in all phases, because he bears the ultimate responsibility for the franchise's performance. If his teams play poorly, the general manager, the team's most visible symbol of authority, takes the heat. If the teams play well, the general manager gets his share of credit—sometimes too much credit. It reminds me of a comedy routine that political impressionist David Frye used to do during the Watergate scandal in the seventies. Frye, impersonating President Richard Nixon at a mock White House press conference, would answer a question about the President's role in the Watergate affair by saying, "I'll take full responsibility—but not the blame. You see, there's a difference. People who are responsible do not lose their jobs. People who are to blame, do."

The best way to keep your equilibrium is to be who you are. It's like Popeye says: "I am what I am and that's all that I am." I keep my perspective because of my belief in my Heavenly Father. So many times in my life as a problem-solver, I found myself alone searching for answers. This may sound righteous or foolish, but it is crystal clear to me that when I asked Him for help He provided me with answers.

I tell my managers and coaches that I have spent almost 30 years evaluating, procuring, and training players, while pursuing better methods of teaching and training. The only personal goal I have as a baseball executive is to be the best ever in player procurement and development.

The general manager's responsibilities are huge. In reality, a baseball franchise is seven small businesses: the major league team, and the six minor league affiliates. Therefore, the general manager must have direct access to and regular communication with the owner to ensure that plans are consistent with the owner's goals and budgetary guidelines.

Every team has certain budgetary constraints. A team in a major financial center or media market—bolstered by strong attendance, lucrative television contracts, advertising revenues, and an owner with deep pockets—may have the resources to sign expensive free agents to fill immediate needs. This has fostered the notion that only the teams with money can win.

Hogwash! I'd rather spend my team's money recruiting and training the best personnel—players, evaluators, managers, instructors, and specialists—and acquiring the latest technologies to help improve our performance. The costs are a lot less and the results are greater. I firmly believe that. And corporations worldwide have shown how to be successful by investing internally on recruiting and training.

For many years some organizations have had affiliations with teams in Puerto Rico, the Dominican Republic, Mexico, and Venezuela. This gives their young players teams to play with in winter ball, while exposing U.S. team officials to the native players on those teams. I think we can expand our affiliations worldwide, now that so many countries are playing baseball. We should definitely have working agreements with the Japanese teams, which in recent years have been conducting regularly scheduled symposiums on training and technology.

Major league teams that play in smaller markets are not the only ones to use money as an excuse for not winning. On the college level I've heard medium- and small-sized schools complain that the larger schools are most successful because they can afford more scholarships. I say, That's not the answer! The answer is in your recruiting. Quality recruiting will beat careless recruiting and frivolous spending every time.

On the high school level, where coaches in all sports are competing for the best athletes, there are coaches who don't take advantage of recruiting and training athletes who participate in other sports at the *same school*. When I coached on the high school level, I always wondered how many young men were not playing baseball simply because we didn't know who the school's best athletes were.

How does the high school baseball coach rectify this? By inviting the school's best athlete to practice with the baseball team. With all the high schools we have in the United States, there must be hundreds of athletes who need only to be asked and encouraged to participate. A good example is Andy Van Slyke, who lettered in basketball, football, and baseball at New Hartford High School in Utica, New York.

Van Slyke thought basketball was his best sport. He was a terrific forward with great jumping ability, and in one season led his league in scoring. His coach, Ed Taylor, was a family friend, and the team drew large, cheering crowds. What could be better? Meanwhile, the baseball team played fewer than 20 games a season because of the climate in upstate New York. But Michael Callan, New Hartford's baseball coach, cultivated a close relationship with Van Slyke and convinced him of his potential as a baseball player. Today Van Slyke is one of the game's best center fielders.

I'm disturbed by the new trend of reducing the general manager's responsibilities, putting the general manager in charge of the major league team only, while the farm director takes care of player development. I believe in specialists, but to run an organization properly you need an overriding vision, and that vision has to come from the general manager. It's as if some owners see their organization as a worm. They chop the worm in half and it grows another head. Then the second worm head has ideas that conflict with the first worm head. And the owners think they'll know what to do when those worms bump heads. This has already happened with the Detroit Tigers, and we've seen the results. And it's happening elsewhere, even with the Yankees.

When I signed with the Yankees I thought my title of senior vice president for baseball operations meant I would be responsible for the baseball operations. The only thing out of the ordinary I asked George Steinbrenner for during our negotiations over my four-year contract was that he retain Bob Quinn, the team's general manager, and have him work on player contracts and administrative matters, which are among his strengths. But as the season began I saw that player development and scouting were the domain of the team's vice president for player development and scouting, who was based at the Yankees' minor league headquarters in Tampa, Florida. Anyone who was hired to work with our minor league teams was hired by the Tampa office, so the senior New York staff had no say in player development.

The scouting department was divided in half. The free-agent scouts, who also covered the minor leagues, were supervised by the Tampa office; the major league scouts were supervised by me. But when it came time for the scouts to turn in their reports, both the free-agent scouts and the major league scouts submitted their information to Tampa first. We in the New York office had to wait until that information arrived by mail or was delivered by the owner.

I felt like I was trying to find a championship down a blind alley, so I continued to travel with the Yankees to make as many firsthand evaluations as I could. Unfortunately, in June Steinbrenner, citing budgetary reasons, pulled our scouts off the road and ordered me to stay in New York, where I "could use the phones to make trades." How parsimonious. The Yankees had $83 million in the bank. By pulling the scouts off the road, Steinbrenner saved approximately $25,000.

In all good franchises, the owner supports and encourages the general manager and his baseball staff. With franchises like the Giants and Mets, the general manager and owner have consistent dialogues so they know what the goals are, and the owner allows his baseball staff to carry out those goals. The trouble comes when the baseball staff has no idea what goals the owner wants to achieve. That wasn't a problem when I worked for Ewing Kauffman.

Working for Charley Finley, on the other hand, was quite an experience. Finley, who owned a profitable insurance company based in Illinois, is a real character—animated, imaginative, fast-paced, feisty, surly, and blunt. If you rambled in a conversation with him, he'd pierce you. But if you presented him with an interesting idea, he wanted to hear more.

Since Finley couldn't be bothered with the various owners' meetings where his presence was required, he'd bring me along, remain in his hotel room, and have me represent him. Being in on those meetings gave me a bird's-eye view of the many facets of the operation of a ball club.

I didn't always agree with Finley's style, but I did like his forward thinking. Finley was the first owner to have his players wear white shoes and multicolored, mix-and-match uniforms. He suggested the use of orange-colored baseballs, believing they would be easier for the players to see. He once had a clock on his scoreboard timing the pitchers between pitches, hoping it would make the pitchers work faster and speed up the game. He urged baseball to play night games during the World Series. He was a proponent of the designated hitter, and in two memorable seasons he used a player of exceptional speed named Herb Washington as a designated runner.

Washington's major league career statistics may be the oddest in the entire *Baseball Encyclopedia*. In 1974 and 1975, Washington appeared in a combined 104 games in the regular season and five in the playoffs without a single at-bat or inning of play in the field. All Washington did was pinch-run. He stole a total of 30 bases and scored 33 runs.

The Oakland A's reflected Finley's personality: arrogant, strong-willed, always ready for combat—with opponents or each other. By the time I hooked up with Finley, his inability to keep pace with baseball's changing marketplace had made him bitter. Finley, who struggled to draw a million fans even when his A's were winning championships, had been trying to move them to Toronto but couldn't get out of his stadium lease. He traded two of his better-paid players, outfielder Reggie Jackson and pitcher Ken Holtzman, to the Orioles at the start of the 1976 season. His goal was to hang on and survive, but his anger sometimes got the best of him.

On June 15, 1976, minutes before the trading deadline expired, Finley sold Vida Blue to the Yankees for $1.5 million, and Rollie Fingers and Joe Rudi to the Red Sox for $1 million each. He wanted to use the $3.5 million he received from those sales to improve his farm system and to sign the remaining players on his major league club. Now $3.5 million doesn't sound like a lot in today's baseball economy, but back then a team could cover its major league payroll and minor league costs for about $5 million total.

After Rudi and Fingers joined the Red Sox I called up infielder/outfielder Wayne Gross from Triple A to replace Rudi, and Steve McCatty, who was our best minor league pitcher, from Double A to replace Fingers.

Since the sale of Rudi and Fingers came when the Red Sox were in Oakland, Boston manager Darrell Johnson decided to keep them on the bench for their first game with the team, because he thought the emotional impact of the situation would affect them negatively.

Many team owners were clamoring for Commissioner Bowie Kuhn to take action against Finley. They felt that not only was Finley dismantling a team that had won five straight Western Division championships, but he was also shifting the balance of power in the Eastern Division to the two wealthiest clubs. The next day Kuhn froze the player sales and summoned Finley to his office. Two days later Kuhn, citing his authority to protect the best interests of baseball, voided both deals and ordered Blue, Fingers, and Rudi to return to the A's. Finley was enraged. When reporters asked him about Kuhn's decision, he responded, "I've decided one thing. If that man had a brain in his head, he'd be an idiot."

Finley, who was prepared to file a lawsuit against Kuhn, also decided that he would not allow the three players to play for the A's, saying their status was "in limbo" until the matter was resolved in the courts. So we played with 22 players for a while. Even when another player on the A's got hurt, reducing the roster of able-bodied players to 21, Finley still wouldn't budge.

On June 23 American League President Lee MacPhail ordered Finley to use Blue, Fingers, and Rudi in games. Two days later Finley let the three players suit up and sit in the dugout, but he still wouldn't let them play. On June 26 pitcher Jim Todd, the A's player representative, told Finley the team—which was in the thick of the Western Division race—would strike the following day and not play the scheduled game against the Twins if Finley did not let Blue, Fingers, and Rudi play.

Finley told Todd he'd suspend every player who went on strike—even though MacPhail said the league wouldn't honor those suspensions—and was set to promote the entire Triple A team in Tucson, Arizona, to the major leagues. Meanwhile, the Tucson Toros were scheduled to play a road game in Salt Lake City. The game had been heavily promoted—proceeds were going to be donated to charity—and 10,000 tickets had been sold. So the Salt Lake City owner told Finley he'd file suit if the Tucson players were called away.

There was so much tension in the air the next day. Neither Finley nor the players had budged. I had no idea if we'd play or forfeit the game. Hours earlier, I got a call from Bobby Bragan, who was then the president of the National Association of Professional Baseball Leagues, which supervises the minor leagues. Bragan asked, "Is it true that Charley's really going to call up the whole Triple A team?" Before I could utter a sound, Bragan answered his own question: "Knowing Charley, I guess it is true."

Finally, as the umpires walked toward home plate to receive the lineup cards from the managers, Finley instructed the public-address announcer to say that Blue, Rudi, and Fingers would be reinstated and that the game would be played under protest. We beat the Twins, 5–3. Rudi went oh-for-four, Blue didn't pitch, and Fingers got a save.

We finished the season in second place, two and a half games behind Kansas City. I'll always wonder if we could have done better had Finley allowed a full complement of players to play.

Following the 1976 season, Finley told me the Pirates were interested in trading with us for our manager, Chuck Tanner, who had a year remaining on his contract. He said that Harding Peterson, the Pirates' new general manager, who was replacing the retiring Joe Brown, wanted to pick a new manager. Finley said to me, "I have a chance to get $100,000 or Manny Sanguillen from the Pirates for Tanner." I was shocked. I couldn't believe my old club would offer money or a player for a manager.

Since our catcher, Gene Tenace, was about to sign with the Padres as a free agent, we needed a catcher to replace him. Finley asked me what I thought he should do. I thought the whole thing was unbelievable, so I replied, "Charley, there's a saying you've always told me that I'm going to repeat to you now: 'Pigs get fat. Hogs go to market. Which do you want to be, a pig or a hog?' " Finley was so excited that I remembered this saying of his that he answered, "Well I'll bet you a steak dinner I can get both." And days later, he did. I'm still stunned.

But Finley's a choirboy compared to George Michael Steinbrenner. If I'd paid more attention to Steinbrenner's first and middle initials—G. M.—I would have known what was in store for me. Steinbrenner's need to win is matched by his need to control people and events. My telephone rang every day, before, during, and after games, long-distance from his office or his home in Tampa. For weeks after I traded for Jesse Barfield, who struggled at the plate during that period, he'd call long-distance and yell, "I told you that was a bad trade! I told you so!"

If a player—any player—made a mistake during a game, that familiar voice on the other end of the line would scream, "I want him traded right now. Release him on the spot. Send him to Columbus. Just get him out of my sight!" If during a game the home-plate umpire's ball-and-strike calls seemed questionable, that familiar voice on the other end of the line would yell, "Those umpires are squeezing us," and demand we send staff interns down behind home plate and chart every pitch. The next day Bob Quinn would deliver a videotape of the game to the American League president's office. Quinn made so many trips with videotapes each year that, as he walked through the doors of the league offices, the league staff would remark, "Here comes Metro-Goldwyn-Mayer again."

I fielded so many long-distance phone calls that one time, when I was summoned to the dugout phone while talking during batting practice with Ira Berkow of *The New York Times*, Berkow wondered who was on the other end. I told him, "One thing's for sure. It isn't Alexander Graham Bell."

Steinbrenner has some good points. He is as demanding of himself as he is of others. He is a marvelous recruiter. He pays his people quite well, and rewards them for loyalty. He has the competitiveness of a warrior. The problem is he wages too many wars on too many fronts, which lead to too many changes. His belief that his players and staff need constant, negative discipline destroys the type of positive atmosphere a team needs to do its best year after year.

I honestly cannot tell you what goals the current Pirates ownership hopes to achieve, because I had so little access to it. The current ownership group consists of 12 owners: nine corporations and three individuals. There is no majority owner to set the franchise's policies and guidelines. Instead, the ownership group gives that authority to the chairman of the board, who in 1987 retired as the chairman and chief executive officer of the Westinghouse Electric Corporation, and the team president, a managing partner in a Pittsburgh law firm. These two men represent the owners at the various major league owners' meetings, but do not have a dime invested in the franchise.

The only Pirates owner I had regular conversations with was Eugene Litman, a real estate developer, and that was because he attended every home game. If any of the other owners came to a game, our conversations were brief and informal. Otherwise, the only times I dealt directly with the ownership group were every three months for 20- to 30-minute presentations. And sometimes many of the owners weren't even present.

In these presentations each person made a formal recitation from a prepared script, outlining the profits gained or losses incurred by his sector during the quarter. These meetings are restrictive and stilted, with no room for spontaneous discussion and meaningful exchanges, so unlike the openness of meetings with baseball people.

The Pirates' management structure is also restrictive. Instead of the conventional, pyramid-shaped management structure, the Pirates have set up a family tree of sorts. The team management is divided into "sides," a term I detest because it fosters competition rather than increasing cooperation. The business side (responsible for ticket sales, advertising, and marketing) and the baseball side are separate entities that report to the team president, who reports to the chairman of the board, who in turn reports to the 12 owners. The general manager, the person responsible for developing and manufacturing the franchise's product, has a relatively small role in the corporate pecking order. In my first two seasons I was supposed to report to Malcolm Prine, the team president and chairman of the board. But when the coalition divided that position in two after Prine left, I never knew to whom I was supposed to report.

Over time, I got the feeling that the team president and the chairman of the board were more interested in the franchise's profit margin than in winning a championship. At the end of August in 1988, with another month remaining in the season, the chairman of the board boasted to an audience at a Rotary Club luncheon that the team was about to turn a profit of $3 million. Meanwhile, the team itself was engaged in a battle for the National League's Eastern Division title.

The chairman and the team president have been frequently quoted as saying, "We believe baseball has to be operated as a business." Baseball is a business, all right, but the business is entertainment, not widgets. Your product is people, who perform before an audience of millions, not inanimate manufactured goods churned out on an assembly line. Your labor costs in baseball will be high, because your workers have a specialized skill and a powerful union. The better your team plays, the more your player payroll will rise because of such market forces as free agency, salary arbitration, and collective bargaining.

The Pirates were in an enviable position in 1988, finishing second in the National League's Eastern Division while having the National League's lowest player payroll ($6.5 million). If that formula could be bottled and replicated year after year, and all other conditions remained the same— that is, no other team in the division improved—then in 1994 the Pirates could pay off the remainder of the $25 million the city of Pittsburgh loaned to the team for operating expenses as part of the purchase.

Has the Pirates' coalition assumed that all conditions can remain the same? If so, they've made a grave error. The 1989 season was clear evidence of that. After finishing second in 1988, the Pirates fell to fifth in 1989, with a record of 74-88.

Player agent Dick Moss raised an issue worth pondering during his contract negotiations on behalf of client Andy Van Slyke in January 1989. Moss, quoted in *The Pittsburgh Press,* said, "The question to be determined is whether the club is determined to be run like a competitive club with the goal of winning a pennant, or if they just want to make money and hold down expenses." If they have a myopic view, contented with the short term, their franchise could easily revert to mediocrity.

The key is not whether you overspend or underspend. It's how wisely you invest your time and money. If you funnel your profits into recruiting and training the best available people, you will always come out ahead of the competition.

The Vision of a Winner

The first step in building a championship team is to visualize its components. The first consideration is the ballpark in which your team plays, since you play half your games there. Each stadium has its own characteristics. What works best in Pittsburgh's Three Rivers Stadium, which has an artificial surface and tough, angular outfield sight lines, may not work in New York's Yankee Stadium, a grass field with outfield dimensions that favor left-handed pull hitters. In Houston's Astrodome, where the artificial surface is fast and fly balls don't carry well, you'd want pitchers who can get fly-ball outs. In Chicago's Wrigley Field, an open-air stadium with strong, unpredictable winds that sometimes turn fly balls into home runs or home runs into flyouts, you'd need pitchers capable of getting ground-ball outs.

You've got to prioritize your needs to suit your ballpark, but you can't go overboard. The Red Sox could trap themselves by trying to get home-run hitters to reach the Green Monster in left field at the expense of table setters and hitters with line-drive power.

Some of the same ingredients are necessary wherever you play. In my book, good athletes are essential for the basics: pitching, above-average team speed, and a strong defense up the middle.

The pitcher has a distinct advantage over the hitter: time. By working fast and changing speeds, the pitcher controls the flow of the game and the hitter's reaction time to the pitches. Therefore, you draft and acquire pitchers who throw hard and teach them how to use the entire strike zone, how to change speeds, field their position, and hold runners on base.

You've heard the saying, "A team can never have too many good pitchers." The number one reason for that is the mortality rate for a pitcher's career, which is higher than any other position. If one of your pitchers breaks down, then a second breaks down, where are their replacements going to come from? That's why you must improve the quality of the pitchers throughout the organization.

As we've learned, running speed is the best measure of general athletic ability. Offensively, players who can steal bases change the game's tempo and disrupt the defense. When a player like Vince Coleman leads off the game by reaching first base, many dynamics come into play. The pitcher, catcher, and first baseman have to divide their concentration between Coleman and the hitter at the plate. The catcher may signal for more fastballs than he would with no one on base, in order to receive the ball more quickly and have more time to make a play at second base. When Coleman takes off for second, the infield goes in motion: the first baseman, who'd been holding Coleman on, skips into fielding position; the second baseman or shortstop runs to second awaiting a throw. All this activity gives the hitter a better chance of reaching base. He'll see more fastballs; there will be a hole at either second or short for the batted ball to go through; and with the defense in motion, there's a greater chance for an error.

Speed allows an offense to manufacture a run without getting a hit. Let's say Coleman walks, then steals second. He can advance to third by stealing the base, or by a sacrifice bunt, a long fly ball, or a ground ball to the right side. Once Coleman's on third, he can attempt a steal of home, or score on a bunt, a sacrifice fly, a ground ball (if the infielders are too deep), a wild pitch, or a balk.

Defensively, you can't compromise on speed in your middle infield or in the outfield, especially when you play on artificial turf. Quite simply, speedsters will get to more balls and make more plays than players of average or below-average speed. And if your middle infielders can't turn a double play, you're giving the opponent *four* outs per inning instead of three.

That's only half the battle. Your middle infielders, outfielders, and catchers must have strong throwing arms. Strong arms are even more imperative if your team plays on an artificial surface, because the ball travels faster than on grass; infielders have to play deeper, giving them longer throws. And consider the fact that base runners run faster on an artificial surface. A batter running to first base on synthetic turf reaches first about one- to two-tenths of a second faster than he would on natural grass.

The only absolute in baseball is that each team has 27 outs. The team that wins is the team that doesn't defeat itself by giving its opponent 29 outs or 31 outs. If you have good pitching, speed, and defense up the middle, you will maximize the effectiveness of your pitching and minimize the opponent's scoring chances. This is the quickest way to turn a poor team into a contender. Add to this formula hitters who have a plan of attack before every at-bat and know how to execute it, and you are on the threshold of a championship.

Let's look at the idea of not defeating yourself from a different perspective. In every other sport, the team with the ball is the team on offense. Question: When the pitcher has the ball and the hitter's at the plate, which one is *really* on offense? I guess it depends on who's pitching and who's hitting. If Nolan Ryan's on the mound and has two strikes on a hitter who has no plan of attack—a hitter of habit—I think you can say that *Ryan* is on offense and the hitter's on defense. Conversely, if Tony Gwynn is at bat against a pitcher who doesn't know how to use the strike zone, Gwynn's on offense.

Mr. Rickey once said that before the hitter gets into the box and before the pitcher gets his sign, one of them has subconsciously given in to the other. So again I ask you, which side is the offense?

Taking this thought further, when the hitter puts the ball in play, does the defense become the offense? Unless the ball's hit over the wall or hit for a ground-rule double, the defense has possession of the ball and controls the outcome of the play. If the defense knows how to execute, while the runner doesn't know how to run the bases properly, the defense scores an out. If the hitter runs the bases properly, while the defense can't execute routine plays, then the hitter is the offensive weapon.

This, my friends, is what baseball truly is: a contest between two sides over time and space. The side that understands this best, practices properly, is prepared, and is able to adjust to the changes in time over the fixed spaces—home plate to the mound, base to base—wins.

The Baseball Staff

Since I'm always in a hurry to turn a franchise into a winner, I need a staff than can keep pace with me, so I scout for people who can handle the responsibilities I delegate to them with efficiency, vigor, and vision.

There are two kinds of staff people: form people and content people. In the business world the form person, who says all the right things and has a great-looking resume, will starve you to death. The content person is the true producer. Maybe his paperwork is messy, but he'll close a deal every time.

When the general manager trains his staff people properly, one of the subtle goals he achieves is to teach them how to think for themselves. Sounds like a contradiction, doesn't it? But we in society train our children to please us, from infancy on. They grow up trying to please their mothers and fathers, their teachers, and, later, their employers. That system of "pleasing" others retards their creativity. As employees, they wind up needing detailed explanations of exactly how the employer wants a task done. If they do a poor job, their defense will be, "But that's the way *you* said you wanted it done." Or we train them to become form people. They say all the right things, but they produce nothing.

As a company manager, I train my personnel, lay out my goals to give them some direction, and let them take it from there. Then I evaluate their work to see exactly what they've accomplished.

I expect my staff, from the team offices down to the field and through the minor leagues, to conduct their personal lives with decorum, as an example to our players. I will not tolerate extramarital affairs or alcohol abuse. If our organization is spending so much time and energy working on ways to help the players grow as people, I cannot allow a single person on my staff to undo that.

Every general manager needs an assistant GM who knows how to negotiate contracts and has complete command of baseball's intricate rules for player transactions. I also have my assistant cross-check the work of our scouts and further explore new technologies and better methods of recruiting and training.

Next on our flow chart is the director of player development. The director of player development and his staff conduct seminars on our teaching and training methods, supervise their implementation, and monitor the progress of our minor league players.

The scouting director trains our scouts properly, deploys them in territories where they will see the most baseball players, and regularly evaluates their work.

The best way for a scouting director to train his scouts is in the field, where the action is. Ride with your scouts as they make their rounds. While you're in the car, exchange ideas on organizing territories and developing contacts. On the field, look at the same players and tell each other what you see. Learn from each other.

You also need an assistant director of player development and scouting who can process all the information both departments have gathered and make it readily available to the general manager.

I mentioned in an earlier chapter that I feel scouting departments can and should be doubled in size. I also believe the time has come to have people in that department who videotape every minor leaguer and every top prospect who is eligible for the June draft. Rather than rely on verbal reports and written grades and essays alone, we should all be able to see those players. One picture is still worth a thousand words. National Football League teams watch videotapes of the top prospects before they decide on their choices, and so should we. In June 1988, thanks to videotape, I drafted for the Pirates a free-agent left-hander named Bobby Underwood from the University of South Carolina. I'd seen a videotape of a college game Underwood pitched that was televised by ESPN, and was really impressed with his curveball.

Let's turn to the playing field. What I look for in a major league manager is someone who has served an apprenticeship on many levels of baseball, who can teach effectively, who understands the needs of his players and can communicate with them, and who is flexible about new ideas. Game strategy is the most overrated part of the major league manager's job. His job, first and foremost, is managing people. He's got to know what every player can do and use each of them in the situations that offer the best opportunity for success.

Another consideration is the composition of our team. If we have a young team, a veteran manager may not want to go through the years it could take us to contend. If we have a veteran team, it may not respond to a rookie manager.

I hired Jim Leyland to manage the Pirates because he'd

had a wide range of baseball experience—after his minor league playing career he managed successfully in the minor leagues and coached on the major league level—and was willing to endure the tough road we had to hoe.

It's important for a manager to hire coaches who teach and communicate effectively. "I delegate a lot of authority to my coaches," says Leyland. "The best way to put it is like Don Zimmer, the manager of the Chicago Cubs, does. Zimmer says he could go home for five days and his team would still run like clockwork. But if his five coaches went home for five days, there would be total chaos."

To give you an example: Because of Ray Miller's track record, Leyland gives him a wide berth. "Jimmy gives me his opinion of what certain pitchers need to work on, and I take it from there," says Miller. "Earl Weaver of the Orioles was the same way. Weaver told me when I first joined his coaching staff that he really didn't know how to throw a curveball—but he knew what a good one looked like. So when Weaver didn't like the curve he saw one of his pitchers throw, he'd tell me to work with the pitcher on that."

Miller also is responsible for setting up the pitching rotation and keeping records of how many pitches every pitcher on the staff has thrown. "Every 10 days or so I sit down with a sheet of paper and a team schedule and plan out a few possible rotations, figuring in the amount of off-days and the pitchers we may want to use in a series against a particular opponent. I submit that sheet to Jimmy. We'll meet on it the next day. He may say something like, 'Let's go with the first rotation you listed. It looks pretty good.'

"When I get to the ballpark I have another sheet of paper I submit to Jimmy that shows the day's pitcher, the number of days he's had to rest between starts, which day he threw between starts and the number of pitches he threw, how he did in his last outing, and how many innings he pitched that day. This way he gets an idea of how many innings or pitches the pitcher should throw during this day's game.

"I also submit sheets that chart our relievers. On those sheets I include the dates they warmed up in the bullpen, how many times they got up to throw, and how many pitches they threw. There are times when a reliever may not have appeared in our last three games but threw five times in the bullpen yesterday.

"We then go over my lists. He'll tell me which relievers he will try not to use, or not use at all, for the day's game. Because I know his thinking, I can have those relievers prepared in advance."

The general manager's task is to alleviate the pressure on the manager to win, no matter how good or bad the ball club is, because he—like any other person—will perform better if there's less stress.

Ten days into the start of the Pirates' 1986 spring training camp, I surveyed our talent and realized that, on the whole, we stunk. So I called a meeting with the manager and the coaches. I said, "We've got a problem here. This is a bad team. We've got some players that we can't trade because of salaries. So we have got to use every bit of imagination and creativity to see what we can do to improve it."

You should have seen the look of relief on their faces. They knew what I was talking about; they'd seen it for themselves. I decided we would set a simple goal: The Pirates were going to win at least 63 games in 1986 in order to avoid a second consecutive 100-loss season. See, there's a stigma when a team loses 100 or more games year after year. Ninety-nine losses for such a team is a victory.

"In that situation," Leyland recalls, "the Pirates had a manager nobody knew anything about taking over a ball club that couldn't win. I had to believe in my ability to manage. I had to be careful not to take it personally. People talk about statistics. My statistics—the record of the Pittsburgh Pirates—are in the newspapers every day.

"What Syd said to us was a big relief. The fact was, we were going to lose 98 games, but I can't tell you how hard our players and coaching staff worked not to lose 100 ball games. It didn't mean much to anyone else at the time, but when we went back to the clubhouse after that sixty-third win, it was as if we were ready to break out the champagne."

I make it a point to check in with the manager and his coaches every day to discuss the health of the club, what we're doing well, and what they think we can do to improve.

Leyland says, "I don't think anybody gets so smart that they can't listen to what another baseball man sees. Would there have been a problem if Syd Thrift wanted to make out the lineup? Yes. He would've had to get another manager. That's just the way it is. I'm sure most managers would feel this way. But he left those things up to me. If we had a disagreement, we sat down and ironed it out. We brought in the opinions of the coaches. But never once did he interfere with my managing the ball club or second-guess me about why I had a player bunt, why I used a hit-and-run play, or why I pulled a guy from the game. Not once."

I remember stopping by Leyland's office one morning during the middle of that season, following another of our 37 one-run losses that year. Our record of 16-37 in one-run games was the 10th-worst in modern National League history. Ron Scheuler, the team's pitching coach that year, was with Leyland. The two of them hadn't slept a wink. They were the most depressed, worn-out-looking guys I ever saw.

I said, "Do you know what's wrong with the two of you? You're taking these losses personally. What this team needs is better relief pitching. That's my responsibility. You guys shouldn't be staying up all night, because it's my fault and not yours. You've done the best you can with these players. Now go home and go to sleep."

What you want in your minor league managers and coaches are people who see themselves as stewards, responsible for the care of every one of their players, guarding that which has been entrusted unto them. It's like the parable of the sower. The parable asks, Which is more important, the seeds or the soil? It's the soil. Without good soil, the seed doesn't grow. So you need good soil, a good environment to help the players grow.

A good minor league manager or coach will explain to his players in private just how vulnerable a target they become when they make it to the major leagues. Mr. Rickey used to warn his players about "foreign alliances and entanglements." In today's climate, that means alcohol abuse, extortionists, drug dealers, and girls under the age of consent. There's an old truism in baseball: "You can't hoot with the owls and soar with the eagles."

We instruct our minor league managers to have five-minute, nonbaseball conversations with each of their players every day. Get to know them as people. Ask them about their lives and their interests. If baseball comes up, steer the conversation away from it. Let them know you care about them.

Player Development

The time-honored philosophy in player development is that you focus on development over winning; players won't develop properly if they have to concentrate on winning, too.

That philosophy makes no sense to me. Players who grow accustomed to losing find new and more creative ways to lose every day. If you take the emphasis off winning at the minor league level, you're left with a well-developed loser.

A fully developed player knows how to win, because he has been trained to take full advantage of the good information he has been taught. He is the most informed player on the field. He can expand his horizons, because he has all the fundamentals down cold. Today's young player is eager to learn things that can make him a better player. What he doesn't want to hear are old stories. He doesn't care who played in the big leagues 20 or 30 years ago.

Don't get me wrong. I don't believe in putting pressure on a young player, and I know none of us are perfect. I simply feel that winning is a natural progression. When the player arrives in the major leagues, he is expected to know how to win. If he first has to learn how to win on the major league level, that's when he feels pressure.

When I came to the Pirates in 1985, their farm teams had terrible records. In my first meeting with the player development staff, I told them, "You cannot develop players without winning. So from here on, *we will win*." My proclamation left them stunned. You could have become deaf from the thud of their jaws dropping to the table.

Once a losing attitude permeates your minor league system, the owners of the minor league franchises chase them out of their cities and switch their affiliations to other major league organizations. The Pirates' Triple A team had become a vagabond. During my first term with the Pirates, their Triple A team played in Columbus, Ohio. It was then moved to Portland, Oregon. By the time I returned to the Pirates, their Triple A team had settled in Hawaii.

Hawaii is a beautiful place for a vacation, but it is five time zones away from Pittsburgh. Say I wanted to speak by telephone with the Triple A manager. I'd have to wait until four o'clock in the afternoon to get him at 10 A.M. his time. If I had to bring up a player from Hawaii, he would have to fly 10 hours to get to Pittsburgh, then need another day for his internal body clock to acclimate to the time change.

I worked out an agreement for our Triple A club to relocate in 1987 to Vancouver, British Columbia, which brought it two time zones closer to Pittsburgh. In 1988 we moved it to Buffalo, New York, just 216 miles from Pittsburgh. The owners of the Buffalo team, the Rich family, had just built Pilot Field, an impressive stadium that was chosen as the site for the 1988 Triple A All-Star Game. They wanted to provide their fans with an exciting, winning team. Bob Rich, a successful businessman who also has a great interest in new methods of studying and measuring player performance, decided to sign with the Pirates, despite being courted by other teams, because he was impressed by our commitment to winning.

There's only one thing you can't teach a player: experience. I discovered the same thing when I broke in bird dogs for hunting. Of course, human beings are far beyond canines, but the training of bird dogs provides an interesting comparison.

Many years ago I used to break in bird dogs by old-fashioned methods, where you waited about six months, allowing the dog to develop physically and mentally, before you started training him. Then I read a book about hunting dogs written by a chemist in New Jersey. He explored the scientific development of dogs by working with the canine corps and the Institute for the Blind. He learned that a dog's brain is fully developed when he is six weeks old, so a lot of time is lost using the traditional training methods. The doctor trained six-week-old dogs to whoa, stand, sit, heel, and kennel using simple visual and oral commands.

When I hunt I'm always on the move from one field to another. I knew that the biggest waste of a bird hunter's time was getting the dogs to climb into the back of his station wagon or pickup truck. The dogs would bark, run around, anything but climb into the truck. So I used the techniques I had read to train my dogs to load quickly. I drilled them in my backyard. They lined up the way a basketball team lines up for lay-up drills, and at my command they sped toward my station wagon and jumped in the back. As they got better at it, I would sit in my station wagon with the motor running, holler "Load," and drive off. It got to be comical, because when the tailgate was up and I pulled out, the dogs were running so fast that they flew through the air and landed on my roof.

But no matter how disciplined the training, how simple the commands, and how thoroughly you care for their medical needs, you cannot train dogs to hunt. They learn that by experience. At the outset, they pick up a scent and track it, but poof, the quail is already gone. A veteran quail hunter will tell you that the dogs don't become superior hunters until they are five or six years old. When they pick up a scent, they know by the smell whether the quail was at the spot five or 10 minutes earlier. So they circle the area, in wider and wider circles, until they find that quail.

This reminds me of baseball players. You start your teaching and training early, while their minds are receptive. Yet, no matter how complete their training is, they only become better by experiencing it for themselves. When they arrive in the big leagues, they will make—and learn from—their rookie mistakes. On the average, when they get past their third season in the big leagues, they have developed some hunting sense. And that's when they are eligible for arbitration. When they reach their prime, in their sixth year, they can become free agents. Then they really know how to hunt.

I once told Branch Rickey, Jr. that every minor league manager should break in at least one bird dog. He thought it was a great idea. See, it teaches you to communicate simply. You can spew out a hundred sentences of hot air to a player and it won't amount to anything except confusion. If you can use one sentence or one word or one sign, he'll understand you better.

If you and your evaluators believe a minor league player is ready to experience baseball on a higher classification, there is no reason why you can't advance a player two or three levels at a time. When I came to Pittsburgh in 1985, Barry Bonds and John Smiley hadn't played on a level higher than Class A. Yet within two seasons Bonds and Smiley arrived on the major league level, and today they are outstanding major league players.

These decisions are quite often predicated on what you have in your own system. I had advanced Bonds at the start of the 1986 season from Class A to Triple A because we had no championship-caliber outfielders on our Double A and Triple A clubs. To tell you the truth, I didn't plan on bringing Bonds to the major leagues in the middle of the '86 season, but a funny thing happened on my way back from a trip to California.

We had selected an outfielder named Moises Alou, the son of former major leaguer Felipe Alou from Canada (California) College in the January draft that year. According to the rules, we had until May to sign him. For some reason we'd gotten bogged down in the negotiations, so that month I headed to California in a last-ditch effort to sign him. Shortly after I arrived, we were able to agree on a contract.

On my way back to Pittsburgh I stopped off in Phoenix on a Saturday night to see our Triple A club play a game against the Phoenix Giants, the San Francisco Giants' Triple A club. Moises Alou had come with me, because he had a sister who lived there. He arrived at the ballpark, dressed, and took batting practice with our team.

I was sitting in the dugout watching batting practice. The left-handed-hitting Bonds really caught my attention. Bonds, a standout in his collegiate career at Arizona State, was our first choice in the June 1985 free-agent draft. His father, Bobby, had been an outstanding major league player.

During that batting practice Bonds hit 10 balls over the right-field fence. When he came into the dugout, I said to him, "Well, Barry, any left-handed hitter can hit the ball over the right-field fence. Why don't you hit some over the center-field and left-field fences?"

His next time up in the batting cage he hit shots over the center-field and left-field fences. He came back to the dugout, smiled, and said, "That's what you wanted, right?"

I then talked with several of the scouts who were on hand. They told me that after a slow start Barry was burning up the league. It got to the point where the other teams were pitching around him.

Before the game I asked him to sit down with me. I said, "Barry, you're closer to the big leagues than you'll ever know." He had a look of doubt on his face. I repeated myself more forcefully. "I'm telling you now: You're closer to the big leagues than you think."

As I watched the game from behind home plate I started thinking about the outfielders we had in Pittsburgh. I realized, Goodness! This kid has more talent by far than any of my major league outfielders.

I knew it would be a risk bringing him up to the big leagues, because he'd had only one and a half seasons of minor league ball. But they were pitching around him, so staying down there was a waste of his time. And, I thought, he's grown up in a baseball environment, has played college baseball, and has the emotional makeup to handle the pressures of the major leagues. I wrestled with this for six innings.

In the seventh I decided I was going to take that risk. I went into our dugout and told the manager, Tommy Sandt, to remove Bonds from the game immediately and get him a plane ticket to Pittsburgh. So here I had dropped off Alou, picked up Bonds, and headed home.

I couldn't wait to put Bonds on the Pirates' roster. It was then that I learned how important it is to have someone on your staff who knows the transaction rules cold.

Since it was still the weekend and our offices were closed, I called the league office myself, activating Bonds and sending outfielder Trench Davis to the minors. The next day, our public relations department announced the transaction.

That Monday I learned I could not send Davis to the minor leagues until he cleared waivers, since he had already used up his minor league options. So I put Davis on waivers, and it wasn't until Thursday of that week that I could play Bonds. From Monday to Thursday, the media had fun with my mistake. Boy, did I look stupid.

I might have had egg on my face, but I told Bonds he

didn't lose a thing. He could take batting practice with the team, observe games for three days, and go on from there.

At the outset he struggled at the plate, his batting average fluctuating between .220 and .240. But I could see he was making progress. He was making the adjustments, and making them fast. He was figuring those pitchers out. He had good swings. He hit a lot of line drives that were caught for outs, but he hung in there and didn't get down in the mouth. He showed that strong character necessary to be a big league player.

I clearly remember Bonds's first five major league home runs. Each one was hit to the opposite field, which is a real display of power.

As I toured the minor leagues at various times during the '86 season, I saw John Smiley, a left-hander on our Prince William (Class A) team in the Carolina League, pitch on three occasions. Smiley's manager, Rocky Bridges, had converted him from a starting pitcher into a first-rate short reliever and was really enthusiastic about his progress. Bridges said he thought Smiley was a better reliever at that moment than Gary Lavelle, who during the seventies and eighties was a top left-handed major league reliever.

After my second visit in August, I came back to Pittsburgh and told Jim Leyland, "John Smiley is the most gifted left-handed pitcher I've seen in years, and I'm seriously thinking about bringing him up to the major leagues in September. I know I'm going to shock a lot of people by having him make the jump from A ball to the majors, so I'm going back to see him one more time, when Prince William plays its last series in Hagerstown, before I make my mind up."

Before Prince William's game I asked Bridges on what level he thought Smiley could pitch next year. Bridges looked at me for a minute. "You know, Smiley is a tough kid," Bridges said. "He doesn't get scared. I think moving him to Triple A is a possibility."

Smiley was terrific in the game I saw him pitch. The following day, which was Prince William's final game of the season, I told Bridges, "Rocky, I've thought about what you said, and I'm going by what I've seen. I've made a decision. After tonight's game, I want you to tell John Smiley he's coming to the major leagues tomorrow."

Rocky was stunned. Then he flashed his toothless smile and said, "You know what? Smiley just might make it."

Smiley, given the opportunity to get his feet wet in the major leagues, worked long and hard with pitching coach Ray Miller and has become one of the premier left-handed starting pitchers in the National League.

Praising and Scolding

We have got to train ourselves as baseball people to "accentuate the positive" and "eliminate the negative." That's always been one of my favorite songs. You can't build anything on negative thinking. You've got to look upon failure as an opportunity to achieve success.

You can win losing. You can actually win a game you've physically lost. It depends on your attitude about tomorrow.

If a short reliever comes into a close game and gives up a game-winning home run, I'll tell him afterwards, "Don't worry, that's just one pitch. If that's the last pitch you're ever going to make in your career, then you'd have a problem. But that wasn't your last pitch. You've got a lot more successful games to look forward to. Look at how many saves and wins you've earned already." He may be startled by what I'm saying, but what I'm trying to do is bring his focus back to the positive aspects.

See, the outcome may be beyond your control, but the method you use to go after it isn't. If you've worked hard to develop your physical and mental abilities to their fullest, your method will bring you success more often than not.

Say you're a lawyer. You take on a case, do extensive research, argue the case as best you can. But the jury decides against your client. You did the best job you could, so you really didn't fail. But if you took the verdict personally, you would see it as a failure.

The most delicate part of a general manager's job and a manager's job is praising and scolding. Sometimes I'll use a parable to convey a message that praises and scolds. I recall in the spring of 1986 how many of the Pirates' players were moaning and grumbling about not wanting to play on our team, so during training camp I assembled the players and told them the parable about the little bird from up North. Here's how it goes:

There was this little bird flying in the rain from the North to the South. As he crossed Delaware, he encountered a cold front that changed the rain into sleet. Ice formed on his wings as he struggled toward Maryland. His wings got so heavy that he fell to the ground and landed in the middle of a barnyard.

In that barnyard was a big pile of fresh cow manure, and he fell in the middle of that pile of fresh cow manure. It was dark in that fresh pile of cow manure, but it was also warm. The little bird thawed out. He felt so good he started singing and chirping at the top of his voice.

An old barnyard cat heard the little bird's song, and when he identified which pile he was in he went over, scooped him out, and ate him.

The moral of that story is: If you're warm and comfortable and you're covered in manure, keep your mouth shut.

Old Rick Reuschel, our best pitcher, and the other players fell to the ground in laughter. When the laughter died down, I said, "Gentlemen, there's a message in that parable for you to learn today. If you're warm and you're comfortable, keep your mouth shut. I don't want to hear about all this 'I don't want to be in Pittsburgh' talk. All you've got to do is tell me quietly and I will make certain that you're traded.

"Greater players than you will ever be have played in Pittsburgh. So until you can prove to me and this manager and this staff that you belong and deserve to be there, then the jury's out on you. And I hope to the Lord that you're capable of playing to my expectations of a major league team."

One of the finest books I've read on the art of praising and scolding is *The One Minute Manager*, by Kenneth Blanchard, Ph.D., and Spencer Johnson, M.D. For their "One Minute Praising" and "One Minute Reprimand," the authors advise you to let people know up front how they are doing; praise or scold immediately; make your praise or criticism specific; tell them how you feel about what they did; stop for a moment to let them feel what you feel; and shake hands or touch them in some way to let them know you're on their side.

I appreciate these tactics, because I believe that a person should gain something from criticism as well as praise. One of the best examples of the "One Minute Reprimand" was an encounter Jim Leyland had with Jim Gott shortly after I traded for him on August 3, 1987. When Gott joined our club, Leyland and I told him we had him scheduled to start a game the following Friday night.

"I hadn't been pitching very much," Gott remembers, "so I asked if they could please let me pitch in relief for a couple of games. They agreed to work me into a game.

"That first night, Doug Drabek was pitching a great game against the Chicago Cubs. I thought I wasn't going to be called upon, so I started throwing in the bullpen, just to get some work in. Ray Miller watched me throw and suggested some minor adjustments.

"We get to the eighth inning. I had just stopped throwing. Drabek ran into some difficulties, so a call came from the dugout, asking for Brett Gideon to warm up. But Gideon was having trouble getting his arm loose. I'm the only pitcher who's warmed up and ready to pitch. Ray told Jim Leyland, 'He's been throwing well. Let's go ahead and put him in the game.'

"The next thing I knew, I was coming into a game with two outs, runners on first and third, and we're ahead, 4–2. The first batter I faced, Brian Dayett, got a jam-shot single. Then it's 4–3, with runners on first and third. I struck out Dave Martinez to end the inning, and retired the side the next inning to get my first save.

"The next night I sat in the bullpen thinking, I'm glad I saved the game last night but, please, let's not try this again. I still have my start on Friday.

"What happened? I was called into that game, too, in a hold situation. I pitched two scoreless innings and was re- moved from the game.

"That Thursday Jim and Syd told me, [former Pirate] 'Don Robinson had been the stopper. He was a veteran, which gave the younger guys in the bullpen a role model. Now we have no veterans in the bullpen. You've done a good job in relief, so we'd like you to take on that role. We want you to help the younger pitchers so they feel less pressure.'

"I was really excited about my new role. So in the next game I proceeded to give up six singles and four runs in two innings. I blew the save and got the loss.

"I walked into the clubhouse with my head down. Leyland pushed me up against a wall, looked me in the eyes, and said, 'Don't walk around this clubhouse with your head down. We don't give up on anybody around here.' That was exactly what I needed to hear at that time."

Leyland says, "My philosophy is, Be fair and be firm. Scold like a father and hug like a father. I've believed all through my life that this is the best way to get results.

"I try to treat my players like I expected to be treated. If

I messed up and didn't put out 100 percent, I expected to be chewed out. If I did something good, I expected a pat on the back.

"I first saw Jim Gott when I managed the Lakeland Tigers, clear back in 1976–77. I knew what great physical talent he had. And I just was not going to let him feel sorry for himself and worry about whether he was ever going to get another chance. So I wanted to accomplish two things: let him know that he had to be tougher, and assure him that we don't give one-time opportunities here. That's not our style. We believed in him."

There are times the general manager has to send a player to the minor leagues because he's struggling. If you visualize a player's confidence level as a thermometer, from zero at the bottom to 100 at the top, then 50 would be your borderline area. When a player's confidence level drops to 30 or 20, the longer we keep him in the major league environment the more we are causing him to fail.

If I send him to the minor leagues, I first have to make him aware that what I'm doing is not a form of punishment but a reward for future improvement. He's being sent to the minor leagues for a specific purpose: to go into a new environment where there is less stress and strain, to play every day, and to recapture his groove of success, so that when we need him again he'll be ready, in a better frame of mind.

The toughest task in the whole world is releasing a player from your organization. Whether the player's a veteran or a rookie, I get really depressed every time, and I've released many, many players.

Every time a manager has to tell a player that he's being released, I make it my business to be there. I don't want my manager to have to be the bearer of such bad news. I don't think that's fair. And I believe my manager gains some respect for me for being with him in that time of crisis.

I often find myself having to explain the situation to a teammate who's been a close friend of the released player.

The teammate may demand an answer, even if he doesn't really want to hear the truth.

I recall the time I released some players, including short-stop Johnnie LeMaster, in March of 1986. That day I rode over to the Pirate City spring training complex with Reuschel. I knew Reuschel didn't agree with the release of LeMaster, because they were friends and he thought Le-Master was a good shortstop.

I said to Reuschel, "Maybe he's better than the players I'm keeping, but I have to see if these young guys can play. That's the way it has to be."

I also noticed that after I released those veteran players who were making huge sums of money, the younger players responded as though I had signed an emancipation procla-mation for them. They saw that their progress was no longer blocked by those veteran players. They looked relieved and enthusiastic, as if I had just unclogged their arteries, and I would have never sensed that had I not been on the field.

Dealing with the Media

I have great respect for the beat writer, because he's with the team all the time. In many cases he knows more about the team than anyone else. I hate to admit that, but it's true.

I have to cooperate with these writers, because the better informed I keep them, the less likely they are to reach er-roneous conclusions that can negatively affect the players and the manager. I will explain to them why we traded a player or sent a player to the minor leagues, so they'll un-derstand that nothing we do is rash and spontaneous. No mysteries. No untold stories.

See, the world is made up of two kinds of people: the positive people who really want to see others achieve suc-cess, and the people who stop to see the wreck on the high-way. In this world the great preponderance of people stop to see the wreck on the highway. That's reflected in the evening news on TV—this person was murdered here and this car crashed over there and so-and-so was robbed. You have to wait 25 minutes for one halfway-decent story. And in today's sports sections, you'll find more stories about team dissension and contract squabbles and paternity suits and drug problems and other sordid and sorry situations than on the game itself.

I spent three hours at a press conference explaining to the New York media why I traded left-handed pitcher Al Leiter to the Blue Jays for Jesse Barfield, since it seemed odd for us to trade a pitcher when we were thin on pitching ourselves. But we had an immediate priority: Dave Winfield's back injury, which would put him out of action for the entire 1989 season, left us with a gaping hole in right field and in the number-four spot in the batting order. With no enforcer behind Don Mattingly, I wasn't sure whether he would see a pitch in the strike zone the rest of the season.

Toronto had an abundance of good outfielders—youngsters Junior Felix and Rob Ducey, and veterans George Bell, Lloyd Moseby, and Jesse Barfield. Even with a DH spot, one of those guys would have to sit.

The odd man out was going to be the 29-year-old Barfield, who in 1986 hit 40 home runs and drove in 108 runs but was slowed the next two seasons by an assortment of wrist and knee injuries. Barfield also played an exceptional right field, leading all American League outfielders in assists (71) over a four-year period. I had admired Barfield's talents during my years with the Pirates, but his contract was too rich for that team's payroll.

I started calling Blue Jays general manager Pat Gillick from Opening Day in my pursuit of Barfield. It took us almost a month to agree on the player he wanted from the Yankees. We finally landed Barfield on April 30 for left-handed pitcher Al Leiter.

At the press conference following the trade, the media

made it sound as if by trading Leiter I had committed sacrilege. Leiter, born in Toms River, New Jersey, a short drive from Yankee Stadium, had been selected by the Yankees on the second round of the June 1984 draft. The last left-handed pitching prospect to stick with the Yankees had been Ron Guidry, so the fans and media eagerly awaited Leiter's arrival on the major league level.

During a late-season call-up in 1987, Leiter captured the imagination of the fans with one pitch in a game against the Blue Jays. George Bell, who was enjoying an incredible season in which he would hit 47 home runs and knock in 134 runs, didn't like a particular strike call made by the home-plate umpire. After registering his protest, Bell took his time getting back into the batter's box. Leiter's next pitch was a high-and-tight brushback fastball that sent Bell sprawling to the dirt. The New York fans loved it.

During the 1988 season Leiter developed blisters on his pitching hand, which limited his effectiveness. He won four games and lost four, with an ERA of 3.92 in 57⅓ innings. All through the winter the fans heard and read reports that many teams were after Leiter but that the Yankees refused to let him go. Then I came along and traded him five weeks later.

For two full weeks the media dissected the trade and judged it a poor one on my part. And poor Jesse Barfield, who told the media he had always dreamed of playing for the Yankees, got off to a one-for-22 start.

I'll say now what I said then: Leiter is a fine prospect. Barfield is a fine *player*. The Yankees had a critical need for an every-day right fielder of Barfield's abilities. I didn't trade Leiter to denigrate his talent. If Leiter blossoms into a 20-game winner for the Blue Jays, I'll be happy. Of course, if Barfield plays the way I know he can, I'll be happi*er*.

I've made mistakes dealing with the media. I speak highly of people almost instinctively. In Pittsburgh I praised everyone in our organization, even those I had my doubts about.

In some cases, they lost their perspective because of my good quotes. They got puffed up beyond reality.

I also got so much personal coverage that some Pirates officials believed I was promoting myself, not the team. I knew that wasn't true, but it stung nonetheless. So when I came to New York I decided to keep a low profile. What happened? Some of the New York newspaper writers got angry with me for not talking, so they went elsewhere for information. Sadly, there were plenty of team sources all too willing to dispense confidential—and, at times, incorrect—information. There were times I'd wonder if I'd lost my mind. I'd read in the newspapers about player transactions we were all set to make, moves I'd never even thought about. All those stories were attributed to unnamed sources in the Yankees organization, many of them sources close to Steinbrenner. (During the 1989 season Joe Donnelly of *Newsday* once wrote that Yankee sources are often as close to Steinbrenner as his underwear.)

The most dangerous, injurious things printed are those stories that rely on unnamed sources. Behind a shield of anonymity, team officials can use the press for self-aggrandizement. And since today's front offices are subdivided, the number of unnamed sources multiplies. Think about the harm that does to the player, the team, and the organization. The player and his family are bound to be upset if they hear or read the player's name in trade rumors. If team officials leak information on contract negotiations or brag about profit margins, your players stop thinking about championships and start thinking about their negotiations, renegotiations, and arbitration hearings. The *team* concept is lost. Now the manager can't manage.

These sources can also leak all sorts of malicious, untrue accusations against their department head or a former boss. The more unnamed sources involved, the worse it gets in baseball's small community for the person who stands accused. That person becomes guilty until proven innocent.

That person has to spend time and money clearing his name of false charges, and the more he tries to refute them, the harder it is to put them to rest. I know, because I experienced this firsthand.

When I decided to resign from the Yankees on August 29, I called Steinbrenner in Tampa at 7:15 A.M. and informed him of my decision. I told him my resignation was for personal reasons, and added that I was sick and tired of coming to work every day and having to answer media questions about my job status. I wished him luck and told him he could call me if he needed anything. He was supportive of my decision and effusively praised my work for the Yankees.

I left New York without meeting with the media, because I didn't want to rehash everything. The media asked Steinbrenner whether Jim Bowden's job would be affected by my departure. Steinbrenner assured them that Bowden would stay on for the remainder of the season.

On August 30, Steinbrenner had Bob Quinn fire Bowden.

Over the following days the New York newspapers were chock-full of erroneous stories about my resignation, filled with quotes from sources close to the team. I figured Steinbrenner was irritated by my resignation, because he hates it when people quit on him; he prefers to fire them. I really didn't care what the newspapers wrote.

But a week later Steinbrenner and unnamed sources on the Yankees launched a vicious, groundless rumor designed to discredit me. On September 7, Steinbrenner, appearing on "Live At Five," a news and entertainment program on New York's WNBC-TV, said the Yankees were being investigated by the commissioner's office for having scouting information belonging to the Pirates.

Steinbrenner—and here I'm quoting from a transcript of the broadcast I received from WNBC-TV—said, "I do know that at the scouting meetings, there were discussions concerning whether the Yankees had computer information from the Pittsburgh Pirates system available to them. That question was asked at those meetings. I haven't heard the report out of Chicago, but I will say that the commissioner's office is . . . my understanding is [the commissioner's office is] looking into that as it concerned the Pittsburgh Pirates. Where Syd fits into that I couldn't say because I don't know what that look-see by the commissioner's office will produce. I would hope that it would not be the case, and I have no reason to believe it is. But we will . . . I mean, that [investigation] is ongoing. That is accurate."

The next day the New York *Daily News* ran a story headlined: "Thrift being probed by baseball." In the article, unnamed sources in the commissioner's office confirmed that there was an investigation, and the writer ended his story by recalling something said to him by an unnamed source within the Yankees organization who had said after my resignation: "There is something more to this that will come out but can't be told at this time."

I called the commissioner's office and pressed them for details: What was the investigation about? Who started it? Why hadn't I even once been questioned by baseball's investigators? All they told me was that they were checking any Yankees long-distance phone calls to Pittsburgh, and comparing the players chosen by the Pirates and the Yankees during the June 1989 Amateur Draft for any similarities. So far, they said, they saw no similarities.

That should have exonerated Bowden and me right there. First, all the Yankees' scouting reports were submitted to Tampa, not New York. Second, the Yankees' minor league officials in Tampa conducted the draft. Bowden was in New York with Quinn, keeping apprised of the selections via a conference line with the commissioner's office. I was in Tampa for the opening day of the draft as a spectator, but returned to New York a day later, while the draft was still going on. As a matter of fact, it was the first time in my management career that I hadn't participated in an amateur draft.

On Sunday, September 11, I'd heard from Bowden that Quinn wanted to speak with me. I phoned Quinn that evening. Quinn told me he had a message to deliver from Steinbrenner. He then read aloud from an article in that day's *New York Times*, which quoted an unnamed Yankees source who said that the investigation centered on Bowden, not me. For the record, Steinbrenner commented that he'd be "astonished if Thrift had knowledge of any improper actions."

"That," said Quinn, "is the message GMS wants you to have. I also want you to know that I was not the source for the article."

"Who was the source?" I asked.

"You can guess."

I fired back, "I'm not in a guessing mood."

Quinn answered, "He goes by three initials, and I don't have three initials."

"Are you saying George Steinbrenner is the source?"

"Yes," said Quinn. "That's his style."

Isn't that typical? Steinbrenner thought I'd be comforted to know that he was only accusing a fine young man I'd brought into the organization, not me personally. This just made me madder.

I called the commissioner's office and repeated to them what Quinn had said. They told me that Steinbrenner had made these charges known to Commissioner A. Bartlett Giamatti not long before his tragic death, but that I'd have to wait for a decision until Deputy Commissioner Francis "Fay" Vincent was selected later in the week.

Then came more stories citing unnamed sources about Bowden tapping into the Pirates' computer system and stealing their scouting reports. The tone of a story in the *New York Post* made it seem as if we were guilty. I didn't want to comment publicly on this matter until the investigation was concluded, so as not to give credence to these stories.

It was 11 days from the time the story first broke until the commissioner's office released a statement to the Associated Press and United Press International, stating that there was no evidence of wrongdoing on our part. Those were the worst 11 days of my professional life. I felt like my 30-year reputation in baseball was being permanently tarnished and there wasn't a thing I could do about it. The allegations hurt Bowden as well. He'd lined up an interview with officials at another club, but they backed off as soon as these charges made the newspapers.

The funny thing was, when the wire services wrote about the statement from the commissioner's office clearing us of any wrongdoing whatsoever, they added that unnamed sources in the commissioner's office said it was Steinbrenner who originally brought the charges and asked for the investigation.

The issue of unnamed sources who practice the art of degradation by subterfuge isn't only a problem in baseball. In September 1989, there were articles in *The Washington Post* and in *New York* magazine about how common in the business world the practice of leaking defamatory remarks has become.

I spoke with Fay Vincent about this a few days after his office concluded its investigation. I told him, "In baseball, uniformed personnel have union protection, but what about nonunion personnel? I believe every owner has to be held responsible when careless, damaging statements that affect an employee's future livelihood come out of his team's 'unnamed sources.' When a team is found guilty of tampering with a player under contract to another team, the owner has to pay a $250,000 fine. I think it's just as severe when a team tampers with the reputation of a former front office employee."

I'm not blaming the media for this. They have stories to write and publications to sell. But one thing I find fault with the media about is when a newspaperman or magazine writer prints incorrect information about player salaries and team finances. It's the same principle I have with my own checkbook: If it isn't balanced right to the penny, I get irritated about it. I don't like anyone to guess numbers. And sometimes the writers have a tendency to do that.

When I trade for a player during the season, some writers will publish the gross number of the player's salary, a figure that on the surface makes the trade look like the dumbest thing you've seen in your whole life, when the true cost to your team is the differential between his yearly salary and the amount you're obligated to pay him for the remainder of that season.

Let's say in August you acquire a player making $850,000 a year, and the player you've traded was making $350,000 a year. So the true salary differential, when you calculate what you are paying the new player for the rest of the season and what you no longer have to pay the player you traded, is about $180,000. That's the real effect of the new player's salary on your team budget, not $850,000.

The players have a responsibility to the media as well. They've got to respect the fact that it's the media's job to report on them. They've got to give honest, thoughtful answers, because their words travel across America. The fastest way a player can make the media his enemy is by being uncooperative or rude. I remind every player that one day he might be eligible for the Hall of Fame, but the baseball writers who vote on his induction may continue to carry a grudge.

There is one rule of discretion my manager and I abide by and expect our players to: If you have anything negative to say about a teammate or anyone else in our organization, say it *only* in the clubhouse, behind closed doors, and not in the newspapers. Don't ever show up a member of this organization, because we're not going to show you up.

If after a game a player who hasn't played is sitting in

the corner of the clubhouse with his head down, any good beat writer is going to see it. So the first player he'll interview is that guy. For the good of the team, a player can't show his disgust at not playing. He's got to camouflage it. He can't wear his feelings on his cuff so the whole world can read them.

I tell those players, "You're in a poker game! You're an actor! You have got to make yourself feel good about everything. What's the best way to feel good about yourself in that dugout when you're not playing? Root for your teammates. Don't give them that phony stuff. Sincerely cheer for them and encourage them. The more success you want for them, the more success *you're* going to have."

If a player's had a bad day and feels angry or frustrated, I think his manager should excuse him from meeting with the press and send him home, or have him work out in the weight room. I've often thought it might be a good idea to put speed bags and heavy bags in the weight room and let the player work off his frustration there. Then again, that might scare off the media altogether.

Contracts

There are two types of negotiators: deal makers and deal breakers. The deal makers do their homework, make reasonable proposals, and wrap up negotiations quickly. The deal breakers make unreasonable proposals that insult the other party's intelligence and cause the negotiations to drag on.

I don't begrudge anyone trying to negotiate as high a salary as he can. I simply want to get to the bottom line in a direct and fair manner and wrap up the negotiations as quickly as possible, so I can get back to the business of improving our ball club. Agents know I'm direct and fair, and that I don't like a lot of counterproposals.

The general manager must have his figure ready before he talks with an agent, because when you initiate an offer you've got to be able to substantiate it. You can't just pick a number out of the sky. To calculate a salary, we use a formula that begins with a base salary tied to length of major league service and adds a cash value for production. Jim Bowden also has helped prepare me for contract discussions by grading every player and comparing his grades and salary request with the grades we've given to every other player in the league who plays the same position and is in the same range of age and experience. If we need more information, we can call on Tal Smith, the former general manager of the Astros, who runs a consulting firm that counsels every team in baseball on salary levels and can represent them in arbitration hearings.

When I took over the Pirates, the team led the league in incentive clauses. We were paying out almost $500,000 in weight incentives alone. One player had a weight-incentive clause that paid him $50,000, even though he had never been overweight by even a pound a day in his life.

The only bonus clauses I'll negotiate are awards clauses: X dollars if the player is named the league's Most Valuable Player, X dollars if he wins a Gold Glove, and so forth. If you're going to award bonuses, every player involved should be offered the same dollar amount. I've frequently recommended to the Player Relations Committee that Major League Baseball, not its teams, should give the award-winning players cash prizes. After all, the awards were created by Major League Baseball in the first place.

The agents I deal with appreciate my preparation, my candor, and my refusal to negotiate through the media, which is why so many of them get along well with me. They know that I do not want to have our negotiations resolved by an arbitrator unless I'm forced to. Why? Because arbitration equals failure. Why should I let someone else dictate the amount of money I'm going to pay my player? And why should I be party to a confrontation that will linger in the player's mind?

Arbitration rulings are one reason why player salaries have soared. The primary reason, however, is because of the law in economics of supply and demand. If we had enough of everything, we wouldn't have as many $2 million or $3 million players.

There's another rule in economics known as "the winner's curse." Winning changes your attitude and rationale, so you wind up paying more for a commodity than you would under normal conditions, because of your anticipation. A baseball player starts to look better and better when you're winning. You start thinking you can't live without him. Your ever-rising expectations get too high. So, against your better judgment, you sign him to a lucrative, long-term deal. If you don't win again the next season, and the player performs below expectations, chances are you won't be able to trade him because of that huge contract.

Now you know why I'm so adamant about the value of player procurement and development.

Ticket Sales and Marketing

The business of baseball has become so complex and time-consuming that few general managers have the time to supervise the sale of season's tickets. On the minor league level, however, the general manager must be involved with ticket sales.

The time your ticket department should make its sales push is when the team is playing well. There's a rule of thumb that for every 15,000 season's tickets you sell, you're guaranteed a total attendance of one and a half to two million customers. So if you build on your full-season ticket stock when the team is successful, you've got yourself covered in the event the team has an off-year the following season. In 1988 the Cardinals, who the previous season won the National League championship, drew three million fans, even though they wound up 25 games behind the Mets.

If your ticket department doesn't sell many season-ticket plans, your franchise will always be operating on thin ice; the team has to win or else the fans won't come out. One of the concerns I had and warned the Pirates' officials about was that in 1988 the team had the lowest full-season ticket sales in baseball. I urged them to capitalize on the fan's excitement over the Pirates '88 performance.

Of course, if you can't field a good team, you can't sell season tickets. The Mets have drawn well over two million fans each season since 1985, a season in which they finished right behind the Cardinals in the National League East. Some people may write that off because the Mets play in the nation's largest media market. But from the late seventies to the mideighties, the Mets struggled to top the one million mark in attendance, because they had settled to the bottom of the division while the Yankees, their crosstown rivals, routinely filled their seats because they'd become a fixture in postseason play.

One thing the Pirates have done in recent years that has helped increase ticket sales is conduct off-season player caravans through Pennsylvania, Ohio, and West Virginia. The caravan is a cross between a goodwill tour and a pep rally. Four or five players in rotation, accompanied by the team's community relations director, speak with and sign autographs for fan groups, civic leaders, and local organizations.

Whenever possible, I do all the missionary work I can on behalf of the team, telling the fans and the writers again and again about our commitment to winning. But the most peculiar, poorly timed dog and pony show I was ever involved with came about during the Pirates' spring training in 1986.

My staff and I were conducting organizational meetings on the second day of spring training in preparation for the arrival of the players the following day when I got a call from Malcolm Prine. He said it was imperative that Jim Leyland and I come to Pittsburgh to help sell tickets. I said, "What? In the middle of these important meetings? We're just getting ready to have our first real sessions." Sorry, he replied, but you've got to do this now.

Leyland and I flew out of Sarasota for Pittsburgh that night. Bill Virdon, one of our coaches, would run the camp for the day we would miss.

The next day Leyland and I stood on a downtown street corner in a steady drizzle with the team mascot, the Pirate Parrot—a man dressed in a bird costume. The crowd, if you want to call it that, was sparse. Most of the passersby wondered aloud who those two fools with the bird were.

"Syd and I were not actually selling the tickets," Leyland remembers. "Someone else in the organization did that. He and I and the Pirate Parrot were more or less glad-handing people."

We wandered to different corners, then went into a shopping center and visited its stores. We were introduced as the new manager and general manager of the team. I don't know whether we sold many season tickets; Leyland and I were too tired to count. But I found out then that Pittsburgh was a good city, because if the people could put up with us and wave to us—even though we hadn't played a game yet—that city had to be a good place to work.

In recent years many newspapers and business publications have written articles about good teams, like the Oakland A's, who draw well *because of* improved marketing and ticket sales. They have it backwards! Winning teams sell tickets. The A's, for example, do a great job marketing their team, selling tickets, and keeping their ballpark clean and comfortable, but the fans come out to see Oakland's talented players win championships. And winning teams are built by a well-run front office under the guidance and supervision of the general manager.

In a March 1989 article in *USA Today,* looking back at the Pirates' improvement during my tenure and assessing their future, Jack McKeon put in perspective the notion of marketing as the key to attendance. "Who is 'marketing'? The players are the marketing. The reason [the Pirates] drew [almost] two million people wasn't fireworks or some promotion. It was winning. If the team goes bad, they don't go looking for marketing people."

9 TRADE SECRETS

Trades are fascinating and mystifying. Wherever I go—on radio or TV shows, when I speak with fans or fantasy baseball team owners—people constantly ask me about trades. They wonder how a trade works, when you make a trade, how you decide which player to trade and which one to trade for, and how much a player's salary figures into it.

A trade is born out of need. You and your evaluators have sized up your strengths and weaknesses, present and future. If you don't have the means within your organization to remedy your weaknesses, you've got to look outside your organization. You then size up the strengths and weaknesses of every one of the other 25 major league organizations to see if you can exchange your strengths for theirs.

Though I depend heavily on my scouting department for the good information I need to make trades, I rely on my own observations and judgments first and foremost. I simply feel more comfortable this way. If I can't see a player first-hand, I'll watch him on television or ask my video department for a tape of games he's played in.

I also have a network of baseball people with other organizations whose opinions I respect. Since I am now a writer, I must refuse to reveal those sources.

The input of your major league manager is important, but you can't always go by his instructions. See, the manager can have tunnel vision; he hard-centers his view from the dugout to the playing field. He sees our course of action from his point of view. The danger is when your manager starts downgrading the players we have and covets players on other teams. That distorts his view altogether. The general manager must have a wide-angle view of the entire organization, from the major league club to the rookie leagues.

Former Dodgers executive Al Campanis once told me that in all of manager Walter Alston's 23 years as a manager, he never once asked the Dodgers front office for a player from another team.

I've always been mystified by what another general manager sees in my players. If he likes the players so much, have I missed something? And I am never sure if he knows what I see in his players.

Before I volunteer any information, I like to ask questions. Questions make the other general managers think about the players they have. Questions let them know I've got some common sense. In the real estate business you're always asking questions of the buyers and sellers: What are your goals? How much of a profit are you hoping to net from the sale of your property? How much will you have to pay the Internal Revenue Service if it's an all-cash transaction?

Carefully chosen questions elicit valuable information. If I'm interested in a particular infielder, I may ask the general manager, "How does your infield situation look?" If he tells me about the players he's high on but does not mention the player I'm hoping to acquire, that tells me the infielder is available.

What it comes down to is you're trying to analyze the personalities and preferences of the 25 people you want to do business with. Having made trades with 17 of baseball's 26 clubs—nine in the American League, eight in the National—I've learned the tendencies of every general manager in baseball. Jack McKeon of the Padres and Al Rosen, the president and general manager of the Giants, are a lot like me: concise, direct, ready to do business. When I became general manager of the Pirates my friends in baseball cautioned me that Rosen likes to test the mettle of the rookie general managers. He wants to know if you've done your homework. The more I got to know him, the more I appreciated and respected him.

Dave Dombrowski of the Expos is aggressive and well-organized. Like Rosen, Dombrowski targets his needs and tells you what he will and won't do. What impresses me most about Dombrowski is that he will pay the price to win, even if it means trading away a group of prospects. Dal Maxvill of the Cardinals, who played for me in Oakland, and Mike Port of the Angels are straight shooters who make quick decisions.

Bobby Cox of the Braves, whom I've known for 25 years, is also clear about his needs. But he's so player-development oriented that you can't pry his good prospects from him with a crowbar.

Some general managers feel more comfortable trading for players from their own league. Cleveland Indians president Hank Peters once told me that even if he had good scouting reports on a National League player, he always felt more comfortable if he was able to see the player for himself before he made a trade.

Some are not comfortable unless they acquire an established veteran, while others are willing to gamble on younger players. So I first have to sell myself to them, and they have to sell themselves to make me want to trade with them.

There are other general managers whom I characterize as pulse feelers, always checking this out and checking that out, throwing around the names of players but not truly interested in making a move.

Trades swing to the pendulum of your ball club. If your team has hit rock bottom, chances are you will still have at least one or two marketable players. Therefore, the wisest course of action is to trade one or both for as many good players and prospects as you can get. In a two-for-one or three-for-one deal, you are addressing more needs, so you are maximizing your return. If I can get a general manager to throw in a Double A or Single A player who we have good reports on, our team may come out ahead in the long run.

Once your major league team has become a contender, and you've built your farm system properly, the pendulum swings the other way. You trade two or three players for the type of impact player who fills a critical need and helps take your team to the top.

The reason I've been a successful trader is that I adhere to a basic trading philosophy: If a trade is not beneficial for both teams, it won't work. Period. Sure, it may turn out over time that one team has gotten the better of the trade. But if you try to hustle the other general manager, he will never trade with you again. And if word gets around that you are difficult to deal with, the other general managers will turn their attention elsewhere.

You've got to keep every avenue open, because time and timing are the crucial components of trading. I may spend a year or more trying to work out a deal with another general manager for a player he deems untouchable. All the while he's being courted by a third and perhaps a fourth party. So I've got to be ready at a moment's notice to step in with a better offer. I learned in real estate how quickly people can change their minds and make a deal they'd been against or feel buyer's remorse and convince themselves to back out of a deal. That's why the general manager must have the authority to make a deal, without first having to explain it, deliberate on it, or leave a message on a team official's answering machine and wait until the next day for his return call.

Player injuries can prompt a general manager to shop for a deal, or they can undo a deal entirely. Early in the 1989 season Andre Dawson of the Cubs suffered an injury. Cubs executive vice president Jim Frey called around to see if he could acquire a veteran outfielder to replace Dawson. In our conversations I was pretty sure I could get from him young outfielder Dwight Smith, who'd just been called up from the minors to fill in for Dawson, and relief pitcher Les Lancaster, who'd been languishing at Triple A because, according to press reports, he'd kept an unflattering dart board picturing team officials above his locker. We talked for weeks, and just as it seemed we might have a deal Cubs reliever Calvin Schiraldi got hurt. Frey decided to call up Lancaster, who then reeled off 30 consecutive scoreless innings. That ended that deal.

Once you do complete a trade that's taken months of negotiation, writers and fans jump up and ask, "What took you so long?" The answer is, You can't eat the fruit until it's ripe. You can shake the tree all you want, but if it's not ready to yield fruit you can't eat a single piece.

I find that some fans are bewildered by player contracts. In the retail world, any item offered for sale has a price tag on it. In the baseball world, not a single player has a price tag on him. In reality, it's the player contract that's traded.

However, contract terms are vital, because in today's world they come in all shapes and sizes, with deferred payments, annuities, guarantees, and so forth. When I worked in Pittsburgh, the stringent baseball budget forced me to steer clear of a number of players because of their contracts.

A player making $1.5 million per season would take up 25 percent of my baseball budget. So I had to shop for bargains: talented players who because of injuries or inexperience were paid in a lower strata. I had a little more flexibility with the Yankees. I could trade for championship-caliber players earning championship-caliber salaries.

But no matter where you work, you still have to be prudent, because you're spending the owner's money, not play money.

A hidden trading market is in "six-year" players, players, who've been in the minor leagues for six seasons. If at the end of their sixth season they aren't protected on their teams' 40-man roster, which is due at the end of the season, they are allowed under the terms of the collective-bargaining agreement to become free agents. The concept is that if they've been stuck in an organization for that long without having a real shot with the major league team, they should be permitted to seek employment with another organization.

I don't like to lose anyone without getting a player in return, so my scouts comb the lower minor league levels looking for players in their sixth seasons. In September of 1986 I traded a six-year pitcher named Jeff Zaske to the Texas Rangers for right-hander Randy Kramer.

Kramer, a native Californian, earned all-league and all-central California honors as a high school pitcher. The Padres selected him in the June 1978 draft, but Kramer decided to remain in school. At San Jose City College, Kramer was named Golden Gate Conference Pitcher of the Year in 1982. In his amateur career Kramer threw five no-hitters and one perfect game. The Astros took him in the January 1982 draft, but again Kramer preferred to wait. Five months later he signed with the Rangers, who had drafted him in the June 1982 draft.

From 1983 to 1986 Kramer, used as a starting pitcher, issued a lot of walks, which led to a lot of runs. But Jackie

Bowen, our scout who covered the Carolina (Class A) League, and Steve Demeter, the manager of our Salem team in that league, saw some things in Kramer they liked and recommended we obtain him. In 1987 we converted him to a reliever. Our minor league staff helped him improve to the point where he made the major league club in 1988. And we got him for a player we were going to lose anyway.

Trading six-year players or signing them as free agents is risk-free. The cost of signing them is minimal. If they don't make the team in spring training, you release them. The Montreal Expos made out like bandits in 1988 when they signed infielder Rex Hudler and outfielder Otis Nixon, both six-year players, to major league contracts. The versatile Hudler batted .273, and Nixon stole 46 bases in 90 games.

Every trade has its own set of circumstances and takes on a life of its own. The best way for me to show you how and why I make trades is by breaking them down into priorities and categories that address many of the needs that arise.

Pitching

Good pitching, to paraphrase John Steinbeck, is a pearl of great price. It is *the* hardest area to trade for, because most everyone needs it, and the few who have it are rarely willing to give it up.

Therefore, you've often got to gamble on young, unproven pitchers or veterans who may need a better environment for success. When I took over the Pirates we had two veteran starting pitchers, Rick Rhoden and Rick Reuschel, followed by a lot of question marks. During my first spring training with the Pirates I was making great progress with Clyde King, who was then the Yankees' general manager, on a possible trade we'd been talking about since the winter meetings involving Rhoden. Why would I trade a proven veteran like Rhoden if we needed pitching? Rhoden, a 10-year veteran who'd been with the Pirates five years, asked to be traded, as is his right under baseball's collective-bargaining agreement. And if someone doesn't want to be on our team, then we really shouldn't keep him around.

At the start of the season, with Jim Leyland by my side, I told Rhoden, "If you aren't happy here I'll do the best I can to get you with a winning club. That's who you say you want to be with. In the meantime I want you to give me one hundred percent effort, because if you don't I won't be able to trade you."

In return for Rhoden I wanted right-handed pitchers Doug Drabek and Brian Fisher, plus outfielder Jay Buhner. Lenny Yochim, the Pirates' special assignment scout, liked Drabek's pitching skills and his competitive fire. Fisher, originally drafted as a starting pitcher by the Braves, had pitched well as a reliever in 1985 but was struggling in '86. My sources inside baseball told me Fisher's problems were correctable. Buhner, a strong-armed, right-handed, power-hitting outfield prospect, was a talented guy the Pirates had in their farm system but gave up on. He'd been traded to the Yankees in December 1984 along with shortstop Dale Berra and pitcher Alfonso Pulido for outfielder Steve Kemp, whom I released in 1986, and shortstop Tim Foli, who retired following the '85 season.

The Yankees didn't want to part with Drabek and Buhner. They kept substituting other names, and we were getting nowhere. But they were in a pennant race with the Boston Red Sox, and as the July 31 interleague trading deadline drew closer, Rhoden was too tempting to lose. Rhoden needed only to clear waivers and the deal was done. However, the Phillies, Padres, Angels, and Red Sox put in waiver claims on him. I had to withdraw Rhoden from waivers and keep him for the rest of the season.

During the 1986 World Series the Yankees changed general managers, replacing King with Woody Woodward. I saw Woodward standing in front of a fountain in the lobby of a Boston hotel and figured he was fair game. I went right up to him and said. "Listen, I'm tired of all the Mickey Mousing around. If you want Rhoden, give me Drabek, Fisher, and one more player and we'll have ourselves a deal."

A month later Woodward and I worked out a trade: Drabek, Fisher, and a minor league relief pitcher named Logan Easley for Rhoden, right-hander Cecilio Guante, and left-handed reliever Pat Clements.

How did Guante and Clements wind up in the deal? Woodward didn't want to give up three players for one. Neither Guante nor Clements figured in the Pirates' long-term plans. I told Woody I'd be willing to include Guante in the deal, and he said, "Fine, but I've *got* to have Clements." Since he sounded so anxious, I told him, "Let me think about it. I'll call you in an hour." One hour later, I told Woodward, "Okay." He was so pleased.

I liked the deal because I figured that had we retained Rhoden he probably would have won no more than 15 games, but the three pitchers I was getting were eight years younger than Rhoden and could win 15 games among them. This trade also allowed me to trade $1.125 million in contracts for $327,500.

As it turned out, Drabek, Fisher, and Easley combined for 23 wins in 1987 while Rhoden won 16 for the Yankees, so we gained seven wins and saved $797,500.

By 1988 we'd developed a good, hard-throwing, young starting staff. As we made strides toward contention I thought we could use an off-speed pitcher, preferably a veteran, to give our staff a different look. See, if you have too many pitchers of similar styles, by the second game of a three-game series your opponents have already adjusted their timing to your staff.

I had been talking for a few weeks during the middle of that season with Larry Himes, the general manager of the White Sox, about some possible trades. On August 13, Himes sent us left-handed pitcher Dave LaPoint for righty reliever Barry Jones.

LaPoint, then 29 years old, was in his baseball prime. Even though he was going to be a free agent following the season, I thought we had a lot to gain. LaPoint proved to be a tremendous addition to our starting staff. In his first two starts for us he allowed only one run and seven hits in 14⅔ innings. He wound up with a 4-2 record and a 2.77 ERA.

Once you have a good starting rotation, you've got to have relief pitchers who can keep you in the game and protect a lead. Middle-inning relievers and setup men are a little easier to come by in the trade market, because in quite a few cases those pitchers had not been successful starters or closers. When you acquire such pitchers, you train them to think of themselves as stoppers, which they really are, even though they're not entering the game in the ninth inning. If they can't come into a game and slam the door in the fifth, sixth, or seventh innings, the game is over right there. Of course, a good closer is as hard to acquire as a good starter, so there are times when you trade for a starter or long reliever and train him to assume that role.

In 1986 and '87 the Pirates had to play round-robin in the bullpen. Don Robinson, who began his career as a starter and pitched in the 1979 World Series, had been the bullpen closer since 1984. But in April of 1986 Robinson injured his knee in a game against the Cubs and could not return until June. So Jim Leyland, his coaches, and I were constantly trying different pitchers in that role: Jim Winn, Cecilio Guante, Pat Clements, Bob Walk, Barry Jones, Jose DeLeon, Ray Krawczyk. All the blown leads and one-run losses were undermining the team's confidence—as well as causing Jim Leyland and me a lot of sleepless nights.

I'd also become concerned about Robinson's frame of mind after he returned. He still had a good arm, but he had no luck holding leads. Our fans booed him so often that I believed he needed a fresh start with another team. And I knew that if I didn't trade Robinson this season, he'd become a 10-and-10 man at the end of the year.

In July of '87 Al Rosen, whose Giants were battling the Reds, Astros, and Dodgers for the top spot in the N.L. West, was interested in Robinson, because the Giants' offense had been scoring runs by the truckload but his bullpen was young and inexperienced.

One of the players Rosen offered was Mackey Sasser, a left-handed-hitting catcher in the Giants' system. I'd seen Sasser play against our Triple A team and thought he had good line-drive power. I thought he could bolster the catching position for us. I also was interested in Jim Gott, whose career underscores why every team needs a good scouting department.

At the age of eighteen Gott was selected by the Cardinals on the fourth round of the June 1977 Free Agent Draft. Five seasons later, the Cards left him unprotected in the December 1981 draft and he was claimed by the Toronto Blue Jays.

Though he had an above-average fastball, Gott was inconsistent as a starting pitcher for the Blue Jays. He was traded to the Giants in 1985. Again he struggled as a starter, and the following year he suffered an injury that kept him out of all but two games. In 1987 the Giants used Gott as a long reliever.

But our organization knew some key things about Gott that made him worth trading for. Jim Leyland had seen Gott pitch in the minor leagues and was impressed by his velocity. Our scouts reported that Gott threw a 91-mile-an-hour two-seam fastball, and a 95-mile-an-hour four-seamer. Trouble was, Gott had relied too much on his two-seamer, trying to induce ground-ball outs after he was ahead in the count. We knew that if he threw more four-seamers, especially when he was ahead in the count, hitters would have trouble timing him.

Rosen and I structured a deal that took four days to complete. On July 31, we received Sasser and a cash payment for Don Robinson; on August 3, when Gott cleared waivers, we claimed him for the Pirates.

Don Robinson played a key role as the Giants won their division, while Gott became one of our bullpen closers, saving 13 games in 1987 and 34 in 1988. What would a team normally have to give up for a closer capable of 34 saves?

Gott also became the Pirates' player representative, and I can't tell you what a pleasure it was to have a person of Gott's character and winning spirit representing our players in that position.

Defense Up the Middle

Second base, shortstop, center field, and catcher are the defensive positions you must attend to first if you hope to have good pitching. In filling these positions, if I had to choose between above-average fielders who are average or below-average hitters, or good hitters who are below-average fielders, I'd take the above-average fielders every time. Quite simply, they are involved in so many plays that they can determine the success or failure of your team's pitching staff.

As with any need, you first look within your organization. When shortstop Rafael Santana of the Yankees suffered a season-ending elbow injury during spring training in 1989, fans and the media assumed we'd deal for another shortstop immediately. But having seen rookie shortstop Alvaro Espinoza's smart, sure-handed fielding, we knew he could make important defensive contributions.

When I was with the Pirates, they had a few good-fielding shortstops, like Rafael Belliard and Felix Fermin, on the major league club, and second baseman Jose Lind was making great strides in the minor leagues. But we had to play a shell game in center field, because we lacked players with both speed and strong throwing arms.

I converted Barry Bonds, a natural left fielder, to center when he played at Triple A, because I planned to play him in center with the Pirates until we could acquire one. In left field, Bonds could make great use of his speed in the roomy left-field foul territories of National League stadiums. That's why Tim Raines, Kevin McReynolds, and Vince Coleman, each of whom are capable of playing center field, are used in left. I figured that if we could obtain a center fielder with speed, a strong arm, and a little more experience to captain the outfield, then move Bonds back to left, we'd have the best coverage of left and center fields in the division.

We could have been set at catcher with five-time All-Star Tony Pena. But Pena's huge contract was something the team couldn't afford at the time. And because Pena was one of the few players we had who could command two, three, or maybe even four players in return, I viewed him as a trump card.

If I was going to trade Pena, I'd need a catcher in return, preferably a left-handed-hitting catcher. We had right-handed-hitting Junior Ortiz, a quality backup catcher, so if I could get a good catcher to platoon with Ortiz, we'd be okay behind the plate. I also was hoping to get a third player, possibly a young pitcher, in any deal for Pena.

The Cardinals seemed like the best team to deal with. After going to the World Series in 1985, the Cardinals fell to third place in the N.L. East in 1986. They believed Pena's experience and leadership could help them return to postseason play, and their franchise had the financial resources to handle Pena's contract. So during the summer of '86 I looked closely at the Cardinals and targeted left-handed-hitting Andy Van Slyke, whom the Cards platooned in right field and first base, as the best center fielder we could obtain.

I loved the way Van Slyke ran the bases: good speed, good judgment, and sharp turns rounding the bases. And I had a vivid image of his performance in center field in a series we played against the Cardinals in August of 1986. Van Slyke, substituting for regular center fielder Willie McGee, was able to read the ball on a dead run and make some great plays on shots hit to the alleys. He's always had an outstanding arm, but when he played center he seemed like a different player. He even hit the ball better. I figured that Van Slyke's game improved when he played center because he liked that position better.

I didn't bother asking Dal Maxvill for a left-handed pitcher, because I know how much Whitey Herzog loves them. It would have been a waste of time to ask for young left-hander Joe Magrane.

We had good reports on right-hander Mike Dunne, a sinker-ball pitcher in the Cards' system who had been a member of the 1984 U.S. Olympic Baseball Team. Dunne had pitched below .500 on the minor league level, but our scouts reported that Dunne threw a two-seam fastball only. If he learned the four-seamer, it would be a great complement to his sinker.

Maxvill was willing to part with Van Slyke and Dunne, but we had trouble agreeing on a catcher. I wanted left-handed-hitting Mike LaValliere. My sources told me the Cardinals' pitchers enjoyed working with the 5-10, 190-pound LaValliere. I kept telling Maxvill, "I want the stumpy guy."

On April 1 Maxvill and I consummated that three-for-one trade. It was the best trade I ever made. Though Pena missed six weeks during the regular season because of a hand injury, he rebounded to hit .381 in the 1987 National League Championship Series and .409 in the World Series. Meanwhile, Van Slyke batted .293 with 21 home runs, 86 RBIs, and 34 stolen bases and became one of the best defensive center fielders in baseball. LaValliere hit .300 and won a Gold Glove for his work behind the plate. And Mike Dunne won 13 games with an ERA of 3.03.

Power Hitting

Rarely do minor leaguers who possess home-run power step into the major leagues and hit homers right away. They need time to develop physically and to adjust to major league pitching. That's why the few who can, like Jose Canseco or Mark McGwire of the A's, are so valuable. If you want an established power hitter for the middle of your order, you have to pay a steep price.

With a good scouting department and good teachers, you can gamble on the development of a young, budding power hitter. My first trade of consequence with the Pirates was to reacquire outfielder Bobby Bonilla from the White Sox for pitcher Jose DeLeon.

The first time I saw Bonilla, he was among the group of players who toured with me in the clinics I gave overseas. When I worked him out I saw he had the makings of a fine player. What surprised me was that he seemed sharper and more alert when I worked him out at third base and first base than when he played the outfield. I called the Pirates and urged them to sign him. But when I became the team's general manager in late 1985, they had already submitted their 40-man protected roster for the coming winter meetings and had decided not to include Bonilla. According to the rules, it was too late for us to change our protected list. That was some winter meeting.

During his year with the White Sox, Bonilla, who was 23 years old at the time, hit only two home runs, so I believed I could get him back without giving up too much. Back then DeLeon, who has since blossomed into a top starter with the Cardinals, had the physical tools but lacked the concentration and the confidence needed to win. The previous two seasons DeLeon went 7-13 and 2-19, and I was afraid the longer he stayed with us the deeper his problems would become.

In late June of 1987 Jim Leyland and I decided to make

a move that would have a profound effect on our offense: We benched 34-year-old third baseman Jim Morrison, who in 1986 had a career year—.274, with 23 home runs and 88 RBIs—and moved Bobby Bonilla in from the outfield to be our every-day third baseman. As an outfielder in 1986, the switch-hitting Bonilla hit .240 in 63 games, with one home run and 17 RBIs. As a third baseman, Bonilla wound up batting .300, with 15 home runs and 77 RBIs. He hit 24 home runs and drove in 100 runs in 1988, and had 24 homers and 86 RBIs in 1989.

This brings up an interesting question: Why do some players perform better at a new position? For Bonds, who in 1987 batted .261 with 25 home runs, 59 RBIs, and 32 stolen bases, the return to left field was easy. We pointed out to him that he had the ability to be among the best defensive left fielders in the game, like Coleman and McReynolds and Rickey Henderson. In Van Slyke's case, I think his role as the captain of our outfield gave him a greater feeling of importance to our team. In Bonilla's case, we learned that as an outfielder his mind often wandered, but as an infielder he was more alert, more into the game.

The economic principle of "highest and best use," which I'd learned in real estate, is certainly applicable to baseball players. When I shifted players from one position to another, they often played to their maximum potential. Sometimes those players had previously been assigned to a position that was wrong for them because it didn't use their skills to the fullest. Van Slyke's speed, to take one example, was wasted at first base. Other times a good athlete is unknowingly wronged by his coach just because he can play different positions. When the scouts see him at first base one day, at second base the following day, and in the outfield the next, they may assume he's been cast in this role because he isn't good enough to hold down one position. He is branded as a utility player, and in his professional career he ends up playing everywhere and nowhere.

Not every player responds to a change in position, however. The most notable example was outfielder Amos Otis, who was moved to third base by the Mets early in his career and fell apart at the plate. When the Royals acquired him in 1970, they installed Otis in center field, where he became a perennial Gold Glove winner and a .280 hitter.

Once you have a true power hitter in the cleanup slot, you've got to get others in the five and six spots in the order to support him. I envisioned Jay Buhner taking one of those spots for the Pirates. I chased him for three years and couldn't get him. But if I hadn't gone after him, I might not have obtained Glenn Wilson.

Even though Bonilla is a switch-hitter, the Pirates were vulnerable to left-handed pitching, because the rest of our power came from Bonds, Van Slyke, and first baseman Sid Bream, all left-handed hitters. We began the 1988 season platooning switch-hitter R.J. Reynolds, used from the left side, and right-handed Darnell Coles, whom I had obtained along with left-handed reliever Morris Madden from the Tigers for Jim Morrison in August of 1987.

Both Coles and Reynolds are good players, but neither could consistently generate home-run power. Defensively, we needed someone who could handle right field in Pittsburgh's Three Rivers Stadium. The dimensions—375 feet in right-center, 335 feet at the foul pole—create sharp sight lines that make it difficult to judge fly balls, and the artificial surface causes balls hit in the gaps or down the line to ricochet off the wall.

I had tried to obtain Buhner back in 1986 in the Rhoden deal, and in 1987 I talked with the Phillies about right-handed-hitting Glenn Wilson, one of the best defensive outfielders in the game. The Phillies wanted Mike Dunne or Doug Drabek in return, whom I could not afford to trade at that time. The Phillies, who'd acquired Wilson from the Tigers in 1984, decided to trade him in December 1987 to the Mariners in a five-player deal.

We move ahead to July 1988. The Yankees, looking for a left-handed power hitter, asked me about the availability of Tommy Gregg, a top prospect at Buffalo whom we had called up earlier in the season to fill in for the injured Barry Bonds. They offered Buhner in return. I couldn't believe it! I was finally about to land him.

There was one small hitch in the deal: Gregg's health. A short time earlier Gregg had sustained a stress fracture in his foot and, as a precaution, the Yankees wanted their team doctor to examine him.

Now, I can't tell Gregg what's going on. Anytime you let word of a trade leak, the players in the clubhouse become distracted, and the next thing you know the manager has a problem on his hands. I simply told Gregg we wanted a doctor in New York to give us a second opinion. That wasn't the whole truth, but it wasn't a lie, either.

The Yankees' doctor sent Gregg back to Pittsburgh with a clean bill of health. All I needed to do was wait for Bob Quinn, who was then the Yankees' assistant general manager, to call me.

That night I got a call from one of my baseball sources, who told me there were rumblings in New York that the Yankees were going to trade Buhner to the Mariners for veteran Ken Phelps, another left-handed power hitter. Once I heard that I knew my deal was over, because I understood that the Yankees tended to be more comfortable trading for established players.

At 3:30 the following afternoon I sat with Leyland in his office waiting for Quinn's call. To pass the time, I called my friend Bill Lajoie, the Tigers' vice president and general manager, who'd been traveling with the Tigers during a road trip in California. I said, "Bill, I just want to say hello and see how you're doing."

The first thing Lajoie said was, "Did you hear that the Yankees have just traded Buhner to the Mariners for Ken Phelps?"

I said, "Are you kidding me?"

"No, the trade was just made."

I immediately realized that, with Buhner on the club, Glenn Wilson would probably be available. Wilson, who played for Leyland in the Tigers' system, was only 29 years old and was in the last year of a $700,000 contract. From a business point of view, the Pirates would be obligated during the 1988 season for only a two-month portion of his salary, and I believed we had a chance to sign Wilson for the following season at or a little below his previous salary.

I thought the Mariners might be interested in reacquiring Coles, their first draft choice in 1980. Coles, who could serve as their designated hitter, would be aided in the field by the smaller outfield dimensions—357 to the alleys, 316 to the foul lines—in Seattle's Kingdome.

I said to Lajoie, "Let me ask you the $64 question. You're a good judge of talent. You've seen Wilson play and you had Darnell Coles last year. If you were me, would you trade Coles for Wilson?"

"In your stadium?" said Lajoie. "Yes, I would do it."

I thanked Lajoie, hung up, and called Dick Balderson, who at the time was the Mariners' general manager. Balderson's secretary said, "Would you mind holding for a few minutes? He's on a call to New York now finishing a deal with the Yankees."

While holding I decided to feign ignorance of the deal when I talked to Balderson. If I jumped in and asked for Wilson right away, he'd raise his asking price. About five minutes later Balderson picked up the phone.

"I just made a trade with the Yankees," he said. "I traded Ken Phelps for Jay Buhner and two minor leaguers."

"Is that right? Well, congratulations. Good for you," I said, not once mentioning how close I'd been to getting Buhner. "How are you going to use Buhner?"

"We're going to play him in center field and in right."

"What are you going to do with Glenn Wilson?"

"We'll work him in the lineup in some way."

"Let me ask you a question. Would you trade me Wilson for Darnell Coles even-up?"

"I'd probably do that," said Balderson, "but I'd first need to check with [Mariners owner] George Argyros. I can't reach him, because he's on a cruise ship that doesn't have a ship-to-shore radio. He's going to call in at 6:30 tonight, which is 9:30 your time."

I then called the Pirates' team president and told him we had a fifty-fifty chance of obtaining Wilson.

The Pirates were hosting the Dodgers that night. At about the eighth inning of our game, Balderson called me to confirm our trade. The Mariners, about to begin their game, scratched Wilson from their starting lineup and informed him of the trade. Balderson had one favor to ask: "Could you get Coles here as quickly as possible? Buhner's flight from Rochester [New York] is fogged in."

I summoned Greg Johnson, the Pirates' public relations director, and asked him to prepare a press release for the media. I called Leyland in the dugout, told him I'd made the deal, and instructed him not to put Coles in the game so he wouldn't run the risk of an injury. Then I asked Charlie Muse, the team's traveling secretary, to arrange a red-eye flight for Coles.

We beat the Dodgers by a score of 3–2 and moved within one-half game of the Mets. As soon as our game ended—at 10:30 P.M.—I dashed to the clubhouse, asked the media to wait outside, and spoke with Coles for about 10 minutes. It was our team policy to inform a player about a trade before he heard it from the media.

At 11:15 I noticed R.J. Reynolds watching the sports report on a television in the clubhouse. Reynolds is a warm, funny person who makes friends easily, and he seemed truly upset that Coles had been traded. I asked Reynolds what was troubling him.

"Darnell and I had become good friends," he said. "I know

it can be a mistake in our business to get close with people, because trades are a part of the game, but I'm really going to miss him."

"I understand how you feel," I said. "I just don't want the media to think we have problems on this team."

Reynolds smiled. "Nah, there are no problems on this team."

Coles had just finished his interviews, so I took him aside again for another few minutes. He thanked me for all the support I had given him. We put our arms around each other and I told him, "I'll be rooting for you in Seattle."

Bench Strength

The test of a contender is its depth. You must have players who can step in and play well when other players need rest or have suffered injuries, and you must have veterans who can be called on to pinch-hit when the game is on the line.

One of the keys to the success of the Oakland A's in 1988 and '89 was depth. Outfielder Stan Javier and infielders Mike Gallego and Tony Phillips were always ready when manager Tony La Russa needed them. While other pennant hopefuls use injuries as a crutch, you never heard La Russa or general manager Sandy Alderson complaining about that, even when they lost Jose Canseco for the first half of the '89 season. Their bench players stepped in and picked up the slack.

When the 1989 Yankees left spring training without a right-handed power hitter, I acquired Steve Balboni from the Mariners for a minor league pitcher who did not figure in our long-term plans. I envisioned Balboni platooning as the designated hitter and filling in at first base for Don Mattingly. The media laughed when the trade was made because, six years earlier, the Yankees had considered Balboni one-dimensional and traded him to Kansas City, and here

I brought him back to fill Dave Winfield's home-run shoes. As it turned out, in 300 at-bats Balboni hit 17 home runs, which tied outfielder/DH Mel Hall for third best on the club, and drove in 59 runs, the fourth best total on the team. What's wrong with those numbers?

In 1988 I believed it was bench strength that separated the Pirates from the Mets in the Eastern Division race. We opened the season lacking veteran players who could pinch-hit in pressure situations or spell our young regulars. We'd been asking such youngsters as John Cangelosi, Orestes De-strade, and Randy Milligan to take on veteran roles.

By not filling those areas, Leyland could not afford to rest Bonds, who was suffering from a knee injury, Van Slyke, or Bonilla. So as the summer wore on, that trio wore down. We started scoring fewer runs, which put more pressure on those players and on our pitching staff.

That August I obtained outfielder Gary Redus from the White Sox for catcher/first baseman/outfielder Mike Diaz. Diaz, a right-handed hitter of some power, was a popular member of the Pirates. His teammates gave him the nickname "Rambo" because of his muscular physique. I liked his enthusiasm for the game and his honesty. I used to call him "Syd" Diaz because he negotiated his own contract directly with me, without employing an agent. Diaz was not a good fielder, so I thought he might flourish in the American League as a DH. Following the season Diaz accepted a huge offer to play in the Japanese leagues.

Though Redus was 31 years old, our scouts said he had the body of a 26-year-old. Redus has good speed and knows how to steal bases. In fact, at the time, Redus was fifth among the all-time leaders in stolen-base percentage. He is a right-handed hitter who had batted leadoff in the past, which allowed Leyland to rest Bonds. Not only did Redus perform well when called on in 1988, but in 1989, when a number of Pirates players went down with injuries, Redus batted .283 and stole 25 bases in 98 games.

Three days after acquiring Redus I made my wildest trade ever: To bolster our bench, I acquired a 10-year veteran for a bedridden prospect.

The Braves were interested in Tommy Gregg and I was interested in 32-year-old Ken Oberkfell. Oberkfell, a lifetime .280 hitter, would give us an experienced left-handed bat off the bench. He could play third or second, which would give some rest to Bonilla and Lind, and was capable of playing shortstop if needed. And he had been in two World Series with the Cardinals, so he could impart that knowledge to our younger players, who had never been in a major league pennant race before.

But the deal was fraught with obstacles. Problem Number One: Gregg had injured himself again. This time he sprained his back stepping into a pothole while catching a ball in a game against the Reds' Triple A team in Nashville. He was hospitalized for three days while the doctors checked to make sure he hadn't injured a vertebra or a disc. The doctors told us Gregg would be sidelined for two weeks. I gave Bobby Cox a full account of Gregg's injury, which he confirmed with the doctor in charge of Gregg's care.

Problem Number Two: I could not accommodate Oberkfell's contract, which ran through 1989, into our team budget. So Cox and I agreed that the Braves would pay $400,000 to offset the Pirates' cost. That allowed me to stay within our $6.5 million baseball budget, still the lowest in the league.

Problem Number Three: Gregg had to clear waivers before we could consummate the deal. I worried that if I put Gregg on waivers alone, another team might claim him and screw up our deal. So Cox and I hatched a plan where I would put five players, including Gregg, on waivers as camouflage.

It worked.

Oberkfell came in hitting line drives right away and had a positive influence in the clubhouse. The following season, the Pirates dealt him to San Francisco, where he became the pennant-winning Giants' top left-handed pinch hitter.

A Change of Scenery

There are instances when it's in the best interests of both the player and his club for him to be traded. If a player doesn't want to be with us, I don't want his disenchantment to affect our other players.

Only once have I ever traded a player just to be rid of him. In 1986 during spring training I sent first baseman Jason Thompson to the Expos. We received Ben Abner and Ronnie Giddens, but, with all due respect to those two gentlemen, I would have taken anybody. I didn't care. Once upon a time Thompson had been a home-run threat, but his skills had eroded and he had become an extremely well-paid malcontent. All he talked about was his fervent desire to be traded from the Pirates. I granted his wish.

In most cases, you decide that the player needs a new environment to succeed only after you've tried every way you can to help him. When we traded Jose DeLeon and Don Robinson, it was because their growth as players was stunted in our environment. Why? That's a tough question to answer, because every team and every person is different. My best guess is that many players impose tremendous pressure on themselves during a cold spell, which, instead of propelling them forward, holds them back. What I do know is that the longer those players remain in that environment, the more of a disservice you're doing to their careers. And from a business standpoint, the more they fail, the lower their trade value becomes.

You'd be hard-pressed to find a more dedicated, diligent, spirited player than third baseman Mike Pagliarulo. When he was with the Yankees he practiced so hard and so often that he'd even go into the clubhouse between at-bats and hit off a batting tee. He averaged 21 home runs in his first four seasons, but tailed off to 15 in 1988. During the 1989 season he struggled even more, incurring the wrath of the fans and the owner, and became a platoon player. In July I traded Pagliarulo to San Diego for pitcher Walt Terrell and a player to be named later.

Before the trade was announced to the media I called Pags and explained why the trade was made. Aside from our need for starting pitching, I told him that he would be moving to a ballpark that favored power hitters and would be managed by Jack McKeon, who would stick by him and help him return to form. He understood what I was saying and thanked me for my candor.

In San Diego, Pags joined another former Yankee, Jack Clark, who'd also been struggling until the last two months of the season. The San Diego media speculated that Clark had spent most of that year in what they termed "Yankee Detoxification."

Who Is the Player to Be Named Later?

Fans are always mystified by trades that include a player to be named later. Who is he? Why can't he be named right away?

There are a smorgasbord of combinations that lead to this. Sometimes it's pretty simple: The player traded from one league to the other hasn't cleared waivers, which may take another 72 hours. According to baseball's rules, you can't have a player to be named later in a trade between teams in the same league; otherwise you'd be playing against your own player.

Other times, both parties agree on a framework—two players for one, four for two—but can't agree on a minor league player to be included in the deal. So the team that owes the player will submit to the other team a list of three or four or six minor league players to choose from, and both sides agree on the amount of time, whether it's 30 days or 90 days or even 180 days, for that choice to be made. This gives the team owed a player more time to evaluate the players on the list.

Both parties write a clause into the trade's paperwork that makes the team that owes a player pay a specified amount of money to the team owed a player if they can't come to an agreement over the time frame.

Contractual Roadblocks

In today's baseball marketplace you have to memorize the collective-bargaining agreement and read the fine print in every player contract.

After six years in the major leagues, a player whose contract has expired can file for free agency. After 10 years in the majors and five with the same team, he can veto a trade. Then there are some players who have no-trade clauses written into their contracts, and others who have a list of teams they'd approve a trade to.

Having been boxed in with Rick Rhoden, I learned I must prepare well in advance for 10-and-five players. I don't like the fact that I can't always do what's in the best interests of our team until the 10-and-five man says okay, but rules are rules.

Let me give you an example of how one player who has a no-trade clause can change the look of a ball club. At the start of the 1989 season, Rickey Henderson's agent asked the Yankees to begin discussions on a new contract. Henderson's contract was to expire following the '89 season, at which time he would have qualified as a 10-and-five man. We had three options: re-sign Henderson; trade him; or allow him to sign with another team following the season.

If Henderson were to play out his contract and sign with another club, the Yankees would have been compensated with draft picks from his new club. This stems from a provision in the 1981 collective bargaining agreement, in which players are statistically ranked based on their past two seasons and put into one of four groupings: Type A, Type B, Type C, and No Compensation. If a team signs a Type A player, they forfeit their first-round pick in the next June amateur draft, plus a selection in a round created after the first round. Type B players command a second-round draft pick; for Type C, a selection in a round created after the draft's second round.

Henderson was a Type A free agent, so if we lost him, we'd get two draft picks in return. However, George Steinbrenner decided he would not sign Henderson to a new contract during the season. In his mind, draft choices were not acceptable, so he ordered me to trade Henderson as quickly as possible.

I sought to acquire two hard-throwing starting pitchers to change the look of the rotation, which to that point was dominated by off-speed pitchers, and an outfielder to replace Henderson. The Giants, Dodgers, and Angels were interested in obtaining Henderson, and as reports in the press about Henderson's contract status appeared, more teams called. But Henderson had a no-trade clause, meaning we could not trade him without his written consent. Henderson and I discussed the situation privately, and he told me there was only one team he would consent to be traded to: the Oakland A's. Oakland is his hometown, where his mother lives and his best friends are.

I asked our staff to seal their lips on this turn of events, because if Sandy Alderson found out his team was our only trade market, he might raise his asking price or substitute lesser players from his end. It was a good thing for us that

Alderson doesn't live in New York, because if he did he'd have read that Henderson had vetoed a proposed trade to a National League team, a rumor that somehow found its way into the New York newspapers.

On June 21 we traded Henderson to the A's for outfielder Luis Polonia and two hard throwers—left-hander Greg Cadaret and right-hander Eric Plunk. Polonia, who gets on base, steals, and moves runners, would be a fourth or fifth outfielder on a good club. On the Yankees, he wound up hitting .300 and stealing 22 bases.

The media, aware of our need for starting pitching, criticized this deal, because they perceived Cadaret and Plunk as nothing more than setup men, the way they'd been most effectively used by La Russa. I believed they could be transformed into starters. Both pitchers were eager to pitch more innings than they had in the past. Cadaret pitched well when he joined the rotation after one of our starters suffered an injury. During the last weeks of the season Plunk also was given an opportunity to start. I feel that both pitchers can be consistent winners in the future.

Under the circumstances, which allowed us only one avenue, I think we made the best trade we could. When Alderson and I concluded the trade, I said to him, "Sandy, I've just made you baseball's executive of the year."

He laughed, "Come on, Syd. Don't say that."

I said, "No, I mean it. I told Al Rosen the same thing in 1987 after I traded him Rick Reuschel, and I'm telling that to you now. And I'll be sure to vote for you, too, same as I did for Rosen."

Trading Down the Stretch

The two trading deadlines during the season—July 31 for interleague trades, and August 31 for players to retain postseason eligibility—provide a real incentive for action. The contending teams are far more likely to make trades that they might not have made earlier in the year. That gives the teams not in contention a chance to trade an established player who can help the contender win now—even if his contract is about to expire—for prospects who can help in years to come.

I always prepare for these deadlines, because you never know what opportunities await. Keep in mind that as the contenders are visualizing their postseason rosters, they may be forced to release a player they haven't been able to deal.

During the 1989 season the Expos were interested in the Yankees' hard-throwing right-handed reliever Lance McCullers. McCullers, whom Bob Quinn had acquired from the Padres in a package deal for Jack Clark before the season began, had been ineffective for us. The Expos have an excellent minor league system, so I hoped for one of their prospects in return. Dave Dombrowski and I talked about some possibilities, but couldn't reach anything firm.

Meanwhile, third base had become a real hot corner for us. At the start of the season Tom Brookens, whom I'd acquired from the Tigers at the start of the season, platooned with Mike Pagliarulo. Before we traded Pags, I moved our Triple A shortstop, Randy Velarde, who has good power, to third base, and planned to bring him up to New York as our third baseman after the trade. Shortly after his promotion, Velarde got hurt. Then Brookens got hurt. We put utility infielder Wayne Tolleson, who'd just come off the disabled list, at third and called up third baseman Hensley Muelens from Double A. Neither player was going to help us in the short term; Tolleson couldn't hit for power and Muelens really needed two more years to develop. So as the Yankees fell out of the Eastern Division race in August I combed every major league organization and zeroed in on the best third-base prospects.

Dombrowski, still looking for bullpen depth, asked me about left-hander John Candelaria, a veteran pitcher with postseason experience, who'd just returned from an injury. I told Dombrowski I would not trade Candelaria unless he gave us Mike Blowers, his Triple A third baseman. After thinking about it for two days, on August 28 Dombrowski agreed to my asking price. It was my last—and finest—deal for the Yankees. Blowers, a right-handed hitter with opposite-field power, can be the Yankees' third baseman for years and years to come.

Here's an interesting postscript. McCullers's season took a turn for the better on August 10, when I claimed veteran reliever Goose Gossage on waivers from the Giants. At the start of the season, after Gossage was released by the Cubs, Stan Williams, one of our scouts, worked Gossage out and submitted a favorable report. I called Gossage, and he told me his first preference was to sign with a West Coast team, so I thanked him for auditioning for us and wished him well.

Al Rosen signed him a short time later, after his pitching staff had been depleted by injuries. Gossage pitched well, but by August the Giants needed depth in their starting rotation. Having signed free-agent starter Bob Knepper and needing to clear a roster spot for the impending return of Dave Dravecky, the Giants released Gossage. I asked Rosen for his appraisal of Gossage. He told me the Goose had a good fastball—not his explosive fastball of years earlier but still in the 90-mile-an-hour range.

Gossage is a fierce competitor who had been through the New York grindstone before. I believed he'd improve the chemistry of our team. What I didn't know was the profound, positive effect Gossage would have on McCullers. Gossage took McCullers under his wing, tutoring his willing pupil on the art of pitching and instilling in him the kind of competitive fire a top reliever needs. In short order, McCullers transformed into a much better, more consistent pitcher.

The Chemical Balance

You must always consider the change in team chemistry when you make a deal. Winning personalities are a key intangible in your team's success. I look for that in every player I may trade for, yet I'm always surprised by the magnitude of the contributions a player with a winning attitude makes.

When the Mets acquired Keith Hernandez from the Cardinals in 1983, they knew he had leadership qualities, so they let him exert them. Hernandez not only led by example, but he had a marvelous impact on the Mets' young pitchers. He'd go to the mound and encourage them, fire them up, give them a scouting report on the hitters at the plate or the runner at first base.

Andy Van Slyke is such a professional in all aspects of the game that his presence makes a huge difference on the Pirates' performance. When he suffered a rib-cage injury in 1989, the aura of the team changed.

I knew Jim Gott was a fine person, but I'll never forget how much his winning attitude helped turn around the Pirates' 1987 season.

I'd made so many moves to improve the ball club that season, yet we were still mired in last place toward the end of August. Because of all the trades, the players were tentative, as if they were waiting for another shoe to drop. Only six players remained from the team I'd inherited the season before. Rick Reuschel, whom I traded to the Giants on August 21 for pitchers Jeff Robinson and Scott Medvin, had been a team leader, and his presence was missed. The new players seemed to be more concerned with proving to their new teammates that they belonged with us than on focusing on themselves. Poor Jeff Robinson looked like he was still in a state of shock, because he had never expected to be traded by the Giants.

After talking things over with Leyland and his coaches, I decided to call a team meeting in Pittsburgh to try and stop our poor play once and for all. I told the players, "I'm through trading for the season. The reason I made all of those trades was to bring each and every one of you to the Pirates. You are my diamonds in the rough. I believe in you and I'm going to stick with you. We're going to have a new team picture taken, and all of you are in it."

I then talked to them about the importance of goal setting for successful performance. "We should set a goal for the number of games we're going to win the rest of the way. We have 38 games left. How many games do you think we can win?"

Gott rose and said to the team, "We should have a goal of 25 games."

I said, "That's a great idea, Jim, but it means we'd have to play at a .650 clip the rest of the way, and we haven't even been playing .500 ball to this point. Are you sure 25 games is realistic?"

Gott answered, "I believe it's realistic. If somebody doesn't think so, let him speak up now."

The atmosphere in the locker room was electric. Gott had proclaimed to the team that he belonged, and now the rest of the players felt they, too, belonged. The Pirates had a goal, a focus—the fans called it "The Drive for 25." We counted off every victory—24 to go, 15 to go, and so on. After we won the 25th game, we had a victory party in the clubhouse. We toasted our success with nonalcoholic champagne. The Pittsburgh writers thought we were being foolish, but it really meant a lot to us. And then we closed the season with two more victories against the Phillies and wound up in a fourth-place tie with them. We exceeded our goal.

Those five weeks were terrific for the franchise. The fans

bore witness to our commitment and really got behind the team. I'm sure those five weeks set the tone for the Pirates' great start in 1988. I knew I was getting a talented pitcher in Jim Gott, but I didn't know he would mean so much to our team chemistry. And you can't ask more of a trade than that. Once again, the intangibles prevail!

10 WHY NOT?

I've always cherished a line written by the great playwright George Bernard Shaw in *Back to Methuselah*: "You see things; and you say, 'Why?' But I dream things that never were; and I say, 'Why not?'"

People of vision and dedication have an immeasurable impact on society. They inspire us to pursue our dreams. I can think of so many visionaries who have reinforced my faith in our ability as people to overcome any obstacle. Jim Abbott of the Angels, a left-handed pitcher born without a right hand, never doubted that he could make it to the major leagues. Ted Kennedy, Jr. participates in a number of sporting activities even though his right leg had to be amputated because of cancer.

Sally Ride defied the odds and became the first woman astronaut. Diplomat Ralph Bunche and U.S. Secretary of Defense Cordell Hull had an idea for a United Nations and saw it through. God said, "Let there be light," and inventor Thomas Edison made electric light available to everyone.

Howard Aiken, a mathematician, conceived the first digital computer. Rosa Parks, a black woman in Montgomery, Alabama, galvanized the civil rights movement in the fifties by refusing to sit in the back of a bus. President Jimmy Carter, Egyptian Prime Minister Anwar Sadat, and Israeli Prime Minister Menachem Begin hammered out a peace accord that sought an end to 40 years of hostilities between Egypt and Israel, even though their Arab neighbors were against that initiative.

These people live or lived their lives challenging the whys and achieving the why nots.

What is the roadblock from why to why not? The fear and disbelief of stepping out into the unknown. People have been fearful for a long time. But as Ralph Waldo Emerson once wrote, "Knowledge is the antidote to fear."

By now you know I'm not the man with all the answers, but the one with all the questions. Every day I think of questions, from the practical to the philosophical, that we in baseball need to address and resolve so that our beloved pastime can grow to new heights. I now pose them to you.

Why not have a research and development institute for Major League Baseball?

After my stimulating years at the Royals Academy, I realized the need for a research and development center for baseball subsidized by Major League Baseball, its teams, and its corporate sponsors. The automobile industry has research and development centers. The National Football League studies the performance of its players. We should have the same thing in our billion-dollar industry.

Through my contacts with high school and college players and coaches during my years out of the baseball mainstream, I became convinced that amateur baseball was ready for this concept. In the ensuing years I was exposed to baseball in Latin America and the Scandinavian countries, where baseball players had been thirsting for knowledge. The baseball students who attended the clinics were amazingly attentive, asking one question after another. Jim Thrift and I will never forget how fascinated the Finns were in 1981 just watching us put down baselines on their field.

Because their desire to learn was so strong, I was sure that someday these countries could compete with us on an international level. It dawned on me that an R & D center for baseball could be international in scope.

As I saw it, an international institute of baseball, located next to a two-year or four-year college, could invite players and coaches worldwide to study from and exchange ideas with the institute's baseball staff and experts in an array of fields. The players the institute develops could graduate to professional baseball through a supplemental draft. It would also have a job-placement service for the coaches to find work on the professional, collegiate, and high school levels.

The institute would contain a facility where orthopedists, scientists, and kinesiologists could not only study human performance, but discover and refine new technologies that could help improve it. Staff psychologists could also devise tests and profiles that would give a more accurate assessment of the emotional characteristics needed for winning baseball.

The players would get intensive baseball instruction, vision training, and a comprehensive physical conditioning program. The professors from the adjacent college would teach the players courses geared to their needs: foreign-language classes and cultural studies, public speaking, media relations, nutrition, stress management, drug and alcohol seminars, and vocational training for concurrent and postbaseball careers. Through the involvement of corporate sponsors, the institute would place the players in off-season jobs at various corporate offices worldwide.

There would also be financial-planning classes for the

players and their wives, since more often than not it is the wife who handles the family finances. By trying to remove that pressure from her husband, she is the one who becomes ill when their finances get out of control. Don't think I'm joking. The wife of one of the Pirates players actually developed ulcers because of this stress.

The baseball staff would conduct daily seminars and think-tank sessions for the coaches, and classes on player procurement and development for those who wish to become team executives. See, in pro baseball's antiquated system, front office people are inbred. Either you've played pro baseball or are connected to someone who works in baseball operations. That's why the same people are recycled so often. In our institute, people who aspired to hold those positions—whether they'd played the game or not—would be properly trained and placed in jobs in the major leagues or on the international level through our job-placement service.

There also would be a vision-training program for umpires. Now I don't mean to be disrespectful to umpires, but their job is based on visual assessments. People talk about adopting the NFL's use of instant replays. That would be totally unnecessary if an umpire had trained and improved his visual acuity, contrast sensitivity, and depth perception.

Much of this dream came to fruition in 1989. Buffalo Bisons owner Bob Rich, who following the 1988 season had purchased the Wichita, Kansas (Double A), minor league team and the Wichita-based National Baseball Congress, the country's oldest and most prestigious tournament, told me in a telephone conversation that he'd been thinking about an international R & D center, too. Rich, who has the intelligence, vision, business acumen, and love for baseball necessary for such an ambitious project, asked me to formulate plans and serve as the institute's director. I arranged for the use of the facilities at Wichita State University, and in July 1989 the International Baseball Institute was born.

The Institute held two three-day sessions over one week, and what a week it was! Attending the two three-day sessions were college and high school players, coaches and Olympic delegates from the U.S., the Bahamas, Spain, France, Italy, Korea, Austria, Switzerland, Holland, and Australia. (Australia is baseball's newest frontier. More and more major league organizations, seeing the growth in recent years of the caliber of play and quality of instruction, have been drafting Australian players and setting up affiliations for their minor league players to play winter ball there.)

Our faculty was first-class. Gene Stephenson, the head baseball coach at Wichita State, coordinated the instruction, and was assisted by Dennis Rogers, Cal State-Fullerton's assistant baseball coach. Stephenson and Hal McRae, a great hitter in his major league career, and now the Montreal Expos' major-league batting coach ran our hitting instruction. Steve Boros was our infield and baserunning instructor. Hal Baird coordinated the pitching instruction, assisted by Brent Kemnitz, an assistant coach at Wichita State. John Scolinos was in charge of baseball fundamentals. Tony Guzzo, the head baseball coach at Virginia Commonwealth University, was the catching instructor. Bill Arce, chairman of the International Sports Group, coordinated our international teams. Mackie Shilstone coordinated our conditioning program. Dr. Bill Harrison was our visual-systems analyst, and Dr. Tony Stellar and Alan Blitzblau were our computer/video analysts.

Here are the courses we taught:

1. Technological analysis of baserunning performance
2. The aerodynamics of pitching
3. Instructing the instructors—a coach's seminar
4. Advanced hitting technology
5. Fielding proficiency
6. Bunting varieties and techniques

7. Catching strategies and mechanics
8. Body conditioning and nutrition for baseball players.

We also had a tournament called the International Friendship Cup, made up of the National Olympic team of Spain; the National team of the Bahamas; Athletes in Action USA Team East; a regional team from Queensland, Australia; and a team called Western Europe United, made up of players from Austria, Switzerland, France, Italy, Holland, and the U.S. Daily highlights of the tournament were broadcast on Spanish National Television.

An R & D center for baseball makes even more sense today, when you consider the billions of dollars Major League Baseball is receiving from its television packages. I'd hate to see all that income eaten up by team operating costs. During my term on Major League Baseball's Umpire Development Committee I spoke with Edwin Lawrence, the executive director; Marty Springstead, the supervisor of American League umpires; and Ed Vargo, Springstead's counterpart in the National League, and they agreed with the value of such a center. I also discussed this with Bart Giamatti before he passed away, and he, too, was receptive to this concept. I truly hope Giamatti's successor, Fay Vincent, picks up the banner.

Why not set up correspondence courses for pro players?

Professional players spend half of their season on the road. The average player looks for innocuous activities—watching television or hanging around the hotel lobby—to pass the time until the team reports to the ballpark. What if he used that time to earn credits toward a degree in a field he could enter during the off-season and after baseball?

Sounds tedious, right? I mean, how many players want to lug around and wade through thick textbooks? It doesn't have to be that way. Many business people who travel earn their master's in business administration using audio- and videotapes provided by the school. There are also cable television systems around the country that air correspondence classes.

I think the players could make their correspondence studies more enjoyable by working in groups. One of the players could be designated as the group leader and conduct informal, one-hour classes. The trainer or the team's public relations director could supervise their work. Not only would it be time well spent, but it would foster a communal, spirited atmosphere.

Why not create a Winning Scorebook for Baseball?

The typical baseball scorebook allows coaches and fans to record the same statistical information they get in a box score. What they're left with is a partial analysis of the players. Baseball writer Thomas Boswell devised his "Total Average" measurements as a way to gauge productivity. The shortcoming in his system is that it relies on information from the box scores.

Dr. Bill Harrison and I have talked about a brave new "Winning Scorebook for Baseball," which would help fans become more aware of the positive contributions scorebooks and box scores omit.

The Winning Scorebook would leave room for the traditional information but also contain spaces for plus and minus ratings in the key categories that are necessary for winning baseball. The players with the highest total points would be considered the most productive.

For example, the batter is at the plate with a runner on second base and nobody out. He hits a ground ball to the right side of the infield so that the runner can advance to third base, where he can score on a fly ball, ground ball, wild pitch, or passed ball. Early in the 1988 season Jose Lind did that 12 times and the Pirates scored nine runs.

Each time he did that, the traditional scorebook showed him as oh-for-one; in the Winning Scorebook, he'd get a plus-one.

In every game there is usually one outstanding defensive play. The traditional scorebook and the box score only acknowledge the putout. In the Winning Scorebook, an infielder who makes a great play from the hole, or an outfielder whose throw holds the runner on second from rounding third and scoring, gets a plus-one.

If the batter failed to advance the runner, or the fielder threw to the wrong base, they would be graded with minus-ones.

Why not have hitters take batting practice at game speed?

Batting practice can be the biggest waste of time if you go about it without a systematic plan that prepares you for live game conditions. Therefore, it seems foolish for a hitter in batting practice to take 20 swings at 75-mile-an-hour fastballs, only to wonder why he can't hit a 90-mile-an-hour fastball during the game.

This is another case of practice making imperfect. Because hitting requires such precise timing and rhythm, anything you do that throws off that timing and rhythm will cause you to fail by your own design.

Seventy-five-mile-an-hour batting practice pitches do nothing but tempt the batter into seeing how many of them he can put into the seats. That causes him to develop an improper swing. He will hitch. He will rock. He will uppercut. And he will carry those flaws into the game. Now what good is that going to do when he's facing Nolan Ryan?

And they say pitchers have the advantage. Yes, they have the advantage—because of the poor preparation of the hitters. Why do you think there were only five .300 hitters in the National League in both 1988 and 1989? Because so many batters waste 100 at-bats—throw them away!—by not devising and practicing a plan in batting practice that will be of value in the game.

We have the greatest athletes playing baseball today, and yet in the last 10 years the pitchers have become better prepared while the hitters are more poorly prepared. You'll never see a pitcher practice all of his warm-up throws at 75 percent of his velocity. He begins his warm-ups at an easy pace and then finishes his throws at game speed.

Why can't a hitter do the same thing? Why not have the last round of batting practice thrown at the same velocities the hitter will see in the game?

Say the hitter knows he's going to face a left-handed pitcher that night who throws an 85-mile-an-hour fastball. Why can't his team employ a left-handed batting-practice pitcher who throws at that same speed? We spend all these millions of dollars on everything else, so why not spend a few extra dollars for a few extra batting-practice pitchers? The most you'd need is four pitchers—two left-handers and two righties—who throw at different speeds.

For those pitchers whose velocity you can't duplicate with a batting-practice pitcher, why not put technology to work? Mike Hall, a former semipro player from Rome, Georgia, has invented a batting practice machine called "The Determinator," through which hitters can practice against televised images of actual pitchers. During the summer of 1989, Hall set up his machine for the Braves in an indoor batting cage in Atlanta-Fulton County Stadium. The batter, taking his stance, looks at a 15-by-15-foot projection screen that's 55 feet away (approximating the distance a pitched ball travels after it leaves the pitcher's hand). There are six holes at different spots on the projection screen; Hall uncovers the one that most closely matches the release point of the pitcher being viewed. The pitcher's motion is projected onto the screen, and when his arm passes the hole, a baseball is propelled toward the hitter by a pitching machine hidden behind the screen. The machine can throw any of seven pitches at speeds up to 104 miles per hour. That's got to be a better way to tune up for facing Dwight Gooden than swinging at some coach's 75-mile-per-hour "fastballs."

Why don't players bunt more?

I am astounded by the lack of bunting skills major league players have. On some teams, when a player is called upon to bunt he reacts as if his hand will break out in a rash if it touches the bat's trademark.

One problem is that players practice incorrectly. If you don't move forward in the batter's box, angle your body so that your front foot points toward the outside upper corner of the box, and hold the bat in fair territory at a 45-degree angle—if you omit just one step in this procedure—you are going to fail in the game.

The other problem is that there are some players who don't practice bunting at all. Believe it or not, that seems directly connected to the rise in baseball salaries. Those players assume that you get paid by the home run, not the bunt. They say to themselves, Bunting is for the singles hitters. I'm macho. I'm a home-run man.

What folly. If it's stats you're after, I say you should focus on attaining a high on-base average, which over the course of a season means more to your team than 15 home runs.

Bunting is a powerful offensive weapon. When executed correctly, it is *the* easiest way to get on base and advance base runners. Mr. Home Run Man may feel so good taking that slow trot around the bases after hitting one out, but if he's in a slump and elects not to bunt his way on base, he's got to feel pretty stupid as he takes that slow walk back to the dugout.

Even the *threat* of a bunt opens more options for hits. If the opposition knows you can bunt, the infielders at the corners will position themselves closer to home plate. That

gives the hitter more holes to shoot for if he pulls his bat
back and swings away.

*Why not weigh the votes for the All-Star Game based on city
population?*

I think fans are entitled to have a voice in the selection
of the teams for the All-Star Game. But two things bother
me about the current process, which excludes managers and
coaches from voting. First, the fans have a tendency to vote
for the players they know, veterans they've seen on television
in postseason play, even if that veteran no longer performs
at his peak. To exclude the young stars from the starting
lineup is unjust.

Think about the National Basketball Association's All-
Star games. I daresay that they generate more enthusiasm
and expectations from basketball fans than baseball's All-
Star games, because the players on the court are the cream
of the crop. If our All-Star Game is second only to the World
Series as baseball's greatest showcase, it's about time we
veer away from the plodding, predictable outcomes of the
past by injecting into it the best players of the current
season.

My other concern is that fans in the larger cities with
winning teams are likely to stuff the ballot boxes for their
favorite home-team players. During my term in Pittsburgh,
it gnawed at me that some of our players deserving of All-
Star honors were bypassed in the voting for the starting
lineup simply because the Pirates are in a smaller market.
They had a smaller voting base and lacked national television exposure.

I propose that each city's votes be tallied in propor-
tion to population. This way, one vote from Pittsburgh,
Seattle, or Minneapolis would equal X number of votes from
Los Angeles, New York, or Chicago. Let's also have our

managers and coaches vote, and weigh their choices more heavily as well.

Why shouldn't baseball telecasters use telestrators to diagram the action, the way they do for football?

The graphics baseball broadcasters display during telecasts are usually statistically oriented: batting averages, averages with runners in scoring positions and less than two outs, batting averages in the month of September in day games on grass fields when the temperature is 50 degrees with a 40 percent chance of showers . . .

That's all well and good for the hard-core baseball fan, but the average housewife is going to feel like she's watching an accountants' seminar. The reason she's bored is that she's not learning any of the things that make baseball exciting.

Instead of the long-winded explanations of the nuances of the game from the so-called color man, why not use an electronic chalkboard to diagram them? What makes John Madden of CBS Sports an outstanding football commentator is that he shows you what he sees.

How can a telestrator be used for baseball telecasts? Let's say the game situation calls for a bunt. If the defense uses a wheel play, the expert commentator could diagram it as he explains it on the replay.

I've heard broadcasters try, with some difficulty, to articulate the timed, measured lead. Say Vince Coleman is on first base. Why not post a small clock at the bottom corner of the screen, the way it's done on boxing telecasts, and actually time the pitcher's delivery, the catcher's throw, and the runner's time to second base.

Why not use a radar gun to show the difference in velocity between the four-seam fastball and the two-seamer? Better yet, use the super-slow-motion camera to show how much more the two-seam fastball falls in the hitter's zone. I can see it on TV, because I know what I'm looking for, and so would a fan once he was shown it.

The super-slow-motion camera can also be used to vividly demonstrate the differences in the start of each batter's swing, his weight shift, the coiling and uncoiling of his mid-section, and the movement of his hands.

The casual fan sometimes assumes that baseball players require less athleticism for their sport than basketball players do for theirs. In fact, the hardest athletic skill is hitting a baseball traveling at 95 miles an hour. I can say that and it may mean nothing to you. Television can show you that and it will astound you.

My point is: You are more likely to remember what you see than what you are told.

Why do some people confuse passion with ego?

I spent some time during the fall of 1988 pondering the word "ego," as used in the phrase, "He's got a big ego."

If ego is self-esteem, I have an ego. If ego means being self-absorbed, refusing to listen to others, I don't have an ego. If ego means having a passion for my work, my family, and my team, then I have a big ego.

We in America need to be passionate for our country to grow, even to survive. We may perceive other people or other races or countries as our enemies, but in reality we are our own enemies. If we don't have passion, we have compla-cency and mediocrity. We have people who want to live off the public trough, people who are trained to do something but paid for doing nothing. That's the most dangerous thing in our society.

I think passion is exciting. It leads to discovery, change, and growth. Some may find passion threatening, particu-larly if they don't want their boat rocked. When you're work-ing with negative, closed-minded people who want to preserve the status quo, they will summon all their energies to undermine you. And if they succeed, they will spend days and months and years harping on you and trying to discredit you instead of focusing on themselves and moving forward.

But my passion for excellence, for perfection, keeps me going. Perfection is an elusive goal in an imperfect world, so I savor those moments of perfection. When Alvaro Espinoza lays down a perfect bunt, when Dave LaPoint uses all his wiles to come back from a three-and-oh count and strike out a batter, when Don Mattingly drives a two-strike pitch to the opposite field, when Jim Gott fires his four-seam fastball up in the strike zone, I feel an inner peace. If I can teach a base runner the timed, measured lead, if I can help a young player under stress by directing him to a visualization expert or a qualified psychologist, I've done my job to perfection.

Perfection doesn't necessarily mean that you have all the answers. One can think he is the discoverer of something, only to learn it had been used 40 years ago. Maybe Branch Rickey knew all about the four-seam fastball. Perhaps Ty Cobb used the timed, measured lead. Perfection is finding practical ideas, evaluating them, using them, and improving on them.

Teamwork—synergism—leads to excellence. That's why I'm so absorbed with all the little things that lead to excellence: players who not only have great athletic ability but a winning spirit and an openness to increasing their net worth; teachers who can simplify the complex and teach at the rate of the learner; scouts who see clearly and evaluate thoroughly; people of initiative, like Jim Bowden, who see a void and find ways to fill it; and all the people outside the baseball mainstream whose knowledge can be transferred and applied to baseball.

Believe me, you don't have to be a dyed-in-the wool baseball fan to make an important contribution to the game. Dr. Joseph Trachtman didn't invent the Accommotrac Vision Tester for baseball. He simply has the vision to imagine all its applications. Dr. John Nash Ott doesn't even follow baseball. He simply has a passion for discoveries that will benefit our health and welfare. If you strive for excellence in your vocation, your discoveries will be used by people of common sense in all walks of life.

If you have a talent for baseball, seek out ways to make yourself even better. I marvel at Tony Gwynn of the Padres. During his childhood, Gwynn and his two brothers went into their backyard and practiced baseball using Wiffle balls and rolled-up socks held together by rubber bands. The 5-11 Gwynn later played baseball and basketball at San Diego State University, and was good enough to be drafted by the Padres and the NBA's San Diego Clippers.

Gwynn was a great hitter in the minor leagues and came to the majors in 1983 swatting one line drive after another. The next season he led the major leagues in batting with a .351 average and helped the Padres reach the World Series.

After the 1984 World Series, at a high point in his success as a professional, Gwynn took stock of himself. He realized that his defensive play in right field was lacking, so he went back to his coaches at San Diego State for help. Every day the coaches hit hundreds of fly balls to every part of right field—down the line, in the gaps—plus ground balls and line drives, until Gwynn felt he had conquered his deficiencies. He also learned to compensate for his throwing arm, which is just average, by releasing the ball more quickly, or by taking a few steps back on a fly ball, then running under it, catching it, and making his throw at full momentum.

In 1986, 1987 and 1989 Gwynn was awarded Gold Gloves for his outfield excellence.

Following the 1986 season, Gwynn, who had stolen 37 bases that year despite a lack of raw speed, set a goal of stealing 50 bases in 1987. Gwynn tried a variety of methods to strengthen his legs. He experimented with a most unusual technique: roller-skating up a hill across the street from his home in Poway, California. Talk about uphill battles! When he realized that all this method did was strain his ankles and hamstring muscles, he scrapped it and went on to a new approach.

Gwynn recruited Padres coach Greg Riddoch to tutor him on the art of base stealing. Riddoch taught Gwynn how to take a proper lead and used videotapes to show him all the tip-offs to look for in a pitcher's motion.

In 1987 Gwynn stole 56 bases.

Satisfied? Not Tony Gwynn. He and his wife, Alicia, set up a room in their house they call "Video Central." It has two television sets and five videocassette recorders hooked up to cable TV and their 10-foot satellite dish. They tape every baseball game that's televised, including Yankees and Red Sox games, because Gwynn likes to study the hitting forms of Don Mattingly and Wade Boggs.

Once they have a Padres game on tape, they edit Gwynn's performance against every National League team onto individual videocassettes. So before a game against, say, the Dodgers, Gwynn will watch the videocassette labeled "Dodgers" and review his batting approach, his stealing leads, and the pitchers' pickoff moves.

To Gwynn, each success provides him with a new starting point in his quest to be the best outfielder in baseball, the smartest base runner, and the first player since Ted Williams to hit .400 in a season.

That's what baseball—and life—are all about.

In his commencement address in May of 1932 to the students at Oglethorpe University in Atlanta, President Franklin D. Roosevelt made an eloquent observation about the need for change and growth in America. I believe his words can be applied to baseball as well.

Roosevelt said, "The country needs and, unless I mistake its temper, the country demands bold, persistent experimentation. It is common sense to take a method and try it: If it fails, admit it frankly and try another. But above all, try something."

INDEX